MW00562435

Roman Lives

Ancient Roman Life
as Illustrated by Latin Inscriptions

FOCUS CLASSICAL SOURCES

Roman Sport and Spectacle • Anne Mahoney • 2001
Roman Religion • Valerie Warrior • 2002
Roman Lives • Brian Harvey • 2004

Roman Lives

Ancient Roman Life
as Illustrated by Latin Inscriptions

Brian K. Harvey

focus an imprint of
Hackett Publishing Company, Inc.
Indianapolis/Cambridge

A Focus book

Focus an imprint of
  Hackett Publishing Company
Previously published by R. Pullins Co.

Copyright © 2004 Brian K. Harvey
All rights reserved

Cover Image: Tombstone of three members of the freedman family of the Vibii
(*CIL* 6.28774), Vatican Museums, Rome. Scala/Art Resource, NY

ISBN 1-58510-769-8

Library of Congress Cataloging-in-Publication Data
Harvey, Brian K.
 Roman lives : ancient Roman life as illustrated by Latin inscriptions / Brian K.
Harvey.
    pages cm. — (Focus classical sources)
 English and Latin
 Includes bibliographical references.
   ISBN 978-1-58510-769-8 (paperback)
 1. Rome—Civilization. 2. Inscriptions, Latin—Rome. 3. Epitaphs--Rome. I. Title.
 DG78.H36 2015
 937—dc23   2015015048

Interior and Cover Design by Linda Robertson

19 18 17 16 15   2 3 4 5 6

TABLE OF CONTENTS

Tomb of the freedman C. Cuspius Cyrus, necropolis outside the Porta Nuceria, Pompeii. *Photo courtesy of the Ministero per i Beni e le Attività Culturali Soprintenza Archeologica di Roma.*

PREFACE

An extremely diverse population inhabited the Roman Empire. As with any complex society, ancient Rome functioned with a wide-ranging group of inhabitants, from the highest-ranking political leader to the humblest salesman on the street. Too often, in the study of Roman history and literature, the focus remains on the Roman elite, and the student loses sight of other members of society.

The limited picture of Roman society provided by extant literary sources can be balanced by examining other sources, however; in particular, we are fortunate to have a wealth of evidence for the lives of the ancient Romans in the form of inscriptions (the study of inscriptions is called epigraphy). An inscription is any carved, scratched or painted document that has been preserved directly from antiquity on some kind of durable material like stone, metal or terracotta. Inscriptions had a wide range of functions. Government documents were generally inscribed on bronze tablets and posted in the towns and cities of the empire to make the law or act known to the population. Public (and, less frequently, private) buildings were adorned with dedicatory inscriptions which commemorated the circumstances of their construction as well as the building's sponsor. A milestone marked every mile of the famous road system of Rome in order to tell the traveler the distance to the nearest town in either direction, as well as the name of the emperor who funded that particular road.

Because such a small percentage of the population was literate (perhaps only 5%), the Romans designed their inscriptions to be "readable" by as many people as possible. The Latin on tombstones is relatively simple and formulaic when compared with literary texts. The preponderance of personal names and titles of offices also make them easier to understand. Many also included images of the deceased or things important to him or her. The words themselves embodied a kind of power. Decrees and documents conveyed the wishes of the central government, and their placement in public places served as a constant reminder of the authority of the rulers. Similarly, a lengthy imperial name or aristocratic career inscription could give even an illiterate reader or observer a sense of the importance of that emperor or aristocrat.

Rather than examining imperial inscriptions, however, we will focus here on inscriptions which preserve the individual memory of a diverse range of Roman people. For example, city and town governments honored certain members of their communities by erecting statues to them with an accompanying inscribed base which not only stated the person's name, but also an account of their career and deeds. Another much more common type of inscription is the tomb inscription (also called an epitaph). Although law prohibited burial within the confines of the city itself, tombs were nonetheless highly visible to the city inhabitants and visitors, as they were placed along the roads leading out of the city. In anticipation of their death, families eagerly purchased plots of land along the road; alternatively, they could choose to be buried in a nearby catacomb or necropolis (*e.g.* the still extant "Isola Sacra" necropolis near Ostia, the ancient port city of Rome). Tomb monuments came in all shapes and sizes. Some housed only a single person; others had space for not only the immediate family, but also the family's freedmen and freedwomen.

Also common were burial clubs (*collegia*) organized around military units, professional societies and mercantile guilds. Members paid money to the club who then took care of the burial of its deceased members.

The inscriptions, or epitaphs, on these monuments included more than just the names of those buried inside and their ages at the time of their death. They tell the reader more about the people themselves. As with statue bases, tomb epitaphs attempted to preserve a certain memory of an individual by describing what the person did in life. In most cases, this meant stating the person's occupation, the military unit in which they served, or the posts they held during their political careers. Often, however, the writers included details of their lives such as how they died, what activities they enjoyed during their lifetimes, or how they felt about the members of their families. One soldier, in fact, does not mention himself by name, but believes that his actions in life will remind people of his identity. Unlike the majority of aristocratic literary and historical texts, inscriptions, especially tomb epitaphs, preserve the words and lives of a wide range of social classes, ages and genders. As such, epitaphs are useful and interesting, even if they are poignant and difficult to read at times. Nevertheless, they offer us a privileged glimpse in the lives of the ancient Romans which is not preserved elsewhere.

The current work collects a number of inscriptions that exemplify the people who inhabited the ancient Roman Empire during the first two centuries AD. The catalog of people and occupations is by no means complete, but is intended, rather, to reflect and represent the hundreds of thousands of inscriptions which have been discovered and published over the last several centuries. Inscriptions were chosen which tend to reflect the great diversity of Roman society. Most are tomb epitaphs, but a few examples of statue bases, building inscriptions and ancient graffiti are also included.

The texts in this collection have been organized into some broad social categories. First are examples of members of the senatorial, equestrian, and municipal aristocracies. Texts illustrating various types of priests and religious attendants follow. The next chapter contains numerous examples of men in the military: common soldiers, non-citizen auxiliary soldiers, centurions, and equestrian officers. The next two chapters illustrate the institution of slavery through inscriptions of slaves and freedmen first from the aristocratic households and then from the household of the emperor. A tremendous number of people were required for the day-to-day running of the imperial palace and bureaucracy. The focus then turns to families and private citizens. First are given examples of Roman families celebrated on a single tombstone. Tombstones of children follow. The next chapter includes epitaphs and dedications exemplifying the virtues and occupations of women. The final two chapters illustrate occupations held by members of the lower classes. First there are inscriptions celebrating the lives of entertainers: gladiators, actors and charioteers, followed by texts demonstrating the types of occupations held by members of the lower classes.

READING INSCRIPTIONS

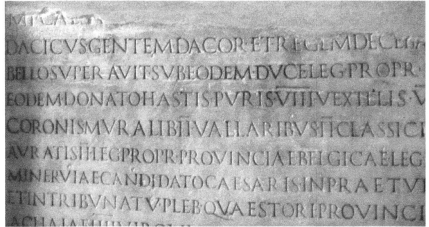

Statue base of an unknown important Trajanic senator (CIL 6.1444; ILS 1022), Capitoline Museums, Rome (courtesy of the Archivio Fotografico dei Musei Capitolini).

    The inscriptions in this collection were written in Latin. The Latin on these stones, however, is not especially difficult to translate. The grammar is typically simple and does not compare in complexity or style to the high literary Latin written by the aristocratic historians and poets of the same period. In fact, a large percentage of the texts consist primarily of names, occupations, and offices. Despite their simplicity, however, reading inscriptions, even in English translation, can be a difficult task, especially for the uninitiated. Although inscriptions tended to use a simple, often predictable, grammatical structure, no punctuation marks help the reader distinguish sentences, phrases, or separate items on a list (such as the various posts held in the course of the subject's public career). Words frequently are split over two lines with no hyphenation to indicate a continuation. Despite that problem, words were frequently divided with a space marked by interpuncts: dots, marks or drawings of ivy leaves chiseled into the stone. The exclusive use of capital letters also makes it difficult to distinguish between proper names and simple words. Another source of confusion is created by the use of capital "V" for both capital "V" as well as capital "U". One of the primary hurdles to reading an inscription is being able to decipher the abbreviations. Because of space and budgetary constraints, much information often had to be squeezed onto a limited space. For this reason, many inscriptions were full of abbreviations.

Despite these difficulties, however, inscriptions were very formulaic in nature; familiarity with Roman epigraphic conventions can make reading ancient Roman inscriptions a relatively easy task. Knowledge of the system of Roman names, an understanding of the typical career patterns, and familiarity with a handful of commonplace abbreviations can greatly facilitate deciphering an inscribed text. Such knowledge comes primarily from reading many similar texts in order to develop a familiarity with all of the characteristic patterns and conventions. Tomb epitaphs are the most common type of inscription, and the most used type in this collection. Therefore, a section on the formulas found on tombstones has been included. There is also an introduction to the way in which Romans of the upper classes described their careers, most notably on tomb epitaphs and statue bases.

In order to facilitate reading, all of the texts in this collection are given with complete transcript, text and translation. The "transcript" gives the text as it appeared on the original stone, metal or other material. The "text" then gives a full Latin version with punctuation and all words unabbreviated. A literal translation of each text has also been given to allow quick and easy access to the information contained in the collection. Additional notes elucidate oddities of the text, and explain the cultural context of the information contained in the inscription.

Roman tombs along the road running north out of Pompeii (the Street of Tombs).

Roman Epitaphs

The earliest Roman epitaphs consisted only of the name of the deceased on a small, one-line plaque located near the place of interment. Eventually, tomb epitaphs included more detailed information on the deceased, as well as details about his friends and family. The following are elements which commonly appear on Roman epitaphs:

- The first common element which often appears is the invocation to the spirits of the dead, "Dis Manibus", often abbreviated as "D M" or "D M S" ("Dis Manibus Sacrum", "sacred to the spirits of the dead.")

- The second common element is personal information regarding the deceased. The description begins by listing the deceased's name following the invocation; the name is usually listed in the Latin dative case. Inscriptions were often dedicated to whole families and therefore include these family members in the dedication. The age of the deceased is generally given next with the formula "qui vixit annos", "who lived ... years". Then the inscription reports the number of years of life (and often the number of months and days as well). The person's occupation or duties, if mentioned, would follow at this point (see below for career inscriptions). The deceased is also often commemorated in terms of specific virtues and other flattering adjectives, *e.g.* "bonus" ("good") or "bene merens" ("well-deserving"). Sometimes the circumstances of death are given. Other formulae that frequently appear include "hic situs est (H S E)", "is buried here", and "ossa sita sunt (O S S)", "the bones are buried here".

- A third common element of the typical epitaph is a list of the inscription's dedicants. The dedicants would usually include family members, but friends or co-workers are also commonly seen. The dedicants' relationship to the deceased is usually given as well. Sometimes the epitaph notes that its creation was required by the deceased's will (*testamentum*). Verbs indicating dedication also appear, for example "dedit" ("gave"), and "dedicavit" ("dedicated").

Tombstone dedicated to the woman Florentina by her husband Philetaerus, imperial freedman paedagogus *(CIL 6.7767), National Museum of Rome at the Baths of Diocletian, Rome*

- A description of the place of burial also sometimes appears. The Latin words for tomb or burial appear with details about the burial spot. In addition to the name of the burial location, the size of the plot of land on which the tomb stands is sometimes marked out at the end of the inscription with the formula "in fronte ... in agro ..." ("... feet long [i.e., the length of the property frontage], ... feet deep)".

Career Inscriptions

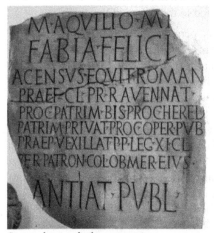

Statue base of the equestrian procurator Marcus Aquilius Felix (CIL 10, 6657; ILS 1387), Capitoline Museums, Rome. Photo courtesy of the Archivio Fotografico dei Museo Capitolini, Soprintenza Archeologica di Roma.

The tombstones of the lower classes were relatively simple affairs. Honorary and sepulchral inscriptions of the upper classes and members of the imperial bureaucracy, however, not only include the usual epitaph elements mentioned above, but also record the complete, often very detailed, public careers of the deceased. In addition to tombstone inscriptions, famous and influential people were honored by the state or their hometowns with statues that included an inscribed base. Aristocrats would sometimes honor themselves on statue bases and building dedications. The following elements were common to career inscriptions:

- The name of the person honored. The name would usually appear in the dative case unless the person was honoring himself. If the stone was recording a dedication made by the person being honored, the name will appear in the nominative.

- The career of the person honored. Offices were listed in chronological order, either in ascending order (from the earliest to the latest office) or in descending order (from latest to earliest office). Without regard to the career order, however, the most prestigious post (for example, consul or town decurion) was often listed first, immediately after the name.

- In the case of honorary dedications and statue bases, the name of the person, or, more often, the political body that dedicated the inscription was stated. Also, certain formulae were commonly used to explain the source of the money used to sponsor the dedication. Common formulaic phrases used to certify that the civic government had granted permission for the placement of the statue or dedication include "publice" ("at public expense"), "de suo" ("out of his own funds"), "decreto decurionum" ("by decree of the decurions") or even "locus datus decurionum decreto" ("place [for the statue or tomb] given by decree of the decurions") and "ex Senatus consulto" ("by decree of the Senate").

Sources of Inscriptions; Abbreviations

The survival of inscriptions from antiquity is very fortunate. Only a small percentage of inscriptions survived the ravages of time. Some were worn down by the ages. Others the ancients re-carved with new inscriptions. In late antiquity and the Middle Ages, large numbers of inscribed stones were reused as building material, either by being incorporated into walls or by being burned for lime. In the Renaissance, the study of Roman inscriptions became popular due to a revived interest in the Classical period. Aristocrats assembled large numbers of inscribed stones for their personal collections. Traveling scholars made their own collections by transcribing the text of the inscriptions they saw on their journeys. In more recent times, archaeology has constantly unearthed a multitude of new stones. In the 19th century, Theodor Mommsen initiated an ambitious project with the goal of assembling all known inscriptions in a single collection of books. The result was a massive series titled the *Corpus Inscriptionum Latinarum* (*CIL*). Volumes began to appear in the 1860s, and new volumes and supplements continue to appear on occasion. At the end of the 19th century, Hermann Dessau published the *Inscriptiones Latinae Selectae* (*ILS*), a selection of about 9,000 texts from the *CIL*. In the late 1800s, French scholars began to publish *L' Année Epigraphique* (*AE*), an annual publication which records all newfound and also recently re-examined inscriptions. The inscriptions in the current collection here have been derived from a combination of the *CIL* and the *AE*. Cross-references are included for those texts that also appear in the *ILS*.

The texts are given according to normal epigraphic conventions. In the

Street of Roman tombs in the Isola Sacra necropolis near Ostia.

transcript or the inscription as it appears on the stone, letters that have been lost due to the breaking of the stone or that are illegible are marked with brackets "[ ]". Any letters that can be restored with some confidence will be included within the brackets. Dashes are used for any part where restoration is not possible ("[---]"). All letters than can be read on the stone will be given in all capitals, just as the original. In the explanatory text that follows the transcript, parentheses are used to fill out the abbreviations, for example "M(arcus)". As with the transcript, brackets are used to mark missing letters due to damage or time. Braces ("{}") are used to demarcate any letters that appear on the stone by mistake, for example "mense{n}s", where "menses" is the correct form. In the translation, the brackets are generally omitted if the text can be restored.

The Roman Name

The Roman man's name has three parts: the *praenomen*, the *nomen*, and the *cognomen*. For example, the orator Cicero's full name was Marcus Tullius Cicero. Marcus is his *praenomen*, Tullius his *nomen* and Cicero his *cognomen*. The *praenomen* was the Roman male's personal name. For the most part, only the immediate family called a person by his *praenomen*. There were only a limited number of *praenomina* which Romans used to name their male children. On inscriptions, the *praenomen* was usually abbreviated. The following is a list of *praenomina* and the abbreviation(s) for each:

Commonly appearing:	Also appearing more rarely:
Gaius (C.)	Aulus (A., Au., Aul.)
Gnaeus (Cn.)	Appius (Ap., App.)
Decimus (D.)	Mamercus (Mam.)
Lucius (L.)	Manius (Mn., Mu.)
Manlius (M'.)	Numerius (N.)
Marcus (M.)	Sergius (S.)
Publius (Pub.)	Servius (Ser.)
Quintus (Q.)	Spurius (Sp.)
Sextus (Sex., Sx., Sext.)	Vibius (V., Vi.)
Titus (T.)	
Tiberius (Ti., Tib.)	

The eldest son in a family generally assumed the same name as his father. Subsequent sons would take a different *praenomen*.

The *nomen* indicated the family to which the person belonged. Every member of the family had the same *nomen*. There were many *nomina*, but some examples include Aelius, Claudius, Cornelius, Flavius, Julius, Junius, Livius, Tullius, and Valerius. In the late Republic and early Empire, people began to add a third name, the *cognomen*, to further differentiate groups or branches within the same family. Although last, these names were not family names (although some only appear with certain *nomina*). The *nomen* continued to be the name shared by the entire family. *Cognomina* were often names that described a particular feature of the first

Interior of a Roman columbarium, *Ostia.*

holder of the *cognomen* (but not necessarily people who inherited that *cognomen* from an earlier member of the family). For example, Cicero means "chickpea", Ahenobarbus means "red-bearded", Quietus means "quiet", and Crassus means "fat". In the second and third centuries, it became common for people (especially senators and equestrians) to have more than one *cognomen*. As with the modern practice of using hyphenated names, a person could keep multiple *cognomina* to show his or her connection with other aristocratic families.

The Roman name also included the person's filiation, an indication of the person's father. For example, the dedicatory inscription on the Pantheon in Rome names Marcus Agrippa "M AGRIPPA L F", "M(arcus) Agrippa, L(uci) f(ilius)", "Marcus Agrippa, son of Lucius". The filiation generally came between the *nomen* and the *cognomen*. Some senators and emperors use this element of their name to trace their lineage back several generations. The following is a list of familial titles and their abbreviations:

F, FIL, filia, filius (son/daughter)
N, NEP, nepos (grandson/granddaughter)
PRON, pronepos (great grandson/granddaughter)
ABN, abnepos (great, great grandson/granddaughter)
ADN, adnepos (great, great, great grandson/granddaughter)

Because their fathers were not Roman citizens, the filiation of slaves, freedmen, and provincials who received the citizenship worked differently and is discussed below.

Upon birth (or the reception of citizenship), Romans were enrolled in one of the thirty-five voting tribes. Inscriptions frequently record the honored person's tribe as a sure indication of their Roman citizenship. Enrolment in a particular tribe had very little to do with where one lived. Instead, children were entered into the tribe of their father and newly enfranchised citizens generally became members of the same tribe as the emperor who granted them the citizenship. The following is a list of the thirty-five tribes and their abbreviations:

Aemilia (Aem.)	Horatia (Hor.)	Romilia (Rom.)
Aniensis (Ani.)	Lemonia (Lem.)	Sabbatina (Sab.)
Arniensis (Arn.)	Maecia (Mae.)	Scaptia (Sca.)
Camilia (Cam.)	Menenia (Men.)	Sergia (Ser.)
Claudia (Cla.)	Oufentina (Ouf.)	Stellatina (Stel.)
Clustumina (Clu.)	Palatina (Pal.)	Sucusana (Suc.)
Collina (Col.)	Papiria (Pap.)	Teretina (Ter.)
Cornelia (Cor.)	Poplilia (Pop.)	Tromentina (Tro.)
Esquilina (Esq.)	Pollia (Pol.)	Velina (Vel.)
Fabia (Fab.)	Pomptina (Pom.)	Voltinia (Vol.)
Falerna (Fal.)	Pupinia (Pup.)	Voturia (Vot.)
Galeria (Gal.)	Quirina (Quir.)	

Women's names originally only had one part: a feminine version of their family's *nomen* (*e.g.*, Aelia, Claudia, Cornelia, etc.). If parents had more than one daughter, the earliest practice was to assign numbers to their names in order to differentiate between the girls (*e.g.* Claudia Prima, Claudia Secunda, Claudia Tertia, etc). As the *cognomen* became more common, daughters' names were distinguished by varying combinations of *nomen* and *cognomina*, rather than by numeration. The *cognomina* were often derived from the mother's or father's family names. A woman did not change her name after marriage.

When a child was adopted into another family, he assumed the full name of his new father, but retained his former *nomen* by converting it into a second *cognomen* by adding "-anus" to the end of it. For example, the future emperor Octavian was named at birth Gaius Octavius (after his father). When Gaius Julius Caesar adopted him, his name was changed to Gaius Julius Caesar Octavianus.

Because the name was such an important mark of status for the aristocracy, names often became very complicated entities. Adoption was very common as childless families chose to adopt rather than allow their family name to disappear. When adoption brought together two important families, the adopted son often combined the majority of his old name with his new name. Also, because wives and mothers sometimes came from more prestigious families than the husbands and fathers, children (and sometimes husbands) would adopt *cognomina* based on the *nomina* of the maternal line. By the height of the imperial period, aristocratic names could be very long indeed. For example, Titus Prifernius Paetus Rosianus Geminus Laecinianus Bassus, a senator from the early second century AD, was the adopted son of Titus Prifernius Paetus. His four other names, however, were meant to preserve a kind of family history (now, unfortunately, lost in obscurity) and allowed his friends to continue to recognize him and call him by his previous

Roman Tombs along the ancient Via Appia, *Rome.*

name. Pliny the Younger, a friend of this man, addressed letters to him simply as "Geminus", probably his original *cognomen*.

Non-Roman citizens (slaves, provincials, foreigners) generally had only one name. When such people received citizenship, they adopted the Roman three-part name. Their original name became their *cognomen* (sometimes in Romanized form) and their *praenomen* and *nomen* were taken from the person who granted them the citizenship. For example, if a man named Publius Cornelius Scipio freed a slave named Botar, Botar's name became Publius Cornelius Botar, freedman of Publius. Imperial freedmen received the *praenomen* and *nomen* of the reigning emperor. While the inscriptions of non-imperial freedmen can be dated only occasionally through knowledge of aristocratic families, imperial freedmen, exhibiting the name of the emperor who freed them, can be dated with relative precision. The following is a list of imperial names from the first two centuries:

> Gaius Julius – Augustus (26 BC – AD 14), Caligula (AD 37-41)
> Tiberius Julius – Tiberius (AD 14-37)
> Tiberius Claudius – Claudius (AD 41-54), Nero (AD 54-68)
> Servius Sulpicius – Galba (AD 68-69; very rare)
> Titus Flavius – Vespasian (AD 69-79), Titus (AD 79-81),
>   Domitian (AD 81-96)
> Marcus Cocceius – Nerva (AD 96-98)
> Marcus Ulpius – Trajan (AD 98-117)
> Publius Aelius – Hadrian (AD 117-138)

Titus Aelius/Aurelius – Antoninus Pius (AD 138-161)
Marcus Aurelius – Marcus Aurelius (AD 161-180), Commodus
   (AD 180-192)
Lucius Aelius/Aurelius – Lucius Verus (AD 161-169); Commodus
   (AD 180-192)
Lucius Septimius – Severus (AD 193-211)
Marcus Aurelius – Caracalla (AD 211-217)

If an imperial freedman has one of these preceding *praenomina* and *nomina*, the reader can be certain that he was freed by one of those emperors, but keep in mind that the inscription could have been erected later than the reign of that particular emperor (thus, the emperor's reign provides a starting point for the earliest possible date for the carving of the inscription in question). Furthermore, the descendants of the imperial freedman would inherit the same *praenomen* and *nomen*, and thus, the name would often continue being used for a long time following the reign of their namesake (although the descendants would not have freedman status indicated in their filiation).

The same naming practice applied to freeborn provincials who received the citizenship either from an emperor's patronage, widespread enfranchisement of a certain geographical region, or through military service in the auxiliaries. Like imperial freedmen, the new citizens assumed the *praenomen* and *nomen* of the reigning emperor. For example, Augustus granted citizenship to a German chieftain named Herman. Herman Romanized his original name and became Gaius Julius Arminius. Arminius was quite famous, because he later led his tribe in revolt against Rome and destroyed three legions with their accompanying auxiliary troops in the Black Forest. In the early third century, the emperor Caracalla passed a law which granted citizenship to all freeborn people of the empire. Because Caracalla's official name was Marcus Aurelius Antoninus, the multitude of people who received their citizenship at that time (or were descended from someone who had) assumed Marcus Aurelius as their *praenomen* and *nomen*.

Roman Emperors to AD 238

Augustus	27 BC – AD 14	Imperator Caesar divi filius Augustus
Tiberius	14-37	Imperator Tiberius Caesar Augustus
Caligula	37-41	Gaius Caesar Augustus Germanicus
Claudius	41-54	Tiberius Claudius Caesar Augustus Germanicus
Nero	54-68	Nero Claudius Caesar Augustus Germanicus
Galba	June, 68-Jan., 69	Servius Galba Imperator Caesar Augustus
Otho	Jan.–Apr., 69	Imperator Marcus Otho Caesar Augustus
Vitellius	Apr.-Dec., 69	Aulus Vitellius Germanicus

		Imperator Augustus
Vespasian	Dec., 69-79	Imperator Caesar Vespasianus Augustus
Titus	79-81	Imperator Titus Caesar Vespasianus Augustus
Domitian	81-96	Imperator Caesar Domitianus Augustus
Nerva	96-98	Imperator Nerva Caesar Augustus
Trajan	98-117	Imperator Caesar Nerva Traianus Augustus
Hadrian	117-138	Imperator Caesar Traianus Hadrianus Augustus
Antoninus Pius	138-161	Imperator Caesar Titus Aelius Hadrianus Antoninus Augustus Pius
Marcus Aurelius	161-180	Imperator Caesar Marcus Aurelius Antoninus Augustus
Lucius Verus	161-169	Imperator Caesar Lucius Aurelius Verus Augustus
Commodus	180-192	Imperator Caesar Marcus Aurelius Commodus Antoninus Augustus
Pertinax	Jan.-Mar., 193	Imperator Caesar Publius Helvius Pertinax Augustus
Didius Julianus	Mar.-June, 193	Imperator Caesar Marcus Didius Severus Julianus Augustus
Septimius Severus	June, 193-211	Imperator Caesar Lucius Septimius Severus Pertinax Augustus
Caracalla	211-217	Imperator Caesar Marcus Aurelius Severus Antoninus Pius Augustus
Geta	211	Imperator Caesar Publius Septimius Geta Augustus
Macrinus	217-218	Imperator Caesar Marcus Opellius Severus Macrinus Augustus
Elagabalus	218-222	Imperator Caesar Marcus Aurelius Antoninus Augustus
Alexander Severus	222-235	Imperator Caesar Marcus Aurelius Severus Alexander Augustus
Maximinus Thrax	235-238	Imperator Caesar Gaius Iulius Verus Maximinus Augustus

THE ARISTOCRACY

The Senatorial Order

By the end of the reign of the emperor Augustus, the senatorial order was comprised of about 600 men and their families who, in conjunction with the emperor, were the primary legislative and governing body in ancient Rome. Entrance to the order remained extremely exclusive throughout Roman history. First, prospective senators were required to have property equaling at least 1,000,000 *sestertii*. Most senators had senatorial parents, but it was also possible to gain admission by being appointed to the Senate by the emperor or by being elected to the quaestorship, the most junior of the senatorial offices. Senators who were granted membership, rather than being born into it, were referred to as *novi homines* ("new men"), and gradually increased their numbers and influence in imperial Rome.

By the second century AD, the career of a senator followed a set course known as the *cursus honorum* ("course of offices"). During his career, a senator was appointed to a series of increasingly more prestigious positions. Young men who aspired to enter the Senate held several posts as they waited for their 24th birthday, the age at which they could run for their first senatorial office. Between the ages of 18 and 20, a young man could expect a post in the viginitivirate, twenty minor administrative posts held for one year. From there, a future senator would be promoted to an army post: namely, the tribunate of a legion (the equivalent to a commissioned officer). Every legion had six tribunes: one of senatorial rank and five of equestrian rank. At the age of 24, men of senatorial families (or those appointed or elected into the Senate) were eligible to run for the initial senatorial office, the quaestorship. Twenty quaestors were elected annually, and were in charge of the administration of state funds.

After the quaestorship, senators were required to wait five years before running for the praetorship, the next major step in the senatorial *cursus honorum*. After holding the quaestorship for a year, however, they were allowed to hold other positions (most notably, the aedileship or tribunate of the plebs), while awaiting the chance to run for praetor. Six aediles (primarily in charge of the upkeep of public property) and ten tribunes of the plebs (protectors of the people's interest within the Senate) were elected annually. Senators from patrician families (the oldest and most prestigious families in the aristocracy) were not eligible to hold four of the six aedile positions or any the tribunates, all of which were reserved for senators of plebeian descent.

At the age of 31, ex-quaestors became eligible for election to the praetorship. Eighteen praetors were elected annually; their main duties concerned the administration of the law courts. Ex-praetors, *i.e.*, those of praetorian rank, became eligible for a number of other posts, including the governorship of provinces. An important innovation of Augustus was the division of the provinces of the empire into two categories: those under the direct jurisdiction of the emperor and those that remained within the realm of the Senate. Augustus chose for himself primarily the provinces which were situated on the dangerous frontiers. This allowed him greater control over foreign policy. Not coincidentally, virtually the entire Roman military was also stationed in these provinces. While the governors of the more peaceful senatorial provinces (*e.g.* Gallia Lugdunensis and Cilicia) continued to be selected by lot (as during the Republic), the emperor personally selected the senators he sent to govern the imperial provinces. Because the emperor selected his own candidates, imperial favor and patronage became important factors at this point in the senator's career. Provinces were further divided into those governed by ex-praetors or ex-consuls. Only ex-consuls were allowed to govern the largest, most dangerous or wealthiest provinces (see below).

A senator normally held his consulship ten or more years after his praetorship. However, many posts would occupy an ex-praetor while he awaited the opportunity to run for consul. Most would command a legion (*legatus legionis*) and govern a province (either in a minor senatorial or imperial province); a number of other positions could be held as well, including civil administrative posts to oversee the state treasury or imperial roads. These posts had a term between one and three years. Senators would hold numerous posts with each usually bringing more responsibility than the one before.

At the age of 42, senators became eligible to be appointed to the office of consul, which was the chief senatorial magistracy of the state. Republican Rome was controlled by two annually elected consuls. Under the emperors, however, more consuls served per year, albeit still in pairs. This change allowed more people to hold the office and thereby created more senators who would be eligible for the offices of consular rank. The emperor and his heirs also frequently held the office. Appointment to the consulship was made exclusively by the emperor. Consulships were of two types: ordinary and suffect. Ordinary consuls entered office on January 1ˢᵗ and gave their names to the year (many inscriptions were dated by consular year). Suffect consuls were replacements made later in the year. By the end of the first century AD, most years saw three or four pairs of consuls. Some senators were favored enough by the emperor to hold the consulship twice

Dedication to the Trajanic senator Lucius Aemilius Karus (CIL 6.1333; ILS 1077), Capitoline Museum, Rome. Photo courtesy of the Archivio Fotografico dei Museo Capitolini, Soprintenza Archeologica di Roma.

or even three times, but most could expect only one consulship and a handful of consular posts.

Senators of consular rank, *i.e.*, ex-consuls, were eligible to hold the most important posts in the empire. As in the case of the ex-praetors, consular senators generally held a number of posts each lasting between one and three years. The most prestigious of these were the governorships of the important imperial provinces in the military zones on the northern and eastern frontiers (*e.g.* Germania, Pannonia and Syria). Consular senators could also be appointed to a number of offices, in which they oversaw various public works such as aqueducts, sewers, and temples. One of the most important of these magistracies was that of prefect of the city (*praefectus urbis*). This official was in charge of the city of Rome while the emperor was away; he also had judicial jurisdiction within the city. The most illustrious consular posts were the proconsulships of Africa or Asia, the two consular senatorial provinces. These particular proconsular positions generally were given to ex-consuls ten or more years after their consulship. A further mark of distinction for consular senators was being appointed to one of the major priesthoods (for example, the augurs, high priests (*pontifices*), and officials in charge of sacred functions and consulting the Sibylline Oracles (*quindecimviri sacris faciundis*).

The inscriptions chosen here illustrate a variety of senatorial careers from the first 250 years of the Empire (from the late 1st century BC to the early 2nd century AD). All demonstrate that the senator gained an advantage from a favorable standing with the emperor, which was a necessity for any senator who hoped to reach the highest rungs of the senatorial ladder. For example, Lucius Munatius Plancus of the first century BC was a friend of Julius Caesar who remained close to the triumvirs and the future first emperor Augustus. The career of the patrician Gaius Ummidius

Durmius Quadratus started off slowly (note the large number of praetorian posts under Tiberius and Caligula before his consulship). Claudius, however, gave him two very important military posts in Illyricum and Syria. Gnaeus Domitius Afer and his brother sided with Vespasian in the civil war of AD 68/69. After Vespasian's victory, the new emperor granted the brothers numerous important posts, especially in the province of Africa. Pliny the Younger, one of the great literati of the early second century AD, never held any post in a major military province, but he did hold numerous important civil assignments. Although he was born an equestrian, his adoptive father's friends in the Senate won him election to the quaestorship. He then came to the attention of the emperor Domitian, who helped him quickly reach the praetorship and make up for lost time. His career slowed down again, however, under Trajan. P. Aelius Hadrianus, who would later become emperor himself, was originally from the same region of Spain as the emperor Trajan. He had a slow career under Domitian and Nerva, when he held a rare three military tribunates before he became quaestor under Trajan. Hadrian remained close to Trajan during both Dacian wars, first as a traveling companion in the court, and then as a legionary commander and provincial governor. After his consulship in 108, Hadrian went on to hold numerous consular military posts (not listed on the inscription), including the governorship of Syria. In these positions, Hadrian was assisting Trajan in the invasion of Parthia. See also, in the section on the equestrian order, the career of Tiberius Julius Celsus Polemaeanus, who was granted senatorial status by Vespasian, and went on to an impressive senatorial career.

1. *L. Munatius Plancus,*
General of the Late Republic

<table>
<tr><td>*CIL* 10.6087; *ILS* 886</td><td>Caieta, Campania, Italy</td></tr>
<tr><td>Plaque on a Mausoleum</td><td>Late Republic/early Augustus</td></tr>
</table>

Plancus was an early supporter of the family of Octavian. During the 50s and early 40s BC, he served under Julius Caesar in the Gallic and civil wars. When Caesar was dictator, he continued to hold high political offices, including the governorship of the newly-formed province of Gaul. After Caesar's death, Plancus invaded the neighboring territory of the Raeti tribe. In 43 BC he joined the cause of the triumvirs: Octavian (the future emperor Augustus), Marcus Antonius (Marc Antony), and Marcus Aemilius Lepidus. When Augustus and Antony came to blows in 31 BC at Actium, Plancus sided with Octavian. In 27 BC, as senator, he initiated the motion in the Senate for Octavian to be named Augustus. Plancus' career exemplifies the heights to which a senator could aspire before Augustus' creation of the empire in 27 BC Plancus was among the last senators not directly connected with the imperial family to receive three supreme acclamations: that of imperator, censor, as well as the right to hold a triumph.

L · MVNATIVS · L · F · L · N · L · PRON
PLANCVS · COS · CENS · IMP · ITER · VII · VIR
EPVLON · TRIVMP · EX · RAETIS · AEDEM · SATVRNI
FECIT · DE · MANIBIS · AGROS · DIVISIT · IN · ITALIA
BENEVENTI · IN · GALLIA · COLONIAS · DEDVXIT
LVGVDVNVM · ET · RAVRICAM

* * *

L(ucius) Munatius L(uci) f(ilius) L(uci) n(epos) L(uci) pron(epos) Plancus, co(n)s(ul), cens(or), imp(erator) iter, VIIvir epulon(um), triump(hator) ex Raetis, aedem Saturni fecit de manibis, agros divisit in Italia Beneventi, in Gallia colonias deduxit Lugudunum et Rauricam.

* * *

Lucius Munatius Plancus, son of Lucius, grandson of Lucius, great-grandson of Lucius,[1] consul,[2] censor,[3] acclaimed triumphant general twice, one of the seven men in charge of religious banquets, triumphed over the Raetii,[4] built the temple of Saturn out of war booty,[5] apportioned territory in Italy at Beneventum,[6] established the colonies of Lugdunum and Raurica in Gaul.[7]

1   Note the lineage. The series of ancestors with the *praenomen* of Lucius indicates that Plancus was the fourth generation of eldest sons.
2   He was consul in 42 BC with the triumvir L. Aemilius Lepidus. Plancus' inscription stresses his consular career and does not mention his career before the consulship.
3   In 22 BC with Paullus Aemilius Lepidus.
4   In 43 BC, after his time as governor of Gaul.
5   Refers to booty taken in the war with the Raeti after Caesar's assassination.
6   Probably in 42 BC when the triumvirs earmarked land belonging to several towns, including Beneventum, for confiscation and re-allocation to soldiers after the civil wars.
7   While he was governor in the 40s BC.

2.   *C. Ummidius Durmius Quadratus, Julio-Claudian Legate*

CIL 10.5182; *ILS* 972   Casinum, Latium, Italy
Statue Base   1st Century AD

Quadratus was an important senator during the Julio-Claudian period. The historian Tacitus describes his actions in the province of Syria during the reign of Nero (*Ann.* 12.45, 48, 54; 13.8-9; 14.26). The inscription generally lists his offices in descending order (from latest to oldest), but some are out of order.

C · VMMIDIO · C · F · TER · DVRMIO
QVADRATO · COS · XV · VIR · S · F
LEG · TI · CAESARIS · AVG · PROV · LVSIT
LEG · DIVI · CLAVDI · IN · ILLYRICO · EIVSD · ET
NERONIS · CAESARIS · AVG · IN · SYRIA · PROCOS
PROVINC · CYPRI · Q · DIVI · AVG · ET · TI · CAESARIS
AVG · AED · CVR · PR · AER · X · VIR · STLIT · IVD · CVRAT
TABVLAR · PVBLICAR · PRAEF · FRVM · DANDI · EX · S · C

* * *

C(aio) Ummidio C(ai) f(ilio) Ter(etina tribu) Durmio Quadrato, co(n) s(uli), XVvir(o) s(acris) f(aciundis), leg(ato) Ti(beri) Caesaris Aug(usti) prov(inciae) Lusit(aniae), leg(ato) divi Claudi in Illyrico, eiusd(em) et Neronis Caesaris Aug(usti) in Syria, proco(n)s(uli) provinc(iae) Cypri, q(uaestori) divi Aug(usti) et Ti(beri) Caesaris Aug(usti), aed(ili) cur(uli), pr(aefecto) aer(arii), Xvir(o) stlit(ibus) iud(icandis), curat(or) tabular(um) publicar(um), praef(ecto) frum(enti) dandi ex S(enatus) c(onsulto).

* * *

To Gaius Ummidius Durmius Quadratus, son of Gaius, of the Teretina tribe, consul, one of the 15 men in charge of the performance of the sacred rites, legate of Tiberius Caesar Augustus of the province of Lusitania,[1] legate of the divine Claudius in Illyricum, legate in Syria of the same emperor and of Nero Caesar Augustus,[2] proconsul of the province of Cyprus, quaestor of the divine Augustus and Tiberius Caesar Augustus,[3] curule aedile, prefect of the public treasury, one of the ten men in charge of hearing legal cases,[4] caretaker of the public records office, prefect for the distribution of grain by decree of the Senate.

1   He was appointed *legatus* of the province of Lusitania late in the reign of Tiberius. He was still legate there in May, 37, when he administered the oath of allegiance on the succession of Caligula (*CIL* 2.172; *ILS* 190). He probably continued in his post under Caligula, but the emperor's name was not included alongside Tiberius' (most likely because of Caligula's infamous *postmortem* reputation).

2   Tacitus indicates that his legateship in Syria began in 51. He died while he was governor (probably before 60).

3   Because both Augustus and Tiberius are mentioned as granting him the position, he probably held it in 14. Tiberius was not deified after his death and is therefore not listed as *divus* on the inscription. When a senator is listed as holding the post of an emperor, it means that he was nominated by the emperor himself, a guarantee of election.

4   The inscription lists no legionary legateship (*legatus legionis*). Either it was omitted for the sake of space or Quadratus did not hold that position. By the end of the first century, however, Senators generally served as regional legate before their praetorship.

Summary of Quadratus' Career

c. AD 10: *Decemvir Stlitibus Iudicandis* (a member of the board of ten men who presided over legal cases which determined whether an individual was considered slave or free).

14: *Quaestor*

16: *Aedilis Curulis* (one of the two senatorial positions as aedile).

c. 21/22: *Praetor*

20s: *Praefectus Aerarii (Saturni)* (prefect of the public treasury, also called the treasury of Saturn, since it was located in the foundation under the temple of Saturn).

20s: *Curator tabularum publicarum* (an officer in charge of the public records office. Tiberius created the office in 16.

20s or 30s: *Praefectus frumenti dandi* (prefect of the distribution of the public grain supply).

30s: Proconsul of the senatorial province of Cyprus; Cyprus was one of the least important of the praetorian imperial provinces.

?-37/38: *Legatus* of the imperial province of Lusitania, in Spain.

Late 30s/early 40s: *Consul Suffectus.*

Reign of Claudius: *Legatus* of the imperial province of Illyricum; Illyricum was an important military province on the Danube, just south of the provinces of Pannonia and Moesia.

51-? (Claudius to Nero): *Legatus* of the imperial province of Syria. Syria was one of the most important provincial commands in the empire. It stood on the border with Parthia and was close to Egypt, the primary supplier of grain to Rome. Only the emperors' most trusted friends and family members held this post.

3.   *Cn. Domitius Afer, Flavian Legate*

CIL 11.5210; *ILS* 990   Fulginia, Umbria, Italy
Marble Tablet   1st Century AD

This tablet is a dedicatory inscription from a statue base erected in Domitius' honor by his hometown of Fulginia, Italy. Domitius was one of the senators who survived the civil wars of 69 by supporting the victorious Flavians. Both he and his brother are also known from the letters of their contemporary, Pliny the Younger. The Domitii remained an important and well-connected family throughout the late first and early second centuries. He adopted his niece, Domitia Lucilla, after his brother's death. Lucilla's daughter married Annius Verus and was the mother of the future emperor Marcus Aurelius.

CN · DOMITIO · SEX · F · VOLT
AFRO · TITIO · MARCELLO

CVRVIO · LVCANO
COS · PROCOS · PROVINCIAE · AFRICAE
LEGATO · EIVSDEM · PROVINCIAE · TVL[LI]
FRATRIS · SVI · SEPTEMVIRO · EPVLONVM
[ITEM] · PRAETORIO · LEGATO · PROVINCIAE · AFR[I]C[AE]
IMP · CAES · AVG · PRAEF · AVXILIORVM · OMNIVM
ADVERSVS · GERMANOS · DONATO · AB
IMP · VESPASIANO · AVG · ET · T · CAESAR · AVG · F · CORONIS
MVRALI · VALLARI · AVREIS · HASTIS · PVRIS · III
VEXILLIS · III · ADLECTO · INTER · PATRICIOS · PRAETORI
TR · PL · QVAEST · PROPRAETORE · PROVINCIAE · AFRIC[AE]
TR] · MIL · LEG · V · ALAVD · IIIIVIR · VIARVM · CVRANDAR · PATRONO
OPTIMO
D · D

* * *

Cn(aeo) Domitio Sex(ti) f(ilio) Volt(inia tribu) Afro Titio Marcello Curvio Lucano, co(n)s(uli), proco(n)s(uli) provinciae Africae, legato eiusdem provinciae Tul[li] fratris sui, septemviro epulonum, [item] praetorio legato provinciae Afr[i]c[ae] imp(eratoris) Caes(aris) Aug(usto), praef(ecto) auxiliorum omnium adversus Germanos, donato ab imp(eratore) Vespasiano Aug(usto) et T(ito) Caesar(e) Aug(usti) f(ilio): coronis murali vallari aureis hastis puris III vexillis III, adlecto inter patricios, praetori, tr(ibuno) pl(ebis), quaest(ori) propraetore provinciae Afric[ae], [tr(ibuno)] mil(itum) leg(ionis) V Alaud(ae), IIIIvir(o) viarum curandar(um), patrono optimo, d(ecreto) d(ecurionum).

* * *

To Gnaeus Domitius Afer Titius Marcellus Curvius Lucanus, son of Sextus, of the Voltinia tribe, consul, proconsul of the province of Africa, legate of the same province while his brother Tullius was proconsul, one of the seven men in charge of public feasts, also[1] praetorian legate of the province of Africa of the emperor Caesar Augustus,[2] prefect of all of the auxiliaries in the war against the Germans, granted military decorations by the emperors Vespasian Augustus and Titus Caesar, the son of the emperor: wall, rampart, and gold crowns, three silver spears, three banners;[3] adlected among the patricians,[4] praetor, tribune of the plebs, pro-praetorian quaestor of the province of Africa, military tribune of the 5th legion Alauda, one of the four men in charge of taking care of the roads; dedicated to their best patron, by decree of the town council.[5]

1   It is possible that the word "FETIALI" was lost in the gap between the end of line 6 and the beginning of line 7. A *fetialis* was one of the minor priesthoods who acted as Rome's representative in diplomacy with other peoples. They also carried out the rituals that ceremonially signaled the start and end of war. There were twenty *fetiales*, originally all of patrician background, but plebeians may have been allowed to join in later centuries.

2   He was in charge of the only legion stationed in North Africa, the 3rd legion *Augusta*. Another inscription dedicated to Domitius indicates that he held this position when he was still merely designated as a future praetor, perhaps about 69. In 68, the commander of the legion, L. Clodius Macer, had attempted to usurp the throne from the recently appointed Galba.

3   The date of the reception of these awards is uncertain, but probably came in 70, after the end of the civil war.

4   By Vespasian *c.* 73, when that emperor accepted the power of a censor to reward his supporters in the civil war.

5   The decurions were the municipal town council whose permission was required for the erection of any public monuments, such as statue bases.

Summary of Afer's Career

Reign of Nero (AD 54-68): *Quattuorvir viarum curandarum* (a member of the board of four men in charge of the upkeep of the roads).

Nero: Tribune of the 5th legion *Alauda*, stationed in Germany Inferior.

Nero: *Quaestor* in the province of Africa. The consular senatorial provinces (Asia and Africa) had their own quaestors.

Nero: Tribune of the Plebs.

69: *Praetor* and praetorian *legatus* of Africa (*i.e.*, *legatus* of the 3rd legion *Augusta*); he seems to have held these two posts together (see note above).

c. 73-75: Prefect of the auxiliaries in Gaul, a post held jointly with his brother.

Reign of Vespasian (AD 69-79): *Consul suffectus*; the date is uncertain, but was probably late in the reign of Vespasian.

c. 82/83: *Legatus* of Africa, held while his brother was the proconsul.

c. 85: *Proconsul* of the senatorial province of Africa.

4.   *Career of Pliny the Younger*

CIL 5.5262; *ILS* 2927	Comum, Po Valley, Italy
Building Dedication	2nd Century AD

This inscription is our best evidence for the complete career of Pliny the Younger, whose public and private letters have been preserved. The original inscription was a large marble slab which was broken into six parts in later times and reused as building material. Transcripts of four of the fragments, then in the Church of S. Ambrosius in Comum, were made in manuscripts in the Middle Ages. Three of those known fragments have since disappeared, leaving only the medieval transcripts as evidence for their contents. Although fragmentary, it is often possible to reconstruct much of the text from the lost fragments.

C · PLINIVS · L · F · OVF · CAECILIVS · [SECVNDVS · COS]
AVGVR · LEGAT · PROPR · PROVINCIAE · PON[TI · ET · BITHYNIAE]
CONSVLARI · POTESTA[T] · IN · EAM · PROVINCIAM · E[X · S · C · MISSVS · AB]
IMP · CAESAR · NERVA · TRAIANO · AVG · GERMAN[ICO · DACICO · P · P]
CVRATOR · ALVEI · TI[B]ERIS · ET · RIPARVM · E[T · CLOACAR · VRB]
PRAEF · AERARI · SATV[R]NI · PRAEF · AERARI · MIL[IT · PR · TRIB · PL]
QVAESTOR · IMP · SEVIR · EQVITVM · [ROMANORVM]
TRIB · MILIT · LEG · [III] · GALLICA[E · XVIR · STLI]
TIB · IVDICAND · THERM[AS · EX · HS · ......] · ADIECTIS · IN
ORNATVM · HS · CCC · [· .... · ET · EO · AMP]LIVS · IN · TVTELA[M]
HS · CC · T · F · I · [ITEM · IN · ALIMENTA] · LIBERTOR · SVORVM · HOMIN · C
HS · XVIII · LXVI · DCLXVI · REI · [P · LEGAVIT · QVORVM · INC]REMENT ·
POSTEA · AD · EPVLVM
[P]LEB · VRBAN · VOLVIT · PERTIN[ERE · ......· ITEM · VIVV]S · DEDIT · IN ·
ALIMENT · PVEROR
ET · PVELLAR · PLEB · VRBAN · HS · [D · ITEM · BYBLIOTHECAM · ET] · IN ·
TVTELAM · BYBLIOTHE
CAE · HS · C

* * *

C(aius) Plinius L(uci) f(ilius) Ouf(entina) Caecilius [Secundus,
co(n)s(ul),] augur, legat(us) propr(aetore) provinciae Pon[ti et Bithyniae]
consulari potesta[t(e)] in eam provinciam e[x s(enatus) c(onsulto) missus
ab] imp(eratore) Caesar(e) Nerva Traiano Aug(usto) German[ico Dacico
p(atre) p(atriae)], curator alvei Ti[b]eris et riparum e[t cloacar(um)
urb(is)], praef(ectus) aerari Satu[r]ni, praef(ectus) aerari mil[it(aris),
pr(aetor), trib(unus) pl(ebis),] quaestor imp(eratoris), sevir equitum
[Romanorum], trib(unus) milit(um) leg(ionis) [III] Gallica[e, XVir
stli]tib(us) iudicand(is), therm[as ex HS ......], adiectis in ornatum HS
CCC [.... et eo amp]lius in tutela[m] HS CC, t(estamento) f(ieri) i(ussit),
[item in alimenta] libertor(um) suorum homin(um) C HS XVIII LXVI
DCLXVI rei [p(ublicae) legavit, quorum inc]rement(a) postea ad epulum
[p]leb(is) urban(ae) volvit pertin[ere ...... item vivu]s dedit in aliment(a)
pueror(um) et puellar(um) pleb(is) urban(ae) HS [D, item bybliothecam
et] in tutelam bybliothecae HS C.

* * *

*Gaius Plinius Caecilius Secundus, son of Lucius, of the Oufentina
tribe,¹ consul, augur, legate with pro-praetorian powers of the province
of Pontus and Bithynia, sent with consular powers to that province, a
position granted by decree of the Senate and approved by the emperor
Caesar Nerva Trajan Augustus Germanicus Dacicus, father of his
country; also caretaker of the course of the Tiber and its banks and of the
sewers of Rome, prefect of the treasury of Saturn, prefect of the military
treasury, praetor, tribune of the plebs, quaestor of the emperor, one of
the six men in charge of a squadron of Roman knights, military tribune
of the 3ʳᵈ legion Gallica, one of the 10 men in charge of hearing legal*

cases, requested in his will that baths be built out of funds equal to [?] sestertii, with 300,000 sestertii added for their decoration ... and that a further 200,000 sestertii be added for their upkeep. Also, he bequeathed to the town (of Comum) 1,866,666 sestertii for the support of 100 of his freedmen, the interest of which amount he wished in the future to be used for a banquet of the urban plebs (of Rome) [...]. Also, while still alive, he gave 500,000 toward the alimenta of boys and girls of the urban plebs,[2] and 100,000 sestertii also a library and for the upkeep of the library.

1   Pliny, born c. AD 62, was originally the son of a L. Caecilius Secundus, but after his father's death he was adopted by C. Plinius Secundus, also known as Pliny the Elder.
2   In the late first and early second centuries, emperors set up a welfare system in which proceeds from the rents on public land was used to provide for orphaned children.

Summary of Pliny's Career

c. 81: *Decemvir Stlitibus Iudicandis* (a member of the board of ten men who presided over legal cases involving the status of slaves).

c. 82: *Legatus* of the 3rd *Gallica*, stationed in Syria.

83 or 84: *Sevir equitum Romanorum* (a position held by young equestrians, especially those with hope of eventually entering the senatorial order).

86/87 (perhaps a few years later): *Quaestor*.

88 or 89: Tribune of the Plebs.

89 or 90: *Praetor*.

96/97 or 98: *Praefectus Aerarii Militaris* (prefect of the military treasury).

98-100: *Praefectus Aerarii Saturni* (prefect of the public treasury).

100: *Consul suffectus*, held in September to October of that year.

103: *Augur* (one of the major priesthoods). This office was open only to ex-consuls.

104/105-106/107: *Curator alvei Tiberis et riparum et cloacarum urbis* (caretaker of the bed and banks of the Tiber and of the city sewers).

109-111 (or 110-112 or 111-113): *Legatus* (governor) of the province of Pontus and Bithynia; the tenth book of Pliny's letters contains Pliny's official correspondence with the emperor Trajan while serving in this position.

5. *The Future Emperor Hadrian*

CIL 3.550; *ILS* 308   Athens, Greece
Statue Base   AD 112

The city of Athens erected this dedication to the future emperor Hadrian in AD 112, five years before he became emperor. It was discovered in the Theater of Dionysius where it had probably stood among the statues of the great patrons and leaders of Athens. The offices are listed in descending order. The text was dedicated in AD 112 when Hadrian was made Archon of Athens. After a relatively slow start (note the unusual number of military tribunates), Hadrian's career demonstrates great imperial patronage, as he held some of the most important posts in the empire. He also stayed in close proximity to his relative and fellow Spaniard, the emperor Trajan. On his deathbed in 117, Trajan adopted Hadrian and named him his successor.

P • AELIO • P • F • SERG • HADRIANO
COS • VII • VIRO • EPVLONVM • SODALI • AVGVSTALI
LEG • PRO • PR • IMP • NERVAE • TRAIANI
CAESARIS • AVG • GERMANICI • DACICI • PANNONIAE
INFERIORIS • PRAETORI • EODEMQVE
TEMPORE • LEG • LEG • I • MINERVIAE • P • F • BELLO
DACICO • ITEM • TRIB • PLEB • QVAESTORI • IMPERATORIS
TRAIANI • ET • COMITI • EXPEDITIONIS • DACICAE • DONIS
MILITARIBVS • AB • EO • DONATO • BIS • TRIB • LEG • II
ADIVTRICIS • P • F • ITEM • LEGIONIS • V • MACEDONICAE
ITEM • LEGIONIS • XXII • PRIMIGENIAE • P • F • SEVIRO
TVRMAE • EQ • R • PRAEF • FERIARVM • LATINARVM • XVIRO • S • I

* * *

P(ublio) Aelio P(ubli) f(ilio) Serg(ia tribu) Hadriano, co(n)s(uli), VIIviro epulonum, sodali Augustali, leg(ato) pro pr(aetore) imp(eratoris) Nervae Traiani Caesaris Aug(usti) Germanici Dacici Pannoniae Inferioris, praetori eodemque tempore leg(ato) leg(ionis) I Minerviae p(iae) f(idelis) bello Dacico, item trib(uno) pleb(is), quaestori imperatoris Traiani et comiti expeditionis Dacicae, donis militaribus ab eo donato bis, trib(uno) leg(ionis) II Adiutricis p(iae) f(idelis) item legionis V Macedonicae item legionis XXII Primigeniae p(iae) f(idelis), seviro turmae eq(uitum) R(omanorum), praef(ecto) feriarum Latinarum, Xviro s(tlitibus) i(udicandis).

* * *

To Publius Aelius Hadrianus, son of Publius, of the Sergia tribe, consul, one of the seven men in charge of public banquets, priest of Augustus, legate of Pannonia Inferior with pro-praetorian powers of the emperor Nerva Trajan Caesar Augustus Germanicus Dacicus, praetor and legate of the 1st legion Minervia at the same time, tribune of the people, quaestor of the emperor Trajan and companion on the Dacian expedition, endowed with military decorations by him (Trajan) twice, tribune of the 2nd legion Adiutrix, loyal and faithful, and of the 5th legion Macedonica, and of the 22nd legion Primigenia, loyal and faithful, one of the six commanders of a contingent of Roman equestrians, prefect of the Latin festival, one of the ten men in charge of the centumviral courts.

Summary of Hadrian's Career

c. 95: Tribune of the 2nd legion *Adiutrix*, stationed in Moesia Superior.

c. 96: Tribune of the 5th legion *Macedonica*, stationed in Moesia Superior.

c. 97: Tribune of the 22nd legion *Primigenia*, stationed in Germania Superior (or perhaps in Inferior). He was there when Nerva adopted Trajan.

101: *Quaestor*.

105: Tribune of the Plebs.

106: *Praetor* and *legatus* of the 1st legion *Minervia*; he held these posts at the same time (an unusual situation). The 1st legion *Minervia* fought in the second Dacian war.

107: *Legatus* of the imperial province of Pannonia Inferior; in 106/107, Trajan divided the military province of Pannonia (a consular imperial province) into two provinces: Superior and Inferior. Superior remained consular, but Inferior became praetorian. Hadrian was the first governor of this new province.

108: *Consul suffectus*.

Between 108 and 117: *Septemvir Epulonum*, one of the major priesthoods held by ex-consuls.

Between 108 and 117: *Sodalis Augustalis*, a minor priestly college instituted by Tiberius following the death of Augustus.

The Equestrian Order

In the early days of the Republic, the equestrians had served as the Roman cavalry. By the late Republic, however, the order was composed of wealthy aristocrats whose money was based in business and trade rather than in property and agriculture. Many worked as government contractors in the provinces where they, for example, collected taxes and oversaw building projects. Augustus began to appoint members of this social class to positions in the Roman military officer corps and the lower levels of the imperial bureaucracy. Like members of the senatorial order, prospective equestrians had to meet a property qualification (probably 400,000 *sestertii*). The number of equestrians was much larger than that of the senators. Many cities in the more Romanized provinces such as Gaul, Asia and Syria were occupied in part by hundreds of equestrian class residents.

In addition to those families with equestrian ancestry, there were three major sources of new equestrians. Many members of the municipal aristocracy in Italy and even in the provinces received equestrian status from the central Roman government as a means of furthering the process of Romanization. Second, children of military veterans were more likely to hold posts as centurions in the legions or the urban garrison of Rome; those who received these positions could be eligible for further promotion to chief centurion, which in turn would allow them to be elevated to equestrian status (see below for more on military promotions and officers). Finally, the children of wealthy freedmen, especially those from the imperial household, increasingly entered the equestrian order during the imperial period. Legally, ex-slaves could not hold office or enter the higher social statuses. The children of freedmen, however, were not bound by such restrictions and could enter a public career if their families were wealthy and enjoyed imperial patronage.

In Rome, there were three categories of equestrians. The first category included the equestrians to whom the emperor had granted the "public horse". They had no official duties but were required, at least during the early empire, to participate in an annual parade of the equestrians. The second category included the four (later five) boards (*decuriae*) of jurors, each 1,000 men strong. The equestrian jurors served in the law courts which tried various civil and criminal cases. The third category was made up of the equestrians who served as high-ranking military officers and civil administrators. With regard to this last category, equestrians were eligible for a wide assortment of posts from the chief centurionate of a legion to the prefecture of the Praetorian Guard.

Unlike the senatorial career, which was designed to be held over a single lifetime, the equestrian career encompassed a very wide range of offices and posts whose duties ran from the very minor positions in the army to some of the most powerful positions in government. Because of the extreme disparity in responsibilities between the lowest and highest tiers, the equestrian career was designed to be furthered over multiple generations. For people that did not achieve equestrian status from birth or imperial prerogative, prospective equestrians would not only act on behalf of their own careers, but also the potential careers of their children and grandchildren. The first generation would take the steps that would put their children into a position to achieve equestrian status. This normally occurred when a soldier who had served in a legion re-enlisted in the hopes of being made a centurion (see the chapter on the military for more details on the centurionate). The second generation would then often begin their military careers at the rank of centurion, often beginning with or reaching the rank of chief centurion, a rank that automatically enrolled him in the equestrian order. From there, the equestrian (or his children) could hope to enter the lowest levels of the imperial equestrian bureaucracy by serving as a junior military officer (tribunes, commanders of auxiliary units). Then they could be promoted to a middle tier position, including the imperial procuratorships (in charge of imperial estates, fleets, and minor provinces) and finally to the high level prefecture (of Egypt, the grain supply, night watch, and Praetorian Guard).

The inscriptions chosen for this collection illustrate careers which span the complete range of the equestrian career. Titus Vennonius Aebutianus was a recipient of the public horse and a juror in Rome. Gaius Baebius Atticus became an equestrian by holding the post of chief centurion in a legion. He advanced rapidly through the junior equestrian military posts and eventually became the procurator of the province of Noricum. He then returned to his hometown and entered the municipal aristocracy. Gnaeus Octavius Titinius Capito and Sextus Afranius Burrus each began their careers as higher-ranking military officers (the typical starting point for sons of equestrians and for municipal aristocrats who wished to

Statue base of the primuspilus and equestrian commander M. Tarquitius Saturninus (CIL 11.3801; ILS 2692), Ostia (courtesy of the Archivio Fotografico della Soprintendenza per i Beni Archeologici di Ostia).

enter imperial service). They then served their time as procurators and eventually achieved the upper echelons of imperial service (Capito as an imperial secretary and prefect of the night watch, and Burrus as praetorian prefect). Tiberius Julius Celsus Polemaeanus, a man from the Greek East, was just beginning his equestrian career when he and his legion acclaimed Vespasian emperor during the civil war of AD 68/69. Vespasian rewarded him with senatorial status, and Polemaeanus went on to hold the highest offices open to Roman senatorial aristocrats. See also the chapter on the Roman army, the inscription of C. Aclutius Gallus, who served as tribune of two legions.

6.   *Titus Vennonius Aebutianus, Equestrian with the Public Horse*

CIL 6.1635; *ILS* 5006; *AE* 1979, 19   Rome
            Tombstone   Unknown

This is an example of an equestrian who not only had been given the *equus publicus*, but also served as a juror in Rome. Aebutianus was originally a member of the municipal aristocracy as shown by his posts in some of the towns of Latium.

> T · VENNONIO · T · F · STELL
> AEBVTIANO · PATRONO · ET
> MVNICIPI · COL · AVG · [T]AVR
> EQ · R · EQ · P · IVD · EX · V · DEC
> SELECTO · CVR · R · P · ALB
> POMPEIANORVM · L · L
> PONTIF · EIVSDE · SACERD
> MVNIA · Q · F · CELERINA · VXOR
> MARITO · KARISSIMO

* * *

T(ito) Vennonio T(iti) f(ilio) Stell(atina tribu) Aebutiano, patrono et municipi col(oniae) Aug(ustae) [T]aur(inorum), eq(uiti) R(omano) eq(uo) p(ublico), iud(ici) ex V dec(uriis) selecto, cur(atori) r(ei) p(ublicae) Alb(ensium) Pompeianorum, L(aurenti) L(avinati), pontif(ici) eiusde(m) sacerd(oti), Munia Q(uinti) f(ilia) Celerina uxor marito [c]larissimo.

* * *

To Titus Vennonius Aebutianus, son of Titus, of the Stellatina tribe, patron and citizen of the colony of Augusta Taurinorum,[1] Roman equestrian with the public horse, selected as juror in the five boards of jurors, caretaker of the state of the Albenses Pompeiani[2] and of the district of Laurentum and Lavinium, priest of the same district;[3] Munia Celerina, daughter of Quintus, his wife, dedicated this to her dearest husband.[4]

1   The modern town of Torino in the shadow of the Alps in northwestern Italy.
2   This was a region in Latium, just south of Ostia (near Laurentum and Lavinium).
3   Municipal magistrates, on the model of the senatorial magistrates in Rome, also held prestigious priesthoods in their towns.
4   Laurentum was on the sea-coast not far from Rome. It was six miles from the town of Lavinium, and the two towns seemed to have shared certain magistrates and priesthoods.

7.   *C. Baebius Atticus, Procurator of Claudius*

CIL 5.1838; *ILS* 1349	Julium Carnicum, Italy
Bronze Tablet from a Statue Base	1st Century AD

This inscription is one of two statue bases with bronze dedicatory tablets (the second tablet has the same text as the current inscription, but is much more fragmentary). Atticus is a good example of a municipal aristocrat who entered imperial service and earned the rank of equestrian. He was originally from the northeastern corner of Italy, in the Alps. After leaving home, he held numerous posts in the provinces around northern Italy. After retiring from service, he returned to his hometown and became a town magistrate. While holding this office, the people of his town honored him with this statue.

C · BAEBIO · P · F · CLA
ATTICO
II · VIR · I · [D] · PRIMOPIL
LEG · V · MACEDONIC · PRAEF
[CI]VITATIVM · MOESIAE · ET
TREBALLI[AE · PRAEF] · [CI]VITAT
IN · ALPIB · MARITVMIS · T[R] · MIL · COH
VIII · PR · PRIMOPIL · ITER · PROCVRATOR
TI · CLAVDI · CAESARIS · AVG · GERMANICI
IN · NORICO
CIVITAS
SAEVATVM · ET · LAIANCORVM

* * *

C(aio) Baebio P(ubli) f(ilio) Cla(udia tribu) Attico, IIvir(o) i(ure) [d(icundo)], primopil(o) leg(ionis) V macedonic(ae), praef(ecto) [ci]vitatium Moesiae et Treballi[ae, praef(ecto) ci]vitat(ium) in Alpib(us) maritumis, t[r](ibuno) mil(itum) coh(ortis) VIII pr(aetoria), primopil(o) iter, procurator(i) Ti(beri) Claudi Caesaris Aug(usti) Germanici in Norico; civitas Saevatum et Laiancorum.

* * *

To Gaius Baebius Atticus, son of Publius, of the Claudia tribe, one of the two town magistrates with jurisdiction,[1] chief centurion of the 5th legion Macedonica,[2] prefect of the cities of Moesia and Treballia,[3] prefect of the cities in the maritime Alps,[4] military tribune of the 8th praetorian cohort,[5] chief centurion a second time,[6] procurator[7] of Tiberius Claudius Caesar Augustus Germanicus[8] in Noricum;[9] the city of the Saevates and Laianci dedicated this.[10]

1   This was the most prestigious post in his hometown, and so was listed first (it was probably also his last office).
2   The chief centurion of a legion held his post for one year. The rank guaranteed admission to the equestrian order, and was the starting point for equestrians who wished to achieve higher military or political

positions. The 5th legion *Macedonica* was stationed in Moesia on the Danube for much of the first century.

3   In the same province in which he had served as centurion.

4   The prefectures of cities were low-level equestrian positions which oversaw the administration of justice in the provinces.

5   The tribunate in the garrison of Rome was a requirement for promotion to higher ranks. By the second century, it was common for young equestrians to hold one tribunate in each of the three corps in Rome: the night watch (*vigiles*), the urban cohorts, and the Praetorian Guard.

6   It was also very common for equestrians who had gained their rank from holding the chief centurionate in a legion to hold a second primipilate (*i.e.*, the post of chief centurion) before advancing to the more prestigious military posts and procuratorships.

7   The three levels of procurators were distinguished by salary. Minor procurators were in charge of the imperial estates and properties, or the minor provincial fleets. They received 60,000 *sestertii* per year. The medium grade procuratorships received 100,000 *sestertii* per year and were responsible for minor provinces (like Noricum and Judea), or major provincial fleets. The highest ranking procurators received 200,000 (or even 300,000) *sestertii* per year. They held only the most important equestrian provinces, and commanded the two fleets at Misenum and Ravenna.

8   The emperor Claudius.

9   He is the first attested governor of the province of Noricum. Atticus skipped a number of posts in the equestrian career (such as command of an auxiliary unit and a lesser procuratorship). This was probably because of Atticus' knowledge of the area. Also, the career structure was not as predetermined in the early first century as it was later.

10   The Saevates and Laianci lived in the Alps in the northwestern portion of Italy, near Noricum, where Julium Carnicum was located.

8.   *Cn. Octavius Titinius Capito, Secretary of Three Emperors*

CIL 6.798; *ILS* 1448   Rome
Marble Tablet   Early 2nd Century AD

This inscription, probably part of a statue base, was discovered near the Circus Flaminius in the Campus Martius. Capito began his career in the military, but quickly was transferred to the imperial court, where he served as an imperial secretary for three emperors: Domitian, Nerva and Trajan. He was known to Pliny the Younger, who called him a "man of letters".

CN · OCTAVIVS · TITINIVS · CAPITO
PRAEF · COHORTIS · TRIB · MILIT · DONAT
HASTA · PVRA · CORONA · VALLARI · PROC · AB

EPISTVLIS · ET · A · PATRIMONIO · ITERVM · AB
EPISTVLIS · DIVI · NERVAE · EODEM · AVCTORE
EX · S·C · PRAETORIIS · ORNAMENTIS · AB · EPISTVL
TERTIO ·IMP ·NERVAE ·CAESAR ·TRAIANI ·AVG ·GER
PRAEF · VIGILVM · VOLCANO · D · D

* * *

Cn(aeus) Octavius Titinius Capito, praef(ectus) cohortis, trib(unus) milit(um), donat(us) hasta pura, corona vallari, proc(urator), ab epistulis et a patrimonio, iterum ab epistulis divi Nervae eodem auctore ex s(enatus) c(onsulto) praetoriis ornamentis, ab epistul(is) tertio imp(eratoris) Nervae Caesar(is) Traiani Aug(usti) Ger(manici), praef(ectus) vigilum, Volcano d(onum) d(edit).

* * *

Gnaeus Octavius Titinius Capito, prefect of an auxiliary cohort,[1] military tribune,[2] granted military decorations: the silver spear and rampart crown,[3] procurator,[4] imperial secretary and in charge of the imperial inheritance,[5] again imperial secretary of the divine Nerva, given by decree of the Senate the insignia of a man of the rank of praetor by the same (Nerva),[6] imperial secretary of the emperor Nerva Caesar Trajan Augustus Germanicus, prefect of the night watch, gave this gift to Vulcan.

1   Capito was prefect of an auxiliary infantry cohort of 500 men. The record of Capito's early offices is abbreviated. For example, he does not indicate in which units he served as prefect.
2   Once again, the legion in which he served has been omitted.
3   The war in which the awards were given is uncertain, but could have been Domitian's war against the Chatti (a Germanic tribe on the Rhine) in 82.
4   The specific duty of his post is not listed. The only information given is that Capito held this required office between his military commands and the higher equestrian posts, as was expected.
5   He held these posts under Domitian whose name was omitted because of the post-mortem condemnation of his memory. The secretariats in Rome were among the highest ranking equestrian posts.
6   Unlike adlection, which brought the equestrian into the senatorial order, insignia merely conferred the honor of praetorian status without making the equestrian an actual senator. Note how Capito continued on his equestrian career after the reign of Nerva.

9. *Sex. Afranius Burrus, Praetorian Prefect of Nero*

CIL 12.5842; *ILS* 1321   Vasio, Gallia Narbonensis
Statue Base   1ˢᵗ Century AD

The praetorian prefect Burrus and the philosopher Seneca were the two most influential courtiers of the early reign of Nero. The people of Burrus' hometown dedicated this statue to him while he was still alive.

VASIENS • VOC
PATRON
SEX • AFRANIO • SEX • F
VOLT • BVRRO
TRIB • MIL • PROC • AVGVS
TAE • PROC • TI • CAESAR
PROC • DIVI • CLAVD[I]
PRAEF • PRAETORI • ORNA
MENTIS • CONSVLAR

* * *

Vasiens(es) Voc(ontii) patron(o), Sex(to) Afranio Sex(ti) f(ilio) Volt(inia tribu) Burro, trib(uno) mil(itum), proc(uratori) Augustae, proc(uratori) Ti(beri) Caesar(is), proc(uratori) divi Claud[i], praef(ecto) praetori, ornamentis consular(ibus).

* * *

The Vocontii of Vasio (dedicated this) to their patron, Sextus Afranius Burrus, the son of Sextus, of the Voltinia tribe, military tribune,[1] procurator of the Augusta,[2] procurator of Tiberius Caesar, procurator of the divine Claudius, praetorian prefect,[3] honored with consular insignia.

1   Like Capito (see above), Burrus' earlier career has been abbreviated in order to focus on his more prestigious later posts.
2   The Augusta, or empress, was Livia, the wife of Augustus and mother of the emperor Tiberius. She received the name of Augusta following the death of Augustus in AD 14. Burrus' duties would have been to oversee her property.
3   The two praetorian prefects were the highest ranking equestrians in the empire. They not only commanded the Guard in Rome, but also served as the emperor's right-hand men. Burrus was praetorian prefect from 51 to 62, and is frequently mentioned in the histories of Nero's reign.

Replica of the statue base of the Neronian praetorian prefect Sex. Afranius Burrus (CIL 12.5842; ILS 1321), Museum of Roman Civilization, E.U.R., Rome.

10. *Ti. Julius Celsus Polemaeanus, Supporter of Vespasian*

ILS 8971; *AE* 1954, 248   Ephesus, Asia Minor
Statue Base   1ˢᵗ Century AD

Celsus exemplifies those who managed to advance from the equestrian to the senatorial order. When the emperor assumed the powers of a censor (as Vespasian did c. AD 73), he had the right to "adlect" equestrians into the Senate at any rank he wished: ex-quaestor (quaestorian), ex-tribune, ex-aedile, ex-praetor (praetorian), or, most rarely, ex-consul (consular). The rank the new senator received meant that he was the equivalent of a senator who had held that post. Polemaeanus was adlected to the ex-aediles, and so was not required to hold the quaestorship, but could go directly to the praetorship as soon as he met the age qualification.

TI · IVLIO · TI · F · COR · CELSO · POLEMAEANO · COS
PROCOS · ASIAE · TRIB · LEGIONIS · III
CYRENAICAE · ADLECTO · INTER · AEDILICIOS · AB
DIVO · VESPASIANO · PR · P · R · LEG · AVG
DIVORVM · VESPASIANI · ET · TITI · PROVINCIAE
CAPPADOCIAE · ET · GALATIAE · PONTI
PISIDIAE · PAPHLAGONIAE · ARMENIAE · MINORIS
LEG · DIVI · TITI · LEG · IIII · SCYTHICAE · PROCOS
PONTI · ET · BITHYNIAE · PRAEF · AERARI · MILITARIS · LEG
AVG PRO · PR · PROVINCIAE · CILICIAE · XVVIR · S · F · CVR

AEDIVM · SACRARVM · ET · OPERVM · LOCORVMQVE
PVBLICORVM · POPVLI ROMANI · TI · IVLIVS · AQVILA
POLEMAEANVS · COS
PATREM · SVVM · CONSVMMAVERVNT · HEREDES · AQVILAE

* * *

Ti(iberio) Iulio Ti(beri) f(ilio) Cor(nelia tribu) Celso Polemaeano, co(n)s(uli), proco(n)s(uli) Asiae, trib(uno) legionis III Cyrenaicae, adlecto inter aedilicios ab divo Vespasiano, pr(aetori) p(opuli) R(omani), leg(ato) Aug(ustorum) divorum Vespasiani et Titi provinciae Cappadociae et Galatiae, Ponti, Pisidiae, Paphlagoniae, Armeniae minoris, leg(ato) divi Titi leg(ionis) IIII Scythicae, proco(n)s(uli) Ponti et Bithyniae, praef(ecto) aerari militaris, leg(ato) Aug(usti) pro pr(aetore) provinciae Ciliciae, XVvir(o) s(acris) f(aciundis), cur(atori) aedium sacrarum et operum locorumque publicorum populi Romani, Ti(berius) Iulius Aquila Polemaeanus co(n)s(ul) patrem suum; consummaverunt heredes Aquilae.

* * *

To Tiberius Julius Celsus Polemaeanus, son of Tiberius,[1] of the Cornelia tribe, consul,[2] proconsul of Asia, tribune of the 3rd legion Cyrenaica,[3] *adlected by the divine Vespasian to the rank of aedile,[4] praetor of the Roman people, imperial legate of the divine Vespasian and Titus of the province of Cappadocia and Galatia, Pontus, Pisidia, Paphlagonia, and Armenia minor, legate of the divine Titus of the 4th legion* Scythica, *proconsul of Pontus and Bithynia, prefect of the military treasury, imperial pro-praetorian legate of the province of Cilicia, one of the 15 men in charge of carrying out the sacred rites, curator of the sacred temples and buildings and of the public places of the Roman people, Tiberius Julius Aquila Polemaeanus, consul,[5] to his father. The heirs of Aquila consummated the work.*

1   His name (Gaius Julius) indicates that he was the grandson (or great-grandson) of a Greek from the East who received his citizenship from Caligula (or, possibly, Augustus). Polemaeanus is known to have been born c. 45 in Ephesus or Sardis.
2   His positions as consul and then proconsul of Asia, which were the peak of his senatorial career, are listed first before the inscription returns to a list of his other posts in ascending chronological order.
3   In AD 69 when he was still an equestrian. This legion was stationed in Alexandria and so was one of the first to acclaim Vespasian emperor during the civil war of 69. It was probably at this time when he was first noticed by Vespasian.
4   In c. AD 73.
5   The family remained important during the reign of Trajan. Polemaeanus' son became suffect consul in AD 110.

Summary of Polemaeanus' Senatorial Career

c. 75: Praetor.

c. 77-79: Legate of the imperial provinces of Cappadocia and Galatia, Pontus, Pisidia, Paphlagonia, and Armenia Minor. He seems to have been *iuridicus* rather than the actual governor. A *iuridicus* was a judge who aided the governor with his judicial responsibilities.

c. 80-82: Legate of the 4th legion Scythica, stationed in Syria.

c. 84: Proconsul of the senatorial province of Pontus and Bithynia.

c. 86-88: Prefect of the military treasury.

c. 89-90: Legate of the imperial province of Cilicia.

92: *Consul suffectus*.

After 92: *Quindecimvir Sacris Faciundis*, one of the major consular priesthoods; this group of fifteen men oversaw religious rituals and consulted the Sibylline Oracles when required.

c. 95: Curator of public works and buildings.

105/106: Proconsul of the senatorial province of Asia.

Municipal Inscriptions

As the Romans conquered first Italy and then the rest of the Mediterranean basin, they promoted the benefits of Roman rule and offered the indigenous peoples the hope of citizenship in exchange for loyalty to the Roman state. In the conquered territories, the Romans endeavored to leave as much of the original infrastructure in place as possible. To hasten the process of Romanization, they granted citizenship and the equivalent of equestrian status to the local aristocracy. The Romanization process also included conferring upon the town a particular status which classified its civic structure in relation to other towns within the empire. The following are the types of urban institutional statuses which were granted during the first three centuries AD:

- *Civitas* (town). A *civitas* was a community which was self-governed with its own town council and magistrates. A *civitas* government was thus the least altered from the original form, and its magistrates were considerably less significant in terms of authority and social status compared to other urban magistrates.

- *Municipium* (municipality). When a city was granted the status of *municipium*, it created a municipal charter based on a single prototype used throughout the empire. The charter established a particularly Roman form of local government. The people in the town were given partial Roman citizenship, called the "Latin rights", and members of the local aristocracy were granted full Roman citizenship after holding a local magistracy.

- *Colonia* (colony). These were towns built either from scratch or over an existing foundation and populated by people with full Roman citizenship. Usually, the land had been confiscated from the indigenous owners and turned over to Roman colonists. During the imperial period, this generally meant soldiers who had been discharged.

In the case of municipalities and colonies, the municipal government which was established by the charter mentioned above mimicked the government structure of Rome (which had a senate presided over by two consuls). Every year two chief town magistrates, the *duoviri*, (or *IIviri*), were elected. They were in charge of presiding over town meetings and councils, the administration of justice, and general control of their town. Inscriptions also mention municipal quaestors (in charge of the town's finances) and aediles (who oversaw the town's food supply, public buildings and roads). A local senate assisted and advised the magistrates. The senate was made up of *decuriones* (the town council), who were former magistrates and other wealthy local aristocrats. For example, it was the decurions, rather than the entire population, who would vote approval for a public building project. The formula "D D", d(ecreto) d(ecurionum) ("by decree of the decurions") is very common at the end of public inscriptions.

This section gives a number of examples of local aristocrats including: an equestrian *duovir* from Venafrum, Italy, a *decurio* from Ostia, a local priest from Spain honored by the provincial council, and an aedile and priest of the imperial cult in Ostia. Also included is Cogidubnus whom Claudius (shortly after the Roman conquest in AD 43) allowed to serve as a "client king" in the area neighboring the southern edge of the new province of Britain.

11.   *C. Aclutius Gallus, Magistrate of Venafrum*

CIL 10.4876; *ILS* 2227   Venafrum, Campania, Italy
Statue Base   1st Century BC/1st Century AD

Gallus is an example of an equestrian who came from the municipal aristocracy. He later returned home to serve as *duovir* after his retirement from imperial service. This inscription was originally a statue base, but the stone was later re-used in the construction of a private house.

C · ACLVTIVS · L · F · TER · GALLVS
DVOVIR · VRBIS · MOENIVNDAE · BIS
PRAEFECTVS · IVRE · DEICVNDO · BIS
DVOVIR · IVRE · DEICVNDO · TR · MIL
LEGIONIS · [PR]IMAE · TR · MILITVM
LEGIONIS · SECVNDAE · SABINAE

* * *

C(aius) Aclutius L(uci) f(ilio) Ter(etina tribu) Gallus, duovir urbis moeni[e]ndae bis, praefectus iure d{e}ic[e]ndo bis, duovir iure d{e}ic[e]ndo, tr(ibunus) mil(itum) legionis [pr]imae, tr(ibunus) militum legionis secundae Sabinae.

* * *

Gaius Aclutius Gallus, son of Lucius, of the Teretina tribe, twice one of the two town magistrates in charge of building the walls,[1] twice prefect with jurisdiction,[2] one of the two town magistrates with jurisdiction,[3] military tribune of the 1st legion,[4] military tribune of the 2nd legion Sabina.[5]

1   The major activity of his tenure must have been the construction of new walls around Venafrum.
2   Prefects were appointed if one or both of the town magistrates died in office. The title "with jurisdiction" is commonly found with the office of *duovir* and probably denotes the full title of the magistracy.
3   This refers to Gallus' first term as *duovir*, after his service as an officer in the imperial army.
4   This was the later 1st legion *Germanica*.
5   The 2nd legion *Sabina* was later renamed the 2nd *Augusta*. Both the 1st and 2nd legions were stationed in the same provinces during the reign of Augustus. They began in Spain, where they participated in the Cantabrian wars (25-19 BC). They were later transferred to the Rhine by Augustus when he attempted to annex Germany between the Rhine and the Elbe.

12.   *M. Annius Proculus, Magistrate of Ostia*

CIL 14.292; *ILS* 6137   Ostia, Latium, Italy
Sarcophagus Inscription   2nd Century AD

By the age of 25, Proculus had become an important leader in the community of Ostia. He was a member of the town council and served as a priest of the imperial cult. This inscription is on the sarcophagus in which Proculus was buried. The sarcophagus was in Pisa at the time of the publication of the *CIL*, but probably originated from Ostia.

D · M
M · ANNIO · M · F · PAL · PROCVLO
DECVRIONI · COL · OST · FLA · DIVI
VESPASIANI · PATRONO · FABRVM
NAVALIVM · OST · VIXIT · ANN · XXV
MENS · VI · DIE · XXVIII · H · IIII

D · M
ANNIAE · IVCVN
DAE · M · ANNI
PROCVLI · MATRIS

* * *

D(is) m(anibus); M(arco) Annio M(arci) f(ilio) Pal(atina tribu) Proculo, decurioni col(oniae) Ost(iensis), fla(mini) divi Vespasiani, patrono fabrum navalium Ost(iensium), vixit ann(os) XXV mens(es) VI die(s) XXVIII h(oras) IIII.

D(is) m(anibus); Anniae Iucundae, M(arci) Anni Proculi matris.

* * *

To the spirits of the dead; to Marcus Annius Proculus, son of Marcus, of the Palatina tribe, member of the town council of the colony of Ostia, flamen of the divine Vespasian, patron of the ship builders of Ostia,[1] lived 25 years, 6 months, 28 days, 4 hours.

To the spirits of the dead; to Annia Iucunda,[2] mother of Marcus Annius Proculus.

1   The members of the guild of the ship builders of Ostia dedicated the inscription (no doubt because of Proculus' patronage). In return, Proculus could expect political support by the guild's members. Many such corporate guilds are known from Ostia, and they often displayed their unified political support for individuals.

2   No father of Proculus is mentioned. Because Proculus was named Annius like his mother, either he did not have a legitimate father or both his mother and father were freedmen of the same patron, also named Annius.

13. *Cn. Numisius Modestus, Influential Provincial in Spain*

CIL 2.4230; *ILS* 6930
Statue Base

Tarraco, Spain
2nd Century AD

Modestus was local aristocrat from the important city of New Carthage (*Carthago Nova* in southeastern Spain). He was later (after he had held all of the municipal magistracies in New Carthage) sent as representative of his hometown to Tarraco, the capital city of the province of Spain (*Hispania Tarraconensis*) and eventually was elected the chief priest (*flamen*) of the imperial cult (see the chapter on Roman religion) for the whole province. In this position, he had the special duty of dedicating some imperial statues. This statue base was erected in Tarraco, the location of the central cult and the statues, rather than Numisius' hometown of New Carthage.

CN • NVMISIO
CN • FIL • SERG
MODESTO
CARTHAG • OMNIB
HONORIB • IN • RE • P • SVA
FVNCTO • ELECTO • A
CONCILIO • PROVINC
AD • STATVAS • AVRANDAS
DIVI • HADRIANI
FLAM • P • H • C
P • H • C

* * *

Cn(aeo) Numisio Cn(aei) fil(io) Serg(ia) Modesto, Carthag(ine), omnib(us) honorib(us) in re p(ublica) sua functo, electo a concilio provinc(iae) ad statuas [c]urandas divi Hadriani, flam(ini) p(rovinciae) H(ispaniae) c(iterioris); p(rovinciae) H(ispaniae) c(iterioris).

* * *

To Gnaeus Numisius Modestus, son of Gnaeus, of the Sergia tribe, from [New] Carthage, endowed with all honors in his hometown,[1] elected flamen *of the divine Hadrian in the province of Hispania Citerior[2] by the provincial council[3], with the special task of dedicating[4] imperial statues;[5] the province of Hispania Citerior dedicated this.*

1   This was a common way to indicate that a person had held the full range of offices in the municipal career: quaestor, aedile, *duovir* and probably a priesthood. Because of the addition of "in re p(ublica) sua" ("in his hometown"), New Carthage is meant rather than Tarraco.
2   The provincial council was based in Tarraco (the inscription's findspot).
3   The Romans instituted provincial councils in every province. The council served as a meeting place for all of the provincials and were major centers for the imperial cult (see the section on Roman religion below). They also organized any embassies to the emperor on behalf of the whole province.
4   The "aurandas" on the stone should probably be seen as "curandas".
5   Imperial statues, especially those reserved for the imperial cult, were held with great reverence. As can be seen here, paying for an imperial statue was a great honor. In fact, the town honored him by giving him his own statue.

14.   *Q. Plotius Romanus*

CIL 14.400; *ILS* 6138   Ostia, Latium, Italy
Statue base   AD 141

Plotius Romanus was a typical member of the municipal aristocracy. He had been recognized in Rome as a member of the equestrian order, he held magistracies in his hometown of Ostia, and he was a priest in the imperial cult. After his death, Ostia decreed that a statue be erected to him at public expense. Romanus' own father paid for the statue himself in the memory of his son.

Q · PLOTIO · Q · FIL
QVIR · ROMANO
EQVO · PVBLICO · EXORN
A · DIVO · HADRIANO
AED · FLAM · ROM · ET · AVG
FLAMINI · DIVI · TITI
HVIC · DECVRIONES
STATVAM · PVBLICE · PONEND
DECREVERVNT
PLOTIVS · NIGER · PATER · HONORE · VSVS
DE · SVO · POSVIT · L · D · D · D

On the Side:

DEDIC · XVI · K · APR
T · HOENIO · SEVERO
M · PEDVCAEO · PRISCINO
COS

* * *

Q(uinto) Plotio Q(uinti) fil(io) Quir(ina tribu) Romano, equo publico exorn(ato) a divo Hadriano, aed(ili), flam(ini) Rom(ae) et Aug(usti), flamini divi Titi; huic decuriones statuam publice ponend(am) decreverunt; Plotius Niger pater honore usus de suo posuit; l(ocus) d(atus) d(ecreto) d(ecurionum).

Dedic(atum) XVI k(alendis) Apr(ilibus) T(ito) Hoenio Severo, M(arco) Peduaeo Piscino co(n)s(ulibus).

* * *

To Quintus Plotius Romanus, son of Quintus, of the Quirina tribe, endowed with a horse at public expense by the divine Hadrian, local aedile,[1] priest in the temple of Rome and Augustus, priest of the divine Titus,[2] the town council decreed that a statue be put up in his honor at public expense; Plotius Niger, his father, taking advantage of his office, put this up at his own expense;[3] the place was given by decree of the town council.

Dedicated on the 16th day before the Kalends of April while Titus Hoenius Severus and Marcus Peduaeus Piscinus were consuls.[4]

1   This statue base was erected when he had only advanced in his career to the office of town aedile. On his tombstone (also preserved in Ostia; *CIL* 14.401), he appears with the same offices. Therefore, he died before he had held the office of *duovir*.
2   See the chapter on Roman religion for *flamines* in the imperial cult.
3   Much of the day-to-day expenses of running a town were assumed by the magistrates currently in office. Although the town council had provided for the statue to be put up at public expense, nevertheless, Romanus' father, holding an unnamed magistracy at the time, paid for it out of his own funds. It is likely that this was a posthumous dedication.
4   March 17th, 141.

15.   *Cogidubnus, King of Great Britain*

CIL 7.11; *AE* 1979, 382   Noviomagus, Britain
Marble Slab; Building Dedication   1st Century AD

Although some foreign kings did not survive the Roman conquest of their former kingdoms, others were rewarded for the support of the Romans by being granted client kingdoms on the frontier of the new Roman province. Such kings helped spread Roman culture and helped create a buffer zone between Roman territory and the tribes further from the Roman border. This practice had been especially useful in the civilized territories of the former Hellenistic kingdoms of the Greek East. Tacitus (*Agr.* 14) places Cogidubnus in this tradition of creating client kings "to make others slaves"; he states specifically that Cogidubnus was granted an independent kingdom in southern Britain in the area around Noviomagus (modern Chichester).

[N]EPTVNO · ET · MINERVAE
TEMPLVM·
[PR]O · SALVTE · DO[MVS] · DIVINA[E]·
[EX] · AVCTORITAT[E · TI] · CLAVD
[CO]GIDVBNI · RE[G · M]AGNI · BRIT
[COLLE]GIVM · FABROR · ET · [Q]VI · IN · E[O]
[SVN]T · D · S · D · DONANTE · AREAM
[---]ENTE · PVDENTINI · FIL

* * *

[N]eptuno et Minervae templum [pr]o salute do[mus] divina[e] [ex] auctoritat[e Ti(beri)] Claud(i) [Co]gidubni re[g(is) m]agni Brit(anniae); [colle]gium fabror(um) et [q]ui in e[o] [sun]t d(e) s(uo) d(ederunt), donante aream [---]ente Pudentini fil(io)

* * *

*Temple to Neptune and Minerva for the well-being of the divine house,[1]
by the authority of Tiberius Claudius Cogidubnus,[2] king of great Britain;
the guild of smiths and its members, gave this out of their own funds;
[...]ens, son of Pudentinus gave the site (for the temple).*

1   The "divine house" is that of the emperor (in this case, Nero).
2   As shown by his name, Cogidubnus was made a Roman citizen by
    Claudius. "By the authority" means that Cogidubnus approved the
    construction of the temple. Tacitus names the client king "Cogidumnus"
    and it is generally believed that the Cogidumnus of Tacitus and the
    Cogidubnus of this inscription are the same person.

RELIGION

The State Religion

The major precept of Roman religion stressed that the gods were everywhere, and the spirits of the gods (*numina*) controlled and explained all natural phenomena. Sacrifice and divination were the two major components of Roman religious ritual. The Romans sought to win over the *numina* by making sacrificial offering appropriate to the particular god or gods whom the participant sought to influence. The worshipers took comfort in the face of unpredictable forces of nature by performing sacrificial rituals to propitiate the *numina*, thereby hoping to persuade the gods to treat pious men more favorably. They would ask for specific blessings, such as providing good weather for growing crops, giving the army an edge in battle, and so on. The Romans also practiced divination, which was either the observation of the flight of birds (augury) or the examination of the entrails of sacrificial animals (haruspicy). Through divination, they sought to determine the will of the gods regarding an impending event or action (such as whether they should go into battle on a certain day). Sacrifice and divination were performed in both public and private spheres.

Roman state religion was concerned primarily with insuring the continued safety and prosperity of the state through public ritualistic religious performances. The majority of public rituals and festivals had their origins in older, more private household cult practices. Just as the family (through the *pater familias*, the father of the family and head of the household) strove to maintain a good relationship with the gods in order to ensure the divine protection of crops, home, and family, so also the priests of the state religion sought the gods' protection for the Roman state and its leaders.

The performance of state cult required the participation of a large number of priests and attendants. In Rome (as well as the other cities of the empire), priesthoods remained almost exclusively in the hands of the aristocracy. There were four major priesthoods, all held by senators of consular rank. The *pontifices* (singular *pontifex*) were the high priests in Roman religion. The chief *pontifex*, the *pontifex maximus*, was the head of the whole state religion. During the Roman imperial period, only the emperor could be *pontifex maximus*. Another important group of priests was the *quindecimviri sacris faciundis* (fifteen men in charge of performing the sacred rites). These priests consulted the books of the Sibyl (these were a series of prophetic books which explained the significance of omens and gave remedies for crises). Also significant were the augurs, who were priests in charge of the practice of official divination referred to as "taking the auspices"; as mentioned above, the practice of augury featured interpreting the significance of the flight patterns of flocking birds. Another group, called the *septemviri epulonum*, incorporated seven priests in charge of organizing public and religious banquets. In addition to the members of the four major priesthoods, one priest, called a *flamen,* was appointed to supervise each of the major cults in Rome.

Some examples of members of the major priesthoods can be found in the previous section, which described members of the senatorial order. These prior examples include Munatius Plancus and Hadrian as *septimviri epulonum*, Ummidius Quadratus as a *quindecimvir sacris faciundis*, and Pliny the Younger as an augur. In addition to the senatorial priests in Rome, some priesthoods in the cities of Italy and outlying provinces were held by equestrians and other municipal aristocrats. The following inscriptions in this section illustrate a variety of priests and attendants involved in Roman state religion.

16.   *Flavia Publicia, Chief Vestal Virgin*

CIL 6.32414; *ILS* 4930	House of the Vestals; Rome
Statue Base	3rd Century AD

The cult of Vesta was one of the oldest and most important in Roman religion. The Vestal Virgins tended the eternal fire of Vesta's hearth and thereby assured the continuation of the empire. Flavia Publicia was the chief Vestal Virgin for a number of years in the first half of the third century. This statue base was erected in her honor and placed in the complex commonly known as the "House of the Vestals" which stood next to the temple of Vesta in the very center of the Roman Forum. A number of Vestal statues surrounded a large, open interior courtyard on the side of the complex closest to the temple.

FLAVIAE · L · FIL
PVBLICIAE · V · V · MAX
SANCTISSIMAE · PIISSIMAEQ
CVIVS · SANCTISSIMAM · ET
RELIGIOSAM · CVRAM · SACROR
QVAM · PER · OMNES · GRADVS
SACERDOTII · LAVDABILI · ADMI
NISTRATIONE · OPERATVR · NVMEN

SANCTISSIMAE • VESTAE • MATRIS
COMPROBAVIT
AEMILIA • ROGATILLA • C • F • SORORIS • FIL
CVM • MINVCIO • HONORATO • MARCELLO
AEMILIANO • C • P • FILIO • SVO
OB • EXIMIAM • EIVS • ERGA • SE
PIETATEM

(on the right side)

COL • V • ID • IVL
DD • NN • I[MP • PHILIPPO] • AVG • II • ET
[PHILIPPO] • CAES • COS

* * *

Flaviae L(uci) fil(iae) Publiciae, v(irgini) V(estali) max(imae), sanctissimae piissimaeq(ue), cuius sanctissimam et religiosam curam sacror(um), quam per omnes gradus sacerdotii laudabili administratione operatur, numen sanctissimae Vestae matris comprobavit; Aemilia Rogatilla C(ai) f(ilia), sororis fil(ia), cum Minucio Honorato Marcello Aemiliano, c(larissimo) p(uero), filio suo, ob eximiam eius erga se pietatem.

col(locata) V id(ibus) Iul(iis) dd(ominis) nn(ostris) i[mp(eratore) Philippo] Aug(usto) II et [Philippo] Caes(are) co(n)s(ulibus).

* * *

To Flavia Publicia, daughter of Lucius, chief Vestal virgin,[1] most venerable and pious; the divinity of the most holy mother Vesta showed her approval of Flavia's most hallowed and devout care of the sacred rites, which she performed through all the grades of the priesthood with praiseworthy management;[2] Aemilia Rogatilla, daughter of Gaius, daughter of Flavia's sister,[3] together with Minucius Honoratus Marcellus Aemilianus,[4] most famous boy,[5] Aemilia's son, dedicated this because of Flavia's exceptional duty toward her sister.

Placed on the 5th day before the Ides of July[6] while our lords the emperor [Philippus] Augustus for the second time and [Philippus][7] Caesar were consuls.

1   There were six Vestal Virgins in office at a time, all of senatorial and patrician background. The chief of these was called the *Vestalis virgo maxima*. Because their ritual demanded absolute purity, the Vestals were bound to an oath of chastity. Vestals found guilty of violating their chastity were buried alive, which was the only acceptable act of atonement to the gods.
2   Vestals held office for a minimum of 30 years. The first ten years, a Vestal learned how to perform the rituals, the next ten years she carried out the rituals, and in the following ten years (and beyond) she trained new Vestals.

3   Publicia's sister would also have been named Flavia (*cognomen* unknown). Based on the name of the child, the father (and husband of Publicia's sister) was named Gaius Aemilius.

4   Publicia's sister had two children: Aemilia and Minucius Honoratus Marcellus Aemilianus. As can be shown by the conversion of the *nomen* Aemilius to an *agnomen*, the son was adopted by a man named Minucius Honoratus Marcellus.

5   After AD 168, this epithet *clarissimus* was used exclusively of those of the senatorial order.

6   July 10th, 247.

7   The names of the two emperors named Philip have been erased, because their memories were condemned (*damnatio memoriae*) after they died in civil war.

17.   *L. Manlius Severus, Sculptor of the Priests of Rome*

CIL 14.2413; *ILS* 4942   Bovillae, Latium, Italy
Tombstone   Unknown

Severus was a town magistrate at Bovillae and served as a priest and a sculptor of priests in the area around Lake Albanum. The cult of Jupiter on the Alban Mountain overlooking the lake was one of the oldest in Roman religion.

D · M
L · MANLIO · L · F · PAL
SEVERO · REGI · SAC
RORVM · FICTORI
PONTIFICVM · P · R · IIII
VIRO · BOVILLENSI
VM · COLLACTANE
O · DVLCISSIMO · ET
INDVLGENTISSIMO
ERGA · SE · FECIT

* * *

D(is) m(anibus); L(ucio) Manlio L(uci) f(ilio) Pal(atina tribu) Severo, regi sacrorum, fictori pontificum p(opuli) R(omani), IIIIviro Bovillensium, collactaneo dulcissimo et indulgentissimo erga se fecit.

* * *

To the spirits of the dead; to Lucius Manlius Severus, son of Lucius, of the Palatina tribe, king of the sacred rights,[1] sculptor of the priests of the Roman people,[2] one of the four town magistrates of the people of Bovillae,[3] dedicated[4] to the sweetest foster-brother[5] and most indulgent toward me.

1   The *rex sacrorum* was a priest in charge of celebrating the rites and organizing the festival calendar. He is called *rex* ("king") because, in Roman political mythology, the *rex sacrorum* assumed the religious duties of the kings after their expulsion at the beginning of the Republic. This office may not have been held in Rome, but rather in the town of Bovillae, in the vicinity of Lake Albanum.

2   As can still be seen in the atrium of the Vestals in Rome, priests sometimes had statues made of themselves for display around the temple. Severus seems to have been a sculptor specifically of priests in Bovillae or perhaps even those from the temple on the summit of the Alban Mountain, by Lake Albanum, where the inscription was found.

3   As a *municipium*, Bovillae had four town magistrates, rather than the two in charge of colonies (such as Ostia).

4   The dedicator is not named.

5   See the section on children for more on foster children.

18.   *C. Curtius Helenus, Lupercus*

CIL 6.32437; *ILS* 4945   Rome
Tombstone   Unknown

Helenus was a *lupercus*. The *luperci* were minor priests in charge of the festival of the Lupercalia, a very old agricultural/fertility cult in Rome. Helenus' tomb inscription is currently in Panormus, Sicily, but probably originated from Rome.

C · CVRTIVS
POST · L · HELENVS
LVPERCVS

* * *

C(aius) Curtius Post(umi) l(ibertus) Helenus, lupercus.

* * *

Gaius Curtius Helenus, freedman of Postumus, lupercus.

19.   *C. Norbanus Quietus, Keeper of the Sacred Chickens*

CIL 6.2200; *ILS* 4961   Rome
Tombstone   Possibly 1st Century AD

Quietus was a freedman of C. Norbanus Flaccus (consul in 15 AD). He was responsible for the care of the sacred chickens used in the taking of the auspices during ceremonies

C · NORBANVS
FLACCI · L
QVIETVS
PVLLARIVS

* * *

C(aius) Norbanus Flacci l(ibertus) Quietus pullarius.

* * *

Gaius Norbanus Quietus, freedman of Flaccus, keeper of the sacred chickens.

20.   *M. Valerius Saturninus, Haruspex*

CIL 6.2164; *ILS* 4951   Rome
Tombstone   Unknown

A *haruspex* was a priest who examined the entrails of animals slaughtered for sacrifice. The purpose was to find omens which would indicate whether or not the gods' favored a proposed action. Saturninus is described as the *haruspex maximus*, chief *haruspex* of his order. He was an equestrian, again demonstrating the preponderance of aristocrats in the major and minor priesthoods at Rome. This tombstone was discovered in the remains of a country villa on the *Via Nomentana*, seven miles outside of Rome.

M' · VALERIO · M' · F
QVIR · SATVRNINO
TRIBVNO
MIL · LEG · III
CYRENEICAE
HARISPICI · MAXIMO

* * *

M(anlio) Valerio M(anli) f(ilio) Quir(ina tribu) Saturnino, tribuno mil(iltum) leg(ionis) III Cyreneicae, har[u]spici maximo.

* * *

To Manlius Valerius Saturninus, son of Manlius, of the Quirina tribe, military tribune of the 3rd legion Cyrenaica,[1] chief haruspex.

1   This legion was stationed in Egypt during the 1st century and Arabia in the 2nd century.

21. *Q. Servilius Auctus, Slaughterer of Sacrificial Animals*

CIL 6.2201; *ILS* 4962   Rome
Tombstone   Unknown

The *victimarius* was an assistant who took the killed sacrificial animals and prepared them for sacrifice. They also removed the entrails for the *haruspices* to investigate. This marble tablet was originally discovered near the Quirinal hill in Rome.

Q · SERVILIVS · Q · L · AVCTV[S]
VICTVMARIVS · FECIT · SIB[I]
ET · ACANIAE · Q · L · LEPIDAE

* * *

Q(uintus) Servilius Q(uinti) l(ibertus) Auctu[s], vict[i]marius fecit sib[i] et Acaniae Q(uinti) l(ibertae) Lepidae.

* * *

Quintus Servilius Auctus, freedman of Quintus, slaughterer of sacrificial animals, made this for himself and for Acania Lepida, freedwoman of Quintus.

22. *Q. Tiburtus Menolavus, Slaughterer of Sacrificial Animals*

CIL 1.1213 and 10.3984; *ILS* 7642   Capua, Campania, Italy
Tombstone   1st Century BC/1st Century AD

The job of the *cultrarius* was probably similar, if not equivalent to that of the *victimarius* in the previous inscription. This inscription is especially old. The letters are reminiscent of the late Republic rather than the Empire. Also, note the "heic", an old form of *hic*, in line 4.

Q · TIBVRTI · Q · L
MENOLAVI
CVLTRARI · OSS
HEIC · SITA · SVNT

* * *

Q(uinti) Tiburti Q(uinti) l(iberti) Menolavi, cultrari, oss(a) h{e}ic sita sunt.

* * *

(Tomb) of Quintus Tiburtus Menolavus, freedman of Quintus, slaughterer of sacrificial animals. His bones are buried here.

The Imperial Cult

The "imperial cult" was a series of rituals which emphasized the centrality of the emperor in government, society and religion. The rituals varied from province to province and even city to city, as municipalities within the diverse geographical regions incorporated various imperial rituals into their own particular religious practices. The imperial cult occasionally included worship of the current emperor directly as a god (especially in the Greek East), but the majority of worship centered on cults of the emperors who had received official deification after their deaths. The imperial cult also included annual vows, which were sacrifices offered to the traditional gods each year asking for protection of the well-being, safety, and health of the ruling emperor. While all priests of every religious cult were expected to make sacrifices and vows on behalf of the emperor, special priesthoods were created which focused solely on the imperial cult. Inside of Rome, priestly colleges known as *sodales* performed rites in honor of the deified emperors (like Augustus, Claudius, Vespasian, and Antoninus Pius).

23.   *D. Lucretius Satrius Valens, Flamen of Nero*

CIL 4.3884; *ILS* 5145   Pompeii, Campania, Italy
Wall Graffiti   1st Century AD

The *flamines* were another group that presided over the imperial cult in a specific temple. Outside of Rome, certain *flamines* worshiped deified emperors, and others were dedicated to honoring the living members of the imperial family. The following was an advertisement for a series of games to be held by a local *flamen* of Pompeii. It was painted on the west wall of the House of the Centenary (*insula* IX.8) in the center of Pompeii. Valens and his son appear on other such advertisements throughout Pompeii.

D · LVCRETI
SATRI · VALENTIS · FLAMINIS · NERONIS · CAESARIS · AVG · FILI
PERPETVI · GLADIATORVM · PARIA · XX · ET · D · LVCRETIO · VALENTIS · FILI
GLAD · PARIA · X · PVG · POMPE · IS · VI · V · IV · III · PR · IDVS · APR · VENATIO
· LEGITIMA
ET · VELA · ERVNT

In small letters inside
the "C" of "Lucreti" in Line 1:

SCR
CELER

In small letters to the
right of "Lucreti" in Line 1:

SCR
AEMILIUS

CELER SING
AD LUNA

* * *

D(ecimi) Lucreti Satri Valentis, flaminis Neronis Caesaris Aug(usti) fili perpetui, gladiatorum paria XX et D(ecimi) Lucreti{o} Valentis, fili, glad(iatorum) paria X pug(nabunt) Pompeis VI, V, IV, III, pr(idie) Idus Apr(iles); venatio legitima et vela erunt.

scr(ipsit) Celer.

scr(ipsit) Aemilius Celer sing(ularis) ad luna.

* * *

Twenty pairs of gladiators belonging to Decimus Lucretius Satrius Valens,[1] priest for life of Nero Caesar, the son of Augustus,[2] and ten pairs belonging to his son, Decimus Lucretius Valens will fight at Pompeii on the sixth, fifth, fourth, third and first days before the Ides of April;[3] there will be a suitable beast hunt[4] and awnings.[5]

Celer wrote this.

Aemilius Celer,[6] special guy, wrote this by the light of the moon.

1   The "D LUCRETI" is written much larger than the rest of the text in order to attract people's attention.
2   As he was the *flamen* of the future emperor Nero when he was still Claudius' heir, it would seem likely that Valens' priesthood fell between AD 51 and 54.
3   April 8th-12th. Note how, because of the Romans' inclusive counting, there is no second day before the Ides of April, only the third day (counting the current day, the intervening day, and the actual Ides) and the day before (*pridie*).
4   For the beast hunts (the *venatio*), see the chapter on the games, below.
5   Many of the nicer amphitheaters in the empire were equipped with awnings that could be spread over the majority of the seating to protect the crowd from the heat of the sun.
6   Celer is known from other similar advertisements around Pompeii.

Foreign Cults

24.   *P. Cornelius Victorinus,*
Priest of Isis and Anubis

CIL 14.4290; *ILS* 4369   Ostia, Latium, Italy
Statue Base   3rd Century AD

By the third century, a number of eastern cults had become accepted in Roman society, even in the West. At Ostia, there were a number of cults of Isis and Anubis, Mithras, and others. The following is a priest of Isis and Anubis in Ostia. Several priests of Isis have been discovered in Ostia, indicating that she probably had a temple in the town (as yet undiscovered or attributed). Victorinus was a city bureaucrat who dedicated a statuette of Mars on horseback, probably in fulfillment of a vow for his recovery from a serious illness. The base was discovered in the Antonine baths in town, although it may have been removed to there at a later time.

P · CORNELIVS · P · F
VICTORINVS
ISIACVS · ET · ANVBIACVS
ET · DECVRIALIS · SCRIBA
LIBRARIVS · COL · OST
SIGNVM · MARTIS · CVM
EQVILIOLO · ISIDI
REGINAE · RESTITVTRICI
SALVTIS · SVAE
D · D

* * *

P(ublius) Cornelius P(ubli) f(ilius) Victorinus, Isiacus et Anubiacus, et decurialis scriba librarius col(oniae) Ost(iensis), signum martis cum equiliolo Isidi reginae restitutrici salutis suae, d(ecreto) d(ecurionum).

* * *

Publius Cornelius Victorinus, son of Publius, priest of Isis and Anubis, record clerk of the office of the town council the colony of Ostia, dedicated this statuette of Mars with a small pony to Isis the queen, restorer of his health,[1] by the decree of the town council.

1   Isis was often worshipped as a goddess of health. In Ostia, she was sometimes called *sancta regina*, sacred queen.

MILITARY

Soldiers in the Legions

The Roman army consisted of two major components of approximately the same numerical strength: the legions and the auxiliaries. The soldiers of the legions were Roman citizens who fought primarily as heavily armed infantry soldiers. The auxiliaries were generally non-Romans who fought as various kinds of light and heavy-armed, missile (arrows, slings and javelins), and cavalry troops.

Each legion was composed of slightly more than 5,000 men divided into ten cohorts. In the case of the second through the tenth cohorts, each cohort was divided into six centuries of 80 men each. The prestigious first cohort was considerably larger with five centuries of 160 men each. In addition to the legionary soldiers, a contingent of 120 cavalry was attached to each legion. Legionaries served for 25 years (20 under Augustus).

Although the common soldier had little hope of promotion to the rank of officer, he did have the possibility of receiving exemption from certain duties, a pay raise, and/or promotion to a position as a member of an officer's staff. First, a soldier could be promoted to exemption from physical duties, a privilege known as *immunis*. From there, they could be promoted to a variety of administrative posts, a promotion which bestowed on them the title of *principalis*. The various administrative posts held by the *principales* qualified the soldier for pay raises, ranging from one and one-half (*sesquiplicarius*), to double (*duplicarius*) or even triple (*triplicarius*) the normal salary. The duties of the *principales* varied from an eagle-bearer (*aquilifer*) to the clerk of the consular commander (*beneficarius consularis*). Other examples of *principales'* posts appear in the section containing auxiliary soldiers: the *duplicarius* Longinus, the trumpeter (*bucinator*) Claudius Ingenuus, and Julius Dexter who was both squad commander (*curator*) and standard-bearer (*signifer*) of his unit. Many of these posts were given to exemplary soldiers who could anticipate a possible promotion to the centurionate,

Tombstone of the eques singularis *M. Aurelius Bithus (CIL 6.3195), Capitoline Museums, Rome (courtesy of the Archivio Fotografico dei Musei Capitolini).*

usually as part of re-enlistment after their official discharge. Military officers are discussed below.

This section also includes the tombstones of an *aquilifer* of the 3rd legion *Augusta* in Africa, the veteran Camulius Lavenus who received military decorations by the vote of his peers, and the veteran Cornelius Verus who had been promoted to double pay before his discharge.

25. *L. Tullius Felix,*
Eagle-Bearer of the 3rd Augusta

CIL 8.2988; *ILS* 2344	Lambaesis, Numidia
Tombstone	3rd century AD

Every legion had a standard topped by a gold eagle (*aquila*). The soldier who carried the eagle standard was called the eagle-bearer (*aquilifer*). Felix, a soldier in the 3rd Legion *Augusta* in North Africa, was an apprentice eagle-bearer (*discens aquilifer*), presumably in training to eventually take over the post from his predecessor. This epitaph, his tombstone, was discovered in the necropolis of that legion. We are fortunate to have another dedicatory inscription which includes a list of the names of those soldiers who had sponsored it. Felix appears on the list and is described as d(iscens) aq(uilifer) (*CIL* 8.2568, line 22).

D · M · S
L · TVLLIO · FELICI
VIXIT · ANOS · XXV
MESES · II · DIES · XVII
DISCENS
AQVILIFERV
LEG · III · AVG · MEMORIE
EIVS · POSVIT · L · BONCIVS
SECVNDVS
AVNCVLO

* * *

D(is) m(anibus) s(acrum); L(ucio) Tullio Felici, vixit an(n)os XXV, me(n)ses II, dies XVII, discens aquilifer(or)u(m) leg(ionis) III Aug(ustae); memori(a)e eius posuit L(ucius) Boncius Secundus, av(u)nculo.

* * *

Sacred to the spirits of the dead. To Lucius Tullius Felix, lived 25 years, 2 months, 17 days,[1] apprentice of the eagle-bearers of the 3rd legion Augusta;[2] in his memory, Lucius Boncius Secundus put this up to his uncle.

1   Being only 25, Felix died before he was discharged.
2   This legion was stationed in Numidia, in Lambaesis, the provenance of the inscription.

26.   *T. Camulius Lavenus, Decorated Veteran of the 3rd Gallica*

CIL 12.2230; *ILS* 2313   Gratianopolis, Gallia Narbonensis
Tombstone   2nd Century AD

Many inscriptions testify to soldiers and commanders who were granted military decorations for actions on the battlefield. Lavenus, however, is the only known example of a soldier who received those decorations by the vote of his comrades.

D · M
T · CAMVL · L · F · LAVENI
EMERITI · LEG · III · GALLIC
HONESTA · MISSIONE · DO[NAT]
AB · IMPER · ANTONINO

AVG · PIO · ET · EX · VOLVMTATE
IMP · HADRIANI · AVG · TOR[QVIBVS]
ET · ARMILLIS · AVRE[IS]
SVFFRAGIO · LEGIONIS
HONORATI · CAMVLIA · SOROR · EIVS
ET · PARTEGORIA · [P]RO[PT]E[R · OB]
MERITA · EIVS · PATRONO · OP[TIMO]
ET · PIISSIMO

* * *

D(is) m(anibus) T(iti) Camul(i) L(uci) f(ili) Laveni, emeriti leg(ionis) III Gallic(ae), honesta missione do[nat(i)] ab imper(atore) Antonino Aug(usto) Pio et ex volu[n]tate imp(eratoris) Hadriani Aug(usti) tor[quibus] et armillis aure[is] suffragio legionis honorati; Camulia, soror eius, et Partegoria [p]ro[pt]e[r ob] merita eius, patrono op[timo] et piissimo.

* * *

To the spirits of the dead of Titus Camulius Lavenus,[1] son of Lucius, veteran of the 3rd legion Gallica,[2] *granted discharge by the emperor Antoninus Augustus Pius, and honored at the wishes of Hadrian Augustus[3] with necklaces and golden armbands according to the vote of his legion; Camulia, his sister, and Partegoria dedicated this to their best and most pious patron on account of his merits.*

1   The editor of the *ILS* notes that the name is corrupt.
2   The 3rd legion *Gallica* was stationed in Syria.
3   These decorations probably came from his participation in quelling the revolt in Judea which led to the destruction of Jerusalem and the establishment of the Roman colony, Aelia Capitolina, in its place.

27. *C. Cornelius Verus, Veteran Settled in Poetovio*

CIL 3.4057; *ILS* 2462   Poetovio, Pannonia
Tombstone   Early 2nd Century AD

One of the benefits soldiers received upon retirement was an allocation of land in a Roman colony. Verus served with Trajan in the Dacian wars and was eventually settled, along with his fellow discharged veterans, in the new colony of Poetovio, in Pannonia. Veteran colonies were an important civilian influence in newly-conquered territories. They also served as a kind of armed reserve which could be called up to protect their territory in the event of enemy invasion or revolt.

C · CORNELIVS · C · F
POM · DERT · VERVS

VET · LEG · II · ADI
DEDVCT · C[OL] · V · T · P
MISSION · AGR · II
MILIT · B · COS
ANNOR · L · H · S · E
TEST · FIER · IVS
HERES
C · BILLIENIVS · VITALIS
F · C

* * *

C(aius) Cornelius C(ai) f(ilius) Pom(ptina tribu) Dert(ona domo) Verus, vet(eranus) leg(ionis) II adi(utricis), deduct(us) c[ol(oniam)] U(lpiam) T(raianam) P(oetovionem) mission(e) agr(aria) II, milit(avit) b(eneficarius) co(n)s(ularis), annor(um) L, h(ic) s(itus) e(st); test(amento) fier(i) ius(sit); heres C(aius) Billienius Vitalis f(aciendum) c(uravit).

* * *

Gaius Cornelius Verus, son of Gaius, of the Pomptina tribe, from the town of Dertona, veteran of the 2nd legion Adiutrix,[1] *settled in the colony of Ulpia Traiana Poetovio[2] with a double allocation of land,[3] served as the clerk of the consular commander, lived 50 years, is buried here; he ordered this to be put up in his will; his heir, Gaius Billienius Vitalis took care of putting it up.*

1   This legion was stationed in Sigdunum, Moesia at the outbreak of the first Dacian war in 101 and in Aquincum, Pannonia in 105 for the second Dacian war. Verus was probably discharged after the conclusion of the second war.
2   Trajan founded the colony of Poetovio during the Dacian wars of the early 2nd century AD. Verus was either an original settler, or less likely, was given land there by a later emperor.
3   As a *beneficarius*, Verus received twice the normal military pay (*duplicarius*), and so also may have received a double allocation of land on retirement.

Soldiers in the Urban Garrison

The emperor Augustus was the first to introduce a sizeable military presence in the city of Rome itself. The new troops in Rome consisted of three separate groups: the Praetorian Guard, the urban cohorts and the night watch (the *vigiles*). All enjoyed the amenities of the City as well as a shorter length of service (sixteen years) than the average legionary, and a more highly esteemed status within the Roman army and society.

28.   *L. Comagius Germanus,*
Soldier of the 9ᵗʰ Praetorian Cohort

AE 1978, 68	Antemnae, Latium, Italy
Tombstone	Unknown

The Praetorian Guard was the most prestigious corps in the Roman military. It was originally composed of nine cohorts of 500 men per cohort, but by the third century, its size increased to ten cohorts with as many as 1,500 men per cohort. The Guard was under the command of the two equestrian praetorian prefects, whose primary duty was to serve as the emperor's military escort in Rome and the provinces.

L · COMAGIVS
L · F · ARN
GERMANVS
CREMONA
MIL · COH · VIIII · PR 7 · CASSI
VIX · ANN · XXX
MILIT · ANN · VIIII
HERED · B · M

* * *

L(ucius) Comagius L(uci) f(ilius) Arn(ensi tribu) Germanus, Cremona (domo), mil(es) coh(ortis) VIIII pr(aetoriae) (centuriae) Cassi, vix(it) ann(os) XXX, milit(avit) ann(os) VIIII, hered(es) b(ene) m(erenti).

* * *

Lucius Comagius Germanus, son of Lucius, of the Arnensis tribe, from the town of Cremona,¹ soldier of the 9ᵗʰ praetorian cohort, century of Cassius,² lived 30 years, served 9 years; his heirs dedicated this to him, well-deserving.

1   A town in northern Italy. Most praetorians were recruited in Italy. Only in the third century did large numbers of soldiers from the provinces begin to serve in the urban garrison (which included the Praetorian Guard).

2   It was common for soldiers to indicate in which century they served. The epigraphic symbol for *centuria* is a character that resembles the number seven.

29.   *…Jllio Quartio, Veterinarian*
of the 1ˢᵗ Praetorian Cohort

AE 1910, 27	Rome
Tombstone	Unknown

The military had its own medical corps. This and the following inscription illustrate members of the medical profession attached to the Praetorian Guard. The presence of cavalry would have necessitated a veterinarian. This inscription, discovered in the necropolis on the Via Salaria in Rome, has been broken in several places, and the beginning of the name has been lost.

[DIS · M]ANIB
[…] LLIO · QVARTION[I]
MEDICO · COH · I · PR
VETERINARIO
VIX · ANN · LXXXV
POSVER · LIB · ME[R?]

* * *

[Dis m]anib(us); […]llio Quartion[i], medico coh(ortis) I pr(aetoriae) veterinario, vix(it) ann(os) LXXXV[…?]; posuer(unt) lib(erti) me[r(enti)?].

* * *

To the spirits of the dead; to […]lius[1] Quartio, veterinarian of the 1ˢᵗ praetorian cohort, lived 85(+?) years; his freedmen put this up to him, deserving(?).

1   The first part of the name has been lost. It is probably either [A]llius or [Ge]llius.

30.   *C. Terentius Symphorus, Surgeon of the 4ᵗʰ Praetorian Cohort*

AE 1945, 62   Messana, Sicily
Tombstone   Unknown

C · TERENTIO · SYMPHORO
C · TERENTI · SYNTROPHI · FILIO
MEDICO · CHIR · COH · IIII
PRAET · ANN · XXIIX · HVIVS
CVRA · FECIT · ATTICVS

* * *

C(aio) Terentio Symphoro C(ai) Terenti Syntrophi filio, medico chir(urgo) coh(ortis) IIII praet(oriae), ann(orum) XXIIX; huius cura(m) fecit Atticus.

* * *

To Gaius Terentius Symphorus, son of Gaius Terentius Syntrophus, surgeon of the 4ᵗʰ praetorian cohort, 28 years old; Atticus assumed the duty of putting this up.

31.   *Seius Iunior,*
Veteran of the 11th Urban Cohort

CIL 6.2896; *ILS* 2109   Rome
Tombstone   After 160 AD

The urban cohorts were the less prestigious component of the urban garrison. They were originally created after the Praetorian Guard, as an auxiliary to them (although they were paid considerably less). Three and later four cohorts were stationed in Rome to serve as a police force. A few other cohorts were stationed in important cities of the Empire including Ostia (to protect the grain supply) and Lugdunum (the location of an imperial mint in the Julio-Claudian period).

D · M
IVL · C · F · FABIA · ROMA
SEIO · IVNIORI · VETERAN
AVG · MILITAVIT · IN · CHORTE
XI · VRB · 7 · VALERI · ANNIS · X
MISSVS · HONESTA · MISSIO
V · IDVS · IANVARIAS · APPIO
ANNIO · ATILIO · BRADVA
T · VIBIO · VARO · COS · VIXIT
ANNIS · XXXX · DIEBVS · XX
FECIT · IVL · PALESTRICE · CO
IVGI · BENEMERENTI

* * *

D(is) m(anibus); Iul(io) C(aio) f(ilio) Fabia (tribu) Roma (domo) Seio Iuniori, veteran(o) Aug(usti), militavit in c(o)horte XI urb(anae) (centuriae) Valeri annis X, missus honesta mission(ne) V idus Ianuarias Appio Annio Atilio Bradua, T(ito) Vibio Varo co(n)s(ulibus), vixit annis XXXX, diebus XX; fecit Iul(ia) Palestrice co(n)iugi benemerenti.

* * *

To the spirits of the dead; to Julius Seius Iunior,[1] son of Gaius, of the Fabia tribe, from Rome, veteran of the emperor,[2] served in the 11th urban cohort, in the century of Valerius, for 10 years,[3] given honorable discharge on the 5th day before the Ides of January while Appius Annius Atilius Bradua and Titus Vibius Varus were consuls;[4] he lived 40 years, 20 days; Julia Palestrice made this for her well-deserving husband.

1   No *praenomen* is listed for Iunior. He may have had the same *praenomen* as his father, Gaius.
2   The term veteran of the emperor (*veteranus Augusti*) was a term reserved for the veterans from the urban garrison (praetorian and urban cohorts).
3   Ten years was shorter than the usual length of service in the urban garrison. He may have been a transfer from the legions.
4   January 9th, 160.

32.   *T. Avidius Romanus,*
Pump-Operator of the Vigiles

CIL 6.2994; *ILS* 2172   Probably Rome (now in Florence)
Tombstone   Unknown

The *vigiles*, or night watch, were responsible for patrolling the streets at night and putting out fires. There were seven *vigiles* cohorts, probably of 1,000 men per cohort. Unlike the praetorian and urban cohorts, the *vigiles* were primarily freedmen. The *vigiles* cohorts were stationed in individual camps distributed throughout the city to allow for better response to fires. A rotating detachment of *vigiles* was sent to Ostia, Rome's port city, to protect Rome's grain supply against fires. The *vigiles* were under the command of the equestrian prefect of the *vigiles*. See also in the section below on the noteworthy deaths of soldiers the inscription from the 1st century of a praetorian killed while putting out a fire in Ostia.

D · M
T · AVIDI · ROMANI · MILIT
COH · VII · VIG · SIPONAR
7 · LAETORI · AVIDIA
ROMANA
MATER
FILIO · PIENTISSIMO

* * *

D(is) m(anibus) T(iti) Avidi Romani, milit(is) coh(ortis) VII vig(iliae), sip(h)onar(i), (centuria) Laetori; Avidia Romana, mater, filio pientissimo.

* * *

To the spirits of the dead of Titus Avidius Romanus, soldier of the 7th cohort of the night watchmen, pump-operator,[1] in the century of Laetorius; Avidia Romana,[2] his mother, dedicated this to her most dutiful son.

1   Pliny the Younger, in a letter to Trajan on the establishment of a fire brigade in Nicomedia, mentions pumps, "siphones" (*Ep.* 10.33).

2   Because Romanus and his mother have the same *nomen* and *cognomen* and most *vigiles* were freedmen, it would seem that both mother and son received their freedom from a man named T. Avidius. There is no mention of a father (who may have also been a freedman named T. Avidius). Romanus may have been illegitimately born while his mother was a slave and was subsequently freed at the same time as his mother, or the father died before his son.

33.   *Indus, Bodyguard of Nero*

AE 1952, 0148   Rome
Tombstone   1st Century AD

In the Julio-Claudian period, the emperors employed German cavalry to serve as bodyguards. These non-citizen troops from the Rhine provinces complemented the *speculatores* in the Praetorian Guard (see below). The emperor Galba later dismissed them.

INDVS

NERONIS · CLAVDI

CAESARIS · AVG

CORPOR · CVSTOS

DEC · SECVNDI

NATIONE · BATAVVS

VIX · ANN · XXXVI · H · S · E

POSVIT

EVMENES · FRATER

ET · HERES · EIVS · EX · COLLEGIO

GERMANORVM

* * *

Indus, Neronis Claudi Caesaris Aug(usti) corpor(is) custos, dec(uria) Secundi, natione Batavus, vix(it) ann(os) XXXVI, h(ic) s(itus) e(st); posuit Eumenes, frater et heres eius, ex collegio Germanorum.

* * *

Indus, bodyguard of Nero Claudius Caesar Augustus,[1] squadron of Secundus,[2] Batavian by nationality,[3] who lived 36 years, is buried here; Eumenes, his brother and heir, from the association of the Germans, put this up.[4]

1   The emperor Nero.
2   Like the auxiliary cavalry, the German cavalry guard was organized into *alae* and *decuriones*.
3   The Batavians were a Germanic people living in Roman territory on the Lower Rhine. They were famous for their cavalry and were commonly employed in auxiliary units and the Julio-Claudian German bodyguard.
4   It is very possible that Indus was serving in the bodyguard when Galba dismissed it. The association here is either a burial society or an association created to support the soldiers after the bodyguard's dissolution.

Tombstone erected by a military burial society to Indus, German bodyguard of Nero (AE 1952, 148), National Museum of Rome at the Baths of Diocletian, Rome. Photo courtesy of the Ministero per i Beni e le Attività Culturali Soprintenza Archeologica di Roma.

34. *C. Petronius Varia, Bodyguard of Caesar*

CIL 6.1921a; *ILS* 2014	Rome
Tombstone	1st Century AD

The *speculatores* were a sub-division of the Praetorian Guard. Their name literally means "scouts", but the *speculatores*, a cavalry contingent in the Guard, served as the bodyguards of the emperor. They were disbanded sometime in the later first century, perhaps by the emperor Domitian or Nerva. Their function as bodyguards was assumed by the non-citizen *equites singulares Augusti*. This tablet is fragmentary and the left side and the far right margin are lost. The emendations given here are those that appear in the *ILS*.

[C • P]ETRONIVS
[C • F] • FAL • VARIA
[SPEC]VLATOR • CAESAR[IS]
[HORDIO]NIA • T • L • EGIS[TE]
[VX]OR

* * *

[C(aius) P]etronius [C(ai) f(ilius) Fal(erna tribu)] Varia, [spec]ulator Caesar[is]; [Hordio]nia T(iti) l(iberta) Egis[te], [ux]or.

* * *

Gaius Petronius Varia, son of Gaius, of the Falerna tribe,[1] bodyguard of Caesar; Hordionia Egiste, freedwoman of Titus, his wife, put this up.

1   Unlike the German bodyguards, the *speculatores* were Roman citizens
    who had originally been recruited for the Praetorian Guard.

35.   *Aurelius Bitus, Praetorian Cavalry Officer*

CIL 6.2601; *ILS* 2055   Rome
Tombstone   3rd Century AD

Even after the dismissal of the *speculatores*, the Praetorian Guard retained a
cavalry force of as many as 1,000 men. These men were originally recruited as
infantry soldiers but received later promotion to the cavalry (but still remained in
their original units). The stone, a marble tablet from a funerary monument, was
discovered in Rome between the *Via Nomentana* and the *Via Tiburtina*.

D • M • AVR • BITO • EQ • COR • VI • PR
NATIONE • TRAX • CIVES • FILOPO
PVLITANVS • AN • P • M • XXXV • QVI
MIL • AN • XVII • SIC • IN • LEGIONE • I • IT
ALICA • AN • II • IN • COR • II • PRET
MVNIFEX • AN • XIIII • FACTVS
EQ • MIL • MENSES • N • X • FRATRI
DIGNISSIMO • VAL • AVLVSA
NVS • PRET • INCOMPARABILI

* * *

D(is) m(anibus/arco) Aur(elio) Bito, eq(uiti) co(ho)r(tis) VI pr(aetoriae),
natione T(h)rax, civ[i]s [Ph]ilopopulitanus, an(nis) p(lus) m(inus)
XXXV, qui mil(itavit) an(nos) XVII, sic: in legione I Italica an(nos) II,
in co(ho)r(te) II pr(a)et(oriae), munifex, an(nos) XIIII, factus eq(ues)
mil(itavit) menses n(umero) X; fratri dignissimo Val(erius) Aulusanus
pr(a)et(orianus) incomparabili.

* * *

To the spirits of the dead; to (Marcus) Aurelius Bitus, cavalry soldier in the
6th praetorian cohort, Thracian by nationality, citizen of Philippopolis,[1]
who lived 35 years more or less and served 17 years as follows: 2 years
in the 1st legion Italica, 14 years in the 2nd praetorian cohort, and,
having been promoted, ten months in the cavalry; Valerius Aulusanus,
a praetorian, dedicated this to his most worthy and incomparable
brother.[2]

1   Philippopolis was a city in the province of Thrace. By the third century,
    it was common for praetorians to come from sources other than Italian
    stock (as had been the rule in the first two centuries).
2   Probably not a natural brother, but rather a "brother in arms".

36.   *C. Vedennius Moderatus,*
Transferred to the Praetorian Guard

CIL 6.2725; *ILS* 2034   Rome
Tombstone   Later 1ˢᵗ Century AD

Moderatus began his career as a soldier in the 16ᵗʰ legion *Gallica*, a legion stationed on the Rhine. In the civil war of AD 68/69, that legion sent detachments to Italy to help Vitellius in his bid for the throne. After his victory over Otho, Vitellius rewarded some of his soldiers with a transfer to the Praetorian Guard (Tacitus *Histories* 2.94). It is likely that Moderatus' transfer took place at that time. Moderatus' inscription was discovered on the *Via Nomentana*, one of the streets that ran near the *Castra Praetoria*, the praetorian camp in Rome. Many praetorian tombs have been discovered along that road. The stone, a large marble statue base that marked Moderatus' tomb, is broken along the bottom of the inscription.

C · VEDENNIVS · C · F
QVI · MODERATVS · ANTIO
MILIT · IN · LEG · XVI · GAL · A · X
TRANLAT · IN · COH · IX · PR
IN · QVA · MILIT · ANN · VIII
MISSVS · HONESTA · MISSION
REVOC · AB· IMP · FACT · EVOC · AVG
ARCITECT · ARMAMENT · IMP
EVOC · ANN · XXIII
DONIS · MILITARIB · DONAT
BIS · AB · DIVO · VESP · ET
IMP · DOMITIANO · AVG · GERM
[...]
* * *

C(aius) Vedennius C(ai) f(ilius) Qui(rina tribu) Moderatus, Antio (domo), milit(avit) in leg(ione) XVI Gal(lica) a(nnos) X, tran(s)lat(us) in coh(ortem) IX pr(aetoriam), in qua milit(avit) ann(is) VIII, missus honesta mission(e), revoc(atus) ab imp(eratore), fact(us) evoc(atus) Aug(usti), arcitect(us) armament(arii) imp(eratoris), evoc(atus) ann(is) XXIII, donis militarib(us) donat(us) bis ab divo Vesp(asiano) et imp(eratore) Domitiano Aug(usto) Germ(anico) [...].

* * *

Gaius Vedennius Moderatus, son of Gaius, of the Qurina tribe, from Antium, served in the 16ᵗʰ legion Gallica for 10 years,[1] was transferred to the 9ᵗʰ praetorian cohort, in which he served for 8 years, given honorable discharge,[2] recalled by the emperor and was made imperial reservist,[3] builder of the imperial war machines,[4] reservist for 23 years,[5] granted military decorations twice by the divine Vespasian and the emperor Domitian Augustus Germanicus[6] ...[7]

1   He probably enlisted in AD 59/60. The 16th *Gallica* was disbanded after Vespasian's emergence as emperor in 70, after the civil war.

2   Despite his transfer to the Praetorians by Vitellius in AD 69, Vespasian kept him in the Guard after Vitellius was defeated. His discharge would have been in AD 77/78, after the usual eighteen years of service.

3   An *evocatus*, or reservist, was a soldier who returned to the military after his official discharge. Most *evocati* were men who hoped to eventually reach the centurionate or were specialized in some branch of service or administration (as with Verus, who became a military architect).

4   By "imperial war machines", Moderatus probably means artillery: catapults and *ballistae*, but he may have been involved with other building projects such as forts and bridges.

5   Twenty three years is an unusually long time to serve as an *evocatus*. If he did, his discharge would have been 100/101, in the reign of Trajan. If that was the case, it is surprising that Domitian, whose memory was condemned posthumously, would still be mentioned with honor during the reign of Trajan. It is more likely that the twenty-three years is Moderatus' total service (including his time as a legionary and praetorian). A service of five years as an *evocatus* would place his final discharge in the 83. Domitian waged a war against the Germanic Chatti in 82 and 83, for which he received the title Germanicus and a triumph. As Domitian oversaw the operations in person, a sizable portion of the Praetorian Guard would have participated in the war. Moderatus may have retired at the end of that war.

6   The circumstances of Moderatus' first award from the reign of Vespasian are unknown. Military activity continued in the East, in Britain and on the Rhine. The second award must have honored his service in Domitian's war against the Chatti (see previous note).

7   There may have been additional lines below the break in the stone.

Soldiers in the Auxiliary Forces

The auxiliaries (*auxilia*) were soldiers who served in less prestigious units meant to supplement the legions. Auxiliary soldiers at first served 30 years, but that was cut back to 25 years in the Flavian period. At the end of their service, non-citizen auxiliaries received Roman citizenship. Roman citizenship gave its holders many privileges and exemptions. Service in the auxiliaries, therefore, was very attractive to non-citizens in the empire, because it offered one of the only opportunities for social advancement. The auxiliaries were organized either into infantry cohorts or cavalry *alae*. In addition to the cohorts and *alae*, mixed infantry and cavalry cohorts were used in the auxiliary branch of the army, and were referred to as the *cohortes equitatae*.

37. *Longinus, Auxiliary Cavalry Soldier of the Thracians*

AE 1928, 156	Camulodunum, Britain
Tombstone	1st or 2nd Century AD

Cavalry *alae* were 500 men strong, divided into *turmae* (squadrons) commanded by decurions. Auxiliary units often served in provinces far from their native land. Longinus was recruited in his native Thrace, but his unit served in Britain.

> LONGINVS · SDAPESE
> MATYGI · F · DVPLICARIVS
> ALA · PRIMA · T[R]ACVM · PAGO
> SARDI · ANNO · XL · AEROR · XV
> HEREDES · EXS · TESTAM · F · C
> H · S · E ·

> * * *

Longinus Sdapesematygi f(ilius), duplicarius ala(e) prima(e) T(h)[r]acum, pago S[e]rdi(ca), anno(rum) XL, aeror(um) XV; heredes ex{s} testam(ento) f(aciendum) c(uraverunt); h(ic) s(itus) e(st).

> * * *

Longinus, son of Sdapezematygus,[1] receiving double pay[2] in the first ala *of Thracians,[3] from the town of Serdica,[4] lived 40 years, served 15;[5] his heirs took care of putting this up in accordance with his will; he is buried here.*

1   His father has a very foreign-sounding name. It is reminiscent of other names from native tribes on the Danube. The son's Roman name, however, indicates that the family had become more Romanized.
2   Making him a *principales* (see the introduction to this chapter).
3   The first *ala* of the Thracians is mentioned on several military diplomas from Britain of the second century, which recorded soldiers who had received honorable discharge.
4   A town in western Thrace, near the border of Moesia.
5   The "aer(orum)" on the stone would seem to be a mistake for "stipendorum", "years of service".

38. *Claudius Ingenuus, Auxiliary Soldier of the Mauri*

AE 1982, 816	Matrica, Pannonia
Tombstone	2nd or 3rd Century AD

Infantry cohorts were either 500 or 1,000 men strong, divided into centuries like the legions. Ingenuus served in a cohort of 1,000 soldiers originally recruited in Mauretania in North Africa. His name indicates that he or his ancestor received the citizenship from a Julio-Claudian emperor (note the *nomen* Claudius). It is more likely that Ingenuus was born a Roman citizen (note that his name, Ingenuus, is Latin for "freeborn"), since his auxiliary cohort seems to have been created in the reign of Marcus Aurelius or later (since it does not appear on the provincial military diplomas before that time). Over time, the legions increasingly recruited soldiers from more humble backgrounds. The opposite was true of the auxiliaries. An increasing number of Roman citizens began to serve in the cohorts and *alae*. This fact is probably a reflection of the increase in the number of citizens across the empire, especially in the frontier provinces.

D · M

CL · INGENVS

BVC · COH · M · MAVR

ET · FLA · PAVLINA · CO

VIX · AN · XXVI

ET · CL · PAVLINVS

[ET · CL] · INGENVA

[...]

* * *

D(is) m(anibus); Cl(audius) Ingenu(u)s, buc(inator) coh(ortis) m(illiariae) Maur(orum), et Fla(via) Paulina, co(niunx), vix(it) an(nos) XXVI et Cl(audius) Paulinus [et Cl(audia)] Ingenua [...].

* * *

To the spirits of the dead; Claudius Ingenuus, trumpeter[1] of the milliary cohort of the Mauri,[2] Flavia Paulina, his wife,[3] who lived 26 years,[4] Claudius Paulinus and Claudia Ingenua (his children)[5] [...put this up...].

1   Trumpeters also served as staff officers (*principales*) in the military headquarters.
2   As shown by the name, this was an auxiliary cohort of 1,000 men originally recruited in Mauretania. The cohort was stationed at Matrica, in the province of Pannonia, on the Danube, south of Aquincum. A number of inscriptions have been found at Matrica, some datable to the post-Severan period, which record many soldiers and veterans with the imperial *nomina* of Claudius and Aelius.
3   His wife, Flavia, must have been descended from the daughter of someone who received the citizenship from Vespasian.
4   This is probably the age of his wife, not Ingenuus. As auxiliary soldiers served 25 years, Ingenuus would not have been discharged by the time the inscription was dedicated.
5   Note the interesting naming scheme adopted by this family. Both children have the *nomen* of their father: Claudius, but the *cognomina* of both parents are used: the son has his mother's name (Paulinus) and the daughter has the father's (Ingenua).

39. *A Cavalry Soldier Known only by his Deeds*

CIL 3.3676; *ILS* 2558   "Bank of the Danube", Pannonia
Tombstone   2nd Century AD

This inscription appeared in manuscripts beginning in the 9th century and was described as being "on the bank of the Danube". The stone has since been lost. Interestingly, the soldier never gives his name, but expects that he will be remembered for his deeds alone. The event described here, in which the emperor Hadrian witnessed a training exercise of the Batavians, is also mentioned by the historian Dio Cassius (69.9).

ILLE · EGO · PANNONIIS · QVONDAM · NOTISSIMVS · ORIS
INTER · MILLE · VIROS · FORTIS · PRIMVSQ · BATAVOS
HADRIANO · POTVI · QVI · IVDICE · VASTA · PROFVNDI
AEQVORA · DANVVII · CVNCTIS · TRANSNARE · SVB · ARMIS
EMISSVMQ · ARCV · DVM · PENDET · IN · AERE · TELVM
AC · REDIT · EX · ALIA · FIXI · FREGIQVE · SAGITTA
QVEM · NEQVE · ROMANVS · POTVIT · NEC · BARBARVS · VNQVAM
NON · IACVLO · MILES · NON · ARCV · VINCERE · PARTHVS
HIC · SITVS · HIC · MEMORI · SAXO · MEA · FACTA · SACRAVI
VIDERIT · AN · NE · ALIQVIS · POST · ME · MEA · FACTA · SEQVATVR
EXEMPLO · MIHI · SVM · PRIMVS · QVI · TALIA · GESSI

* * *

ille ego Pannoniis quondam notissimus oris inter mille viros fortis primusq(ue) Batavos, Hadriano potui qui iudice vasta profundi aequora Danuvii cunctis transnare sub armis. Emissumq(ue) arcu, dum pendet in aere, telum, ac redit, ex alia fixi fregique sagitta; quem neque Romanus potuit nec barbarus unquam non iaculo miles, non arcu vincere Parthus. Hic situs, hic memori saxo mea facta sacravi. Viderit an ne aliquis post me mea facta sequatur. Exemplo mihi sum primus qui talia gessi.

* * *

I am that one who was very well known on the shores of Pannonia, who was foremost of the 1,000 Batavians in my unit. I was able, with Hadrian looking on, to swim across the wide waters of the deep Danube in all my armor. Also, when an arrow shot from my bow still hung in the air, I shot another arrow and hit the first arrow as it was falling back to the earth. I am the one whom neither Roman nor Barbarian soldier was ever able to best with the javelin, nor could the Parthian best me with the bow. Here I am buried. Here I entrust my deeds to this mindful stone. It remains to be seen whether anyone after me will match my deeds. As the first to do such things, I am an example for the future.

40.   *C. Julius Dexter,*
Veteran of an Auxiliary Cavalry Ala

CIL 8.2094; *ILS* 2518   Thlepte, Numidia
Tombstone   2nd Century AD

Dexter is another example of a soldier who was recruited into the auxiliaries as a Roman citizen. He was a cavalry soldier who advanced to junior officer rank in his unit. After his discharge, he held municipal office in Thlepte, in North Africa, the colony in which he was settled. This inscription was found on the Roman road between Theveste and Capsa on the ancient site of Thelepte.

DIS • MANIBVS
C • IVLIVS • DEXTER • VET • MIL • IN • ALA
EQ • CVR • TVRMAE • ARMOR • CVSTOS • SIGNI
FER • TVR • MILITA • ANNIS • XXVI • DIMIS • EMER
HONESTA • MISSIONE • DVOVIRATV • EGIT • IN • COL
SVA • THELEPTE • VIXIT • AN • LXXXV • HIC • CREMATVS
TVTIA • TERTIA • MARITA • IVLI • DEXTRI • VIX • AN • LXX
HIC • CREMATA • EST

* * *

Dis manibus; C(aius) Iulius Dexter, vet(eranus), mil(itavit) in ala eq(uitum), cur(ator) turmae, armor(um) custos, signifer tur(mae), milita(vit) annis XXVI, dimis(sus) emer(itus) honesta missione, dvoviratu(m) egit in col(onia) sua Thelepte, vixit an(nos) LXXXV; hic crematus.

Tutia Tertia, marita Iuli Dextri, vix(it) an(nos) LXX, hic cremata est.

* * *

To the spirits of the dead; Gaius Julius Dexter,[1] veteran, soldier in a cavalry ala,[2] commander of his squadron,[3] guardian of the armory, standard-bearer of his squadron, served 26 years, honorably discharged, held the position of town magistrate[4] in his colony of Thelepte,[5] lived 85 years; he is here cremated.

Tutia Tertia, the wife of Julius Dexter, lived 70 years, is here cremated.

1   Dexter's name would indicate that he was descended from someone who received the citizenship from Augustus (perhaps as an auxiliary soldier).
2   The specific unit is not given. Dexter is more interested in giving a general record of his military service which had probably ended thirty years before his death.
3   The commander of a squadron (about 30 men) in a cavalry *ala* was called a *curator*.
4   This would seem to indicate that Dexter, by the end of his life, had earned the rank of equestrian, or at least had entered the ranks of the municipal aristocracy in his colony.
5   Trajan founded the colony of Thelepte.

Noteworthy Deaths of Soldiers

The following inscriptions record some soldiers who died while on duty: Flaminius who was killed while serving in Africa with the 3rd legion *Augusta*, Caelius who was killed by the German army of Arminius in the disaster of Quinctilius Varus in AD 9, and an unnamed praetorian who was killed while extinguishing a fire in Ostia.

41. *L. Flaminius, Legionary Killed in Combat*

CIL 8.14603; *ILS* 2305   Simitthu, Africa Proconsularis
Tombstone   Early 1st Century AD

Service in a Roman legion was a long affair. Here, Flaminius recounts his death in battle after having served 19 of his 20 or 25 required years in quiet garrison duty. This inscription was discovered in the necropolis of the 3rd legion *Augusta* outside Simitthu, on the Roman road leading north.

L • FLAMINIVS • D • F • ARN
MIL • LEG • III • AVG
7 • IVLI • LONGI • DILECTO
LECTVS • AB • M • SILANO • MIL
ANNIS • XIX • IN • PRAESIDIO
VT • ESSET • IN • SALTO • PHILOMV
SIANO • AB • HOSTEM • IN • PVGNA
OCCISSVS • VIXIT • PIE
ANNIS • XL
H • S • E

* * *

L(ucius) Flaminius D(ecimi) f(ilius) Arn(ensis tribu), mil(es) leg(ionis) III Aug(ustae), (centuriae) Iuli Longi, dilecto lectus ab M(arco) Silano, mil(itavit) annis XIX in praesidio, ut esset in salto Philomusiano ab hoste{m} in pugna occis{s}us, vixit pie annis XL; h(ic) s(itus) e(st).

* * *

Lucius Flaminius, son of Decimus, of the Arnensis tribe, soldier of the 3rd legion Augusta,[1] *in the century of Julius Longus, chosen in the levy by Marcus Silanus,[2] served garrison duty for 19 years only to be killed by the enemy[3] in battle in the Philomusian territory,[4] lived devoutly for 40 years; he is buried here.*

1 Africa was the only senatorial province to have a legion stationed in it: the 3rd *Augusta*. In the reign of Caligula or Claudius, the emperor removed that legion from the jurisdiction of the senatorial proconsul and handed it over to an imperial legate.

2   M. Julius Silanus was proconsul of Africa between AD 33 and 38.
     He was probably the last proconsul of Africa to command the 3rd
     Augusta.

3   Note the misspelling in the Latin: "hostem" instead of the ablative
     "hoste" after the preposition "ab" and "occissus" with the extra "s"
     instead of "occisus".

4   Not much is known about this region. It was evidently an area close to
     Smitthus.

42.   *M. Caelius, Victim of the Disaster of Varus*

CIL 13.8648; *ILS* 2244   Vetera, Germania Inferior
          Tombstone   Early 1st Century AD

In AD 9, Quinctilius Varus, Augustus' legate of Germany, marched the 17th,
18th and 19th legions (and an equivalent number of auxiliary troops) into a German
ambush in the Black Forest. Most of the expedition was annihilated along with
their commander. Caelius was a centurion in the 18th legion and was killed along
with the majority of his comrades. In the early reign of Tiberius, Germanicus,
the emperor's nephew and adopted son, went to the site and recovered some of
the bones of the dead. He also avenged Roman pride by defeating Arminius, the
German chieftain who had defeated Varus, in a pitched battle (Tac. *Hist.* 1.60).
Above the inscription is a large picture of Caelius. He is shown holding the vine
sapling which was the symbol of the office of centurion. Numerous military
awards (*torques, phalerae,* and a *corona civica*) adorn his cuirass. On either side
of the picture of Caelius are busts of two of his former slaves (freed by Caelius).
Both freedmen are labeled with their names: Marcus Caelius Privatus, freedman
of Marcus and Marcus Caelius Thiaminus, freedman of Marcus.

M · CAELIO · T · F · LEM · BON
7 · LEG · XIIX · ANN · LIIIS
[CE]CIDIT · BELLO · VARIANO · OSSA
[I]NFERRE · LICEBIT · P · CAELIVS · T · E
LEM · FRATER · FECIT

* * *

M(arco) Caelio T(iti) f(ilio) Lem(onia tribu), Bon(onia domo),
(centurioni) leg(ionis) XIIX, ann(os) LIII s(emissis), [ce]cidit bello
Variano, ossa [i]nferre licebit; P(ublius) Caelius T(iti) [f(ilius)]
Lem(onia tribu) frater fecit.

* * *

*Marcus Caelius, son of Titus, of the Lemonia tribe, from Bononia,[1]
centurion of the 18th legion, lived 53 ½ years, died in the war of Varus; it
will be permitted to bury the bones here;[2] Publius Caelius, son of Titus,
of the Lemonia tribe, his brother, made this.*

1   A town in northern Italy.
2   This could refer to Caelius, his freedmen, or both. Many bodies were
    not recovered from the scene of the disaster. The freedmen may have
    accompanied their master to Germany and died there with him. It is
    also possible that the freedmen did not accompany him on his final
    campaign (or were in Rome while Caelius was in Germany). As such,
    they may have still been alive when the tombstone was erected, and
    that the inscription provided for their future burial in the same tomb.

43. *Soldier Killed in Ostia while Extinguishing a Fire*

ILS 9494; *AE* 1912, 250   Ostia, Latium, Italy
Tombstone   1st Century AD

This inscription was put up before Claudius sent a detachment of the *vigiles*
to Ostia to protect the new harbor. Other inscriptions of the 6th praetorian cohort
have been discovered in Ostia; it is possible that the cohort was stationed there
before the construction of the *Castra Praetoria* in AD 23. This tombstone was
found outside Ostia's *Porta Romana*, on the east side of town on the road leading
up the Tiber to Rome.

[.....]V[..]
MILITI · COHOR · VI · PR
OSTIENSES · LOCVM · SEPVLT
DEDERVNT
PVBLICOQ · FVNERE · EFFERVN
DECRERVNT · QVOD · IN · INCENDIO
RESTINGVENDO · INTERIT
IN · F · P · XII
IN · AG · P · XXV

* * *

[.....]v[..], militi cohor(tis) VI pr(aetoriae), Ostienses locum sepult(urae)
dederunt publicoq(ue) funere efferun(t) decre(ve)runt quod in incendio
restinguendo interit; in f(ronte) p(edes) XII, in ag(ro) p(edes) XXV.

* * *

*[...?...],[1] soldier in the 6th praetorian cohort; the people of Ostia gave
him a place of burial and decreed that they grant him a public funeral
and burial, because he died while putting out a fire; this burial plot is 12
feet wide and 25 feet deep.*

1   The top of the stone is illegible, so the name is not known.

Military Officers

The most junior officer of the Roman army was the centurion. A centurion commanded one of the legion's 59 centuries of 80 men each (160 men in the first cohort). The senatorial legionary legates (the commanding officer of a legion) appointed the legionary centurions. Centurions were drawn from the following sources:

- Common soldiers in the legions who had seen long service. Most from this category who previously had achieved the distinction of being declared *immunes* and *principales*. Many also had re-enlisted as *evocati* after their discharge.

- Men of the equestrian order who wished to embark upon a career in the imperial service.

- Centurions and decurions from the auxiliary forces.

- Soldiers from the Praetorian Guard (or, less frequently, from an urban cohort) who had completed their shorter term of service and re-enlisted as *evocati*.

- Sons of centurions.

Each of the six centurions in the 2nd through 10th cohorts had one of the following titles, which are listed in order of ascending seniority: *hastatus posterior, princeps posterior, pilus posterior, hastatus prior, princeps prior* and *pilus prior*. All centurions in these cohorts were of equal rank, although the *pilus prior* was the chief centurion of his cohort. In contrast, the 1st cohort had only five (as opposed to six) centuries, but they were double the size of ordinary centuries. The centurions of the 1st cohort were the most prestigious in the legion. They had titles similar to centurions of the other cohorts, except there was no *pilus posterior*, and the *pilus prior* was called the *primus pilus*. Holding rank of *primus pilus* in the 1st cohort guaranteed entry to the equestrian order.

Above the rank of centurion was the rank of tribune. The legion had six military tribunes, one from the senatorial order and five from the equestrian. The senatorial legionary legate commanded the legion. For examples of the senatorial officers, see the chapter on the senatorial aristocracy. Auxiliary units (cohorts and *alae*) were commanded by equestrian prefects or tribunes. For examples of equestrian officers, see the chapter on the equestrian aristocracy.

The inscriptions in this section illustrate the typical career path of non-senatorial military officers. Caesius Verus rose from the ranks of the Praetorian Guard and, after serving as a *principalis*, eventually reached the rank of centurion. Claudius Vitalis was an equestrian who joined the army. As a career centurion, he moved from legion to legion. Ovinius Rufus and Gavius Silvanus were chief centurions in legions and were then promoted to the tribunates of the garrison of Rome. Tiberius Claudius Maximus led a distinguished career. He started as a legionary cavalry soldier but eventually reached the rank of *decurio* (an officer in an auxiliary *ala*).

44. *M. Caesius Verus, From Soldier to Centurion*

AE 1990, 896   Comana Pontica, Pontus
Tombstone   2nd Century AD

After a privileged career as a praetorian and *evocatus*, Verus was eventually promoted to the rank of centurion.

M · CAESIVS
M · F · POL · VERVS
POLLENTIA · 7
LEG · V · MAC · MILI
TAVIT · IN · COH · IX
PRAETORIA · ANN
XVI · ORDINATVS · TVBI
CEM · ITEM · OPTIO · AD · CAR
CAREM · FACTVS · EST · MILI
TAVIT · EVOCATVS · ANNIS
VII · CENTVRIO · FACTVS
EST · IN · LEG · V · MAC · FVIT · OR
DINE · IN · SEXTA · HASTATVS
POSTERIOR · STIPENDIA · AC
CEPIT · CALIGATA · XVI · EVO
CATIVA · VII · CENTVRIONI
CA · IIII · MILITAVIT · ANNIS
XXVII · VIXIT · ANNIS · XXXXI
M · CAESIVS · ATIMETVS · ET
M · CAESIVS · LIMEN · LIBERTI · ET
HEREDES · EIVS · EX · TESTAMENTO · F · C

* * *

M(arcus) Caesius M(arci) f(ilius) Pol(lia tribu) Verus, Pollentia (domo), (centurio) leg(ionis) V Mac(edonicae), militavit in coh(orte) IX praetoria ann(is) XVI, ordinatus tubicem, item optio ad carcarem factus est, militavit evocatus annis VII, centurio factus est in leg(ione) V Mac(edonica), fuit ordine in sexta hastatus posterior, stipendia accepit caligata XVI, evocativa VII, centurionica IIII, militavit annis XXVII, vixit annis XXXXI; M(arcus) Caesius Atimetus et M(arcus) Caesius Limen liberti et heredes eius ex testamento f(aciendum) c(uraverunt).

* * *

Marcus Caesius Verus, son of Marcus, of the Pollia tribe, from Pollentia,[1] centurion of the 5th legion Macedonica.[2] *He served in the 9th praetorian cohort for 16 years during which he was made trumpeter and later officer in charge of the military prison. He served a further 7 years as reservist.[3] He was then made centurion in the 5th legion* Macedonica *and was the 6th ranking centurion in his cohort.[4] He served as a regular soldier for 16 years, as reservist for seven and as centurion for four. He served a total of 27 years and lived 41; Marcus Caesius Atimetus and*

Marcus Caesius Limen, his freedmen and heirs,[5] took the responsibility of constructing this according to the wishes expressed in his will.

1   A town in Spain, Verus' birthplace. Verus' burial and inscription, however, were in Pontus and Bithynia. A possible reason for the odd location of the inscription is that the legion with which Verus was centurion at the time of his death, the 5th *Macedonica*, was stationed in Pontus and Bithynia. It is known that this legion was transferred from the Danube to the East for the major Parthian wars under Nero, Trajan and Lucius Verus. The pattern of Verus' career suggests he partook in either the wars of Trajan or Verus in the early and middle 2nd century.

2   Marcus lists his most senior position first before recording his entire career from the beginning.

3   Verus continued to serve as an *evocatus* in the hopes of eventually being promoted to the rank of centurion. Because the praetorian term of service was the shortest in the Roman army, most *evocati* came from the praetorians.

4   He was therefore in the most junior centurionate in his cohort.

5   It would appear that Verus died without a wife. His heirs were his freedmen, both of whom bear his *praenomen* and *nomen* (Marcus Caesius).

45.   *Ti. Claudius Vitalis, Career Centurion*

CIL 6.3584; *ILS* 2656	Rome
Tombstone	2nd Century AD

Vitalis was a career centurion. As an equestrian, he entered the army as a centurion and then received numerous transfers from one centurionate to another. Most of his transfers were from one legion to another. Some, however, were within the same legion, which suggests that he was good at a specific job, such as recruiting new soldiers in depleted legions; he thus was transferred to units which required his special expertise.

TI · CLAVDIO · TI · F · GAL · VITALI · EX · EQVITE · R
ORDINEM · ACCEPIT · IN · LEG · V · MAC · SVCCESSIONE
PROMOTVS · EX · LEG · V · MAC · IN · LEG · I · ITAL · DONIS · D
TORQVIB · ARMILL · PHALER · CORONA · VALL · BELLO
DACICO · SVCCESSIONE · PROMOT · EX · LEG · I · ITAL · IN · LEG
I · MINER · ITER · DONIS · D · TORQVIB · ARMILL · PHALER
CORONA · VALL · BELLO · DACICO · SVCCESSIONE · PRO
MOT · EX · LEG · I · MINER · IN · LEG · XX · VICT · ITEM · PROM
IN · LEG · EAD · ITEM · SVCCESSIONE · PROMOTVS · EX · LEG · XX
VICT · IN · LEG · IX · HISP · SVCC · PROMOT · EX · LEG · IX · HISP
IN · LEG · VII · CL · P · F · ITEM · SVCCESSIT · IN · LEG · EAD
MILIT · 7 · IN · II · PR · POST · ANNIS · XI · VIXIT · ANNIS · XLI

* * *

Ti(berio) Claudio Ti(beri) f(ilio) Gal(eria tribu) Vitali, ex equite R(omano), ordinem accepit in leg(ione) V Mac(edonica), successione promotus ex leg(ione) V mac(edonica) in leg(ionem) I Ital(icam), donis d(onato) torquib(us) armill(is) phaler(is) corona vall(ari) bello Dacico, successione promot(us) ex leg(ione) I Ital(ica) in leg(ionem) I Miner(viam), iter(um) donis d(onato) torquib(us) armill(is) phaler(is) corona vall(ari) bello Dacico, successione promot(us) ex leg(ione) I Miner(via) in leg(ionem) XX Vict(ricem), item prom(otus) in leg(ione) ead(em), item successione promotus ex leg(ione) XX Vict(rice) in leg(ionem) IX Hisp(anicam), succ(essione) promot(us) ex leg(ione) IX Hisp(anicae) in leg(ionem) VII Cl(audiam) p(iam) f(idelem), item successit in leg(ione) ead(em), milit(avit) (centurio) in II (cohorte) pr(inceps) post(erior) annis XI, vixit annis XLI.

* * *

To Tiberius Claudius Vitalis son of Tiberius, of the Galeria tribe, from the equestrian order, took a post as centurion in the 5ᵗʰ legion Macedonica.[1] *He then was promoted from the 5ᵗʰ legion* Macedonica *to the 1ˢᵗ legion* Italica,[2] *during which post he was given military decorations for distinguished service in the Dacian War: necklaces, arm-bands, breast-plate ornaments, and a rampart crown.[3] He was then promoted from the 1ˢᵗ legion* Italica *to the 1ˢᵗ legion* Minervia,[4] *with whom he was again given military decorations: necklaces, arm-bands, breast-place ornaments, and a rampart crown in the Dacian war.[5] He next was promoted from the 1ˢᵗ legion* Minervia *to the 20ᵗʰ legion* Victrix[6] *and later was promoted within the same legion. Then he was promoted from the 20ᵗʰ legion* Victrix *to the 9ᵗʰ legion* Hispana.[7] *Next he was promoted from the 9ᵗʰ legion* Hispana *to the 7ᵗʰ legion* Claudia,[8] *loyal and faithful. Later, he was promoted in the same legion and served as centurion in the 2ⁿᵈ cohort as the fifth ranking centurion for 11 years and lived for 41 years.[9]*

1   At this time, the 5ᵗʰ legion *Macedonica* was stationed in Moesia Inferior.
2   The 1ˢᵗ legion *Italica* was stationed in Moesia Inferior.
3   Necklaces (*torques*), arm-bands (*armillae*), and breast-plate ornaments in the shape of round metal disks (*phalerae*) were frequently distributed to soldiers and commanders after the successful completion of a war. They are often represented on tomb portraits of soldiers. The gold rampart crown (*corona vallaris*) was given to the first soldier who gained entrance to an enemy camp by crossing the rampart (the *valla*). These awards probably came at the end of Trajan's first Dacian war (AD 101-102).
4   The 1ˢᵗ legion *Minervia* had been created by Domitian and stationed in the Rhine. In the winter following the first Dacian war, Trajan

transferred the legion to the Danube. Afterwards, it participated in the second Dacian war (AD 105-106).

5   Probably at the conclusion of the second Dacian war.

6   The 20th legion *Victrix* was stationed in Britain.

7   The 9th legion *Hispana* was stationed in Britain. Trajan transferred the legion to Germany Inferior in c. 112/113 to compensate for legions drawn off for the Parthian war. Vitalis may have been in the legion at the time of the transfer.

8   The 7th legion *Claudia* was stationed in Moesia Superior. Part of the legion was taken to Parthia for Trajan's war there in c. 114/115, but it is likely that Vitalis had already retired (or been killed) by that time.

9   His final position was probably 5th ranking centurion in the 2nd cohort (i.e. *princeps posterior*). Eleven years is probably the length of his total service in all of the cohorts mentioned, perhaps ca. AD 100-110.

46.   *L. Ovinius Rufus,*
Tribune of Augustus' Praetorian Guard

CIL 10.4872; *ILS* 2021　·   Venafrum, Campania, Italy
Tombstone   Early 1st Century AD

This is one of the earliest inscriptions which mentions an officer of the Praetorian Guard. He served in the Guard of Augustus.

> L · OVINIVS · L · F · TER · RVFVS
> PRIM · ORDO · COHORTIVM · PRAET
> DIVI · AVGVSTI · PRIM · PIL · LEG · XIIII · GEM
> TRIB · MIL · COHORT · XI · VRB · TRIB · MIL
> COH · [.]III · PRAET · PRAEF · FABR · IIVIR
> L · OVINIO · M · F · TER · PATRI
> M · OVINIO · L · F · TER · VOPISCO · FRATRI
> ALLIDIAE · L · F · RVFAE · MATRI
> PVLLIAE · PRIMAE · VXORI

* * *

L(ucius) Ovinius L(uci) f(ilius) Ter(etina tribu) Rufus, prim(us) ordo cohortium praet(oriarum) divi Augusti, prim(us) pil(us) leg(ionis) XIIII Gem(inae), trib(unus) mil(itum) cohort(is) XI urb(anae), trib(unus) mil(itum) coh(ortis) [ ]III praet(oriae), praef(ectus) fabr(rum), IIvir, L(ucio) Ovinio M(arci) f(ilio) Ter(etina tribu), patri, M(arco) Ovinio L(uci) f(ilio) Ter(etina tribu) Vopisco, fratri, Allidiae L(uci) f(iliae) Rufae, matri, Pulliae Primae, uxori.

* * *

Lucius Ovinius Rufus, son of Lucius, of the Teretina tribe, centurion in the first praetorian cohort[1] of the divine Augustus,[2] chief centurion of the 14ᵗʰ legion Gemina,³ *military tribune of the 11ᵗʰ urban cohort,⁴ tribune of the 3ʳᵈ(?) praetorian cohort, prefect of the engineers, duovir, to his father Lucius Ovinius, son of Marcus, of the Teretina tribe,⁵ to his brother Marcus Ovinius Vopiscus, son of Lucius, of the Teretina tribe, to his mother Allidia Rufa, son of Lucius, to his wife Pullia Prima.⁶*

1   Because the first cohort was the most prestigious, its members are sometimes called "primus ordo".
2   Because Augustus is named *divus*, the inscription must have been put up after his death.
3   In the reign of Augustus, this legion was stationed first on the Danube and then was transferred to the Rhine.
4   Generally, tribunes would begin their career in the urban garrison by commanding a cohort of the *vigiles*. It is possible that Augustus had not yet instituted the *vigiles* at the time of Rufus' promotion.
5   The father does not have a *cognomen* reported. *Cognomina* only began to be widely used in the 1ˢᵗ century BC. Note how his two sons have *cognomina*.
6   This inscription says much about Rufus' family. Rufus was the eldest son of a man named Lucius Ovinius (note the common *praenomen* of father and son). His brother was named Marcus (whose *praenomen* came from his grandfather, see the filiation of the father). Their father was married to a woman named Allidia Rufa whose name was the source of Rufus' own *cognomen*. Rufus' wife was named Pullia Prima, i.e. the eldest daughter of a family named Pullius.

47. *C. Gavius Silvanus, Tribune in the Urban Garrison*

CIL 5.7003; *ILS* 2701   Taurini, Italy
Statue Base   1ˢᵗ Century AD

Silvanus exemplifies the typical career of an officer from the primipilate to the tribunate of the urban garrison. He also received military decorations for his actions during the emperor Claudius' invasion of Britain. Silvanus is known from the histories of Tacitus to have been a member of the conspiracy of Piso, a senator who conspired against Nero, unsuccessfully, in 65 (Tac., *Hist.* 15.50, 60, 61, 71).

C · GAVIO · L · F
STEL · SILVANO
[P]RIMIPILARI · LEG · VIII · AVG
[T]RIBVNO · COH · II · VIGILVM
[T]RIBVNO · COH · XIII · VRBAN
[TR]IBVNO · COH · XII · PRAETOR
[D]ONIS · DONATO · A · DIVO · CLAVD

BELLO • BRITANNICO
[TO]RQVIBVS • ARMILLIS • PHALERIS
CORONA • AVREA
[P]ATRONO • COLON • [D • D]

* * *

C(aio) Gavio L(uci) f(ilio) Stel(latina tribu) Silvano, [p]rimipilari leg(ionis) VIII Aug(ustae), [t]ribuno coh(ortis) II vigilum, [t]ribuno coh(ortis) XIII urban(ae), [t]ribuno coh(ortis) XII praetor(iae), [d]onis donato a divo Claud(i) bello Britannico: [to]rquibus armillis phaleris corona aurea, [p]atrono colon(iae), [d(ecreto) d(ecurionum)].

* * *

To Gaius Gavius Silvanus, son of Lucius, of the Stellatina tribe, chief centurion of the 8th legion Augusta,[1] tribune of the 2nd cohort of the fire brigade, tribune of the 13th urban cohort, tribune of the 12th praetorian cohort,[2] granted military decorations by the divine Claudius for the war in Britain: necklaces, armbands, armor decorations, and a gold crown,[3] the patron of the colony; this was put up by decree of the town council.

1   The 8th legion *Augusta* was stationed on the Danube, but it seems to have sent detachments for the war in Britain under Claudius (AD 43)
2   This is the first datable reference to a 12th praetorian cohort. The emperor Claudius probably increased the size of the Guard from nine to twelve cohorts shortly after his succession.
3   Silvanus probably received these decorations while serving as a centurion of the 8th *Augusta*. It is possible, however, that, as in the case of many chief centurions, posts Silvanus held before that of chief centurion have been omitted, so he may have received decorations as a regular soldier.

---

48.   *Ti. Claudius Maximus, Captor of Decebalus*

AE 1969/70, 583	Philippi, Macedonia
Tombstone	2nd Century AD

This inscription illustrates the career of a lifelong auxiliary soldier and officer. He was a prominent figure in Trajan's Dacian and Parthian wars. Most significantly, he was the soldier who captured and killed the Dacian chieftain Decebalus and brought his head to Trajan.

TI • CLAVDIVS
MAXIMVS • VET
[S] • V • F • C • MILITAVIT
EQVE • IN • LEG • VII • C • P • F • FAC
TVS • QVESTOR • EQVIT
SINGVLARIS • LEGATI • LE

GIONIS · EIVSDEM · VEXIL
LARIVS · EQVITVM · ITEM
BELLO · DACICO · OB · VIRTV
TE · DONIS · DONATVS · AB · IM
P · DOMITIANO · FACTVS · DVPLI
A · DIVO · TROIANO · IN · ALA · SECVD
PANNONIORVM · A · QVO · ET · FA
TVS · EXPLORATOR · IN · BELLO · DA
CICO · ET · OB · VIRTVTE · BIS · DONIS
DONATVS · BELLO · DACICO · ET
PARTHICO · ET · AB · EODE · FACTVS
DECVRIO · IN · ALA · EADE · QVOD
CEPISSET · DECEBALV · ET · CAPVT
EIVS · PERTVLISSET · EI · RANISSTO
RO · MISSVS · VOLVNTARIVS · HO
NESTA · MISSIONE · A · TERENT[IO · SCAV]
RIANO · CONSVLARE · [EXERCI]
TVS · PROVINCIAE · NOV[AE · DACIAE]

* * *

Ti(berius) Claudius Maximus vet(eranus), [s(e)] v(ivo), f(aciendum) c(uravit), militavit eque(s) in leg(ione) VII C(laudia) p(ia) f(ideli), factus qu(a)estor equit(um), singularis legati legionis, eiusdem vexillarius equitum, item bello Dacico ob virtute(m) donis donatus ab imp(eratore) Domitiano, factus dupli(carius) a divo Tr[a]iano in ala secu(n)d(a) Pannoniorum, a quo et fa(c)tus explorator in bello Dacico, et ob virtute(m) bis donis donatus bello Dacico et Parthico, et ab eode(m) factus decurio in ala eade(m) quod cepisset Decebalu(m) et caput eius pertulisset ei Ranisstoro, missus voluntarius honesta missione a Terent[io Scau]riano consulare [exerci]tus provinciae nov[ae Daciae].

* * *

Tiberius Claudius Maximus, military veteran, took care of making this dedication while he was still alive. He served in the cavalry in the 7th legion Claudia *loyal and faithful,[1] was made financial officer of the cavalry, guard of the legionary legate, standard bearer of the cavalry in the same legion, was awarded military decorations by the emperor Domitian for his courage in the Dacian war,[2] was promoted to double-pay grade by the divine Trajan[3] in the second ala of the Pannonians,[4] was promoted to scout by Trajan in the Dacian war,[5] was awarded military decorations twice by Trajan for his courage in the Dacian and Parthian wars,[6] was made platoon officer by Trajan in the same ala because he captured Decebalus and brought his head to Trajan in Ranisstorum.[7] He served voluntarily after he was granted honorable discharge by Terentius Scaurianus, consular commander of the army in the new province of Dacia(?)[8]*

1   The 7th legion *Claudia* was stationed in Viminacium, Moesia Superior. Maximus was therefore a Roman citizen who was originally recruited into the legions. He was also probably recruited as a cavalry soldier, a fact that indicates that he was probably the son of a military veteran. Philippi, Maximus' hometown, was a veteran colony.

2   Domitian fought two wars in Dacia, in 85 and again in 86.

3   The inscription mistakenly refers to Trajan as "Troianos."

4   The second *ala* of the Pannonians was stationed in the new province of Dacia after the Dacian wars. It is possible that Trajan formed the *ala* in preparation for his campaigns in Dacia. As such, Maximus would have been one of the first to be recruited into the new unit.

5   Trajan fought two wars against the Dacians: in 101-102 and again in 105-106.

6   The first award probably came at the end of the second Dacian war. The second came during the Parthian war, fought from 113 to 116.

7   Only the head was brought (not Decebalus alive), because Decebalus is known to have committed suicide rather than fall into the hands of the Romans (Dio 68.14). The scene is commemorated on the top of Trajan's column, where the cavalry are depicted catching up with the fleeing Decebalus.

8   Scaurianus was also the first governor of Dacia after Trajan annexed that province (probably from AD 106 to 110). The new province could also have been Mesopotamia, (which has allowed scholars to hypothesize that Scaurianus was the first governor of that province as well), since Maximus also received awards in the Parthian war. Those second decorations, however, could have come during his voluntary service after discharge.

SLAVES AND FREEDMEN

The institution of slavery was well-established, accepted and widespread in ancient Rome. For the Romans, slave labor was economically advantageous because, after the initial purchase, masters only had to provide room and board for their slaves and did not have to pay wages (although some did give their slaves an allowance, called the slave's *peculium*). Slaves could be of any race, gender or age, as long as they could perform the desired task.

Roman slaves have been divided into two categories: rural and urban. Rural slaves generally had a difficult life of hard labor in the fields of the large agricultural estates, which were owned by the aristocracy. Chain gangs and poor

Tombstone of Cornelia Frontina, wife of an imperial freedman in charge of the main gladiatorial barracks in Rome (CIL 6.10164; ILS 5153), National Museum of Rome at the Baths of Diocletian, Rome (courtesy of the Ministero per i Beni e le Attività Culturali, Soprintendenza Archeologica di Roma).

quality food and lodgings characterized the life of a rural slave. In comparison, urban slaves had a much better life. They were generally associated with the urban villas of the aristocracy. These urban households could be very large, with slaves numbering in the hundreds. The slaves often had very specialized jobs (for example, doorkeeper or cook), which usually gave them more freedom and leisure than their rural counterparts. Also, because they generally lived in closer proximity to the master, urban slaves had a better chance of developing a personal relationship with him or his family, making manumission more likely (although such proximity also exposed them to harsher treatment in the case of a cruel master). By the first century AD, rural slaves declined in number, as the aristocracy now preferred exploiting freeborn tenant farmers, rather than large numbers of unskilled agricultural slaves. While slaves had to be purchased (or be born into slavery) and supported at the master's expense, tenant farmers worked plots of land belonging to the landowner, and gave the owner a significant share of the crops. Such farmers were not purchased and were relatively self-sufficient.

The Romans enslaved people for various reasons, and some were born into slavery. The Roman army would capture slaves following a victory in a foreign war or after quelling a provincial revolt. Such wars, however, were often sporadic and generally gathered uneducated prisoners who were sold as slaves to work on large, rural estates. Piracy, brigandage and even voluntary enslavement provided many urban slaves. Slave traders also reportedly collected children exposed at birth, and raised them as slaves to be sold when they were ready to enter the workforce. Some people, called *vernae*, were born into slavery.

In Roman law and culture, slaves were considered to be sub-human and remained completely within the control of their master. Despite the lowly status of slaves in the Roman world, however, their treatment gradually became more humane. The agricultural chain gangs began to disappear. In the urban sphere, the emperors passed laws prohibiting masters from mistreating and arbitrarily killing their slaves. Also, manumission, by which a slave received his freedom and Roman citizenship, was very common. In fact, a study of the names of the commoners of Rome indicates that the city was heavily populated by freedmen (*liberti*, manumitted slaves) and their descendants.

Few inscriptions about slaves exist, and those that do are for urban slaves. Thus, the inscriptions in this section illustrate urban slaves belonging to wealthy aristocratic masters. They not only document the lives of urban slaves, but also illustrate the high degree of specialization within large, aristocratic households. Some slaves were even literate (e.g. Grapte the secretary, Carpimus, who was in charge of household expenses, and Urbana the pedagogue). Some slaves attended to the physical appearance of the family members (Psamate the hairdresser, Zethus the barber, and Italia the dressmaker), others served as household staff (Mithrodates the baker), and others as property managers (Cero the caretaker, Bathyllus the steward, Musaeaus the *ianitor* (doorkeeper), and Philologus the butler). The relationship between slave and free could be friendly, as illustrated by an inscription of a number of slaves who dedicated an inscription to an imperial freedman. Another inscription records the monetary provision for public slaves, who served the local government officials.

Household Slaves

49.   *Grapte, Secretary*

CIL 6.9540; *ILS* 7397   Rome
Tombstone   1ˢᵗ Century AD

Grapte was a secretary whose primary duties would have been to take dictation from her mistress or to make copies of previously written notes and letters. Her inscription, a small marble slab (*cippus*), was found on the *Via Appia*.

DIS · MANIB
GRAPTE
EGNATIAE · MA
XIMILLAE
A · MANV
CONIVGI · KARIS
SIMAE · C · EGN
ATIVS · AROGVS

* * *

Dis manib(us); Grapte, Egnatiae Maximillae a manu, coniugi [c]arissimae; C(aius) Egnatius Arogus.

* * *

To the spirits of the dead; Grapte, secretary of Egnatia Maximilla;[1] Gaius Egnatius Arogus dedicated this to his very dear wife.[2]

1   Egnatia Maximilla was the wife of Glitius Gallus, one of the people banished following the conspiracy of Calpurnius Piso against Nero. Tacitus (*Ann.* 15.71) mentions that she was very rich, but that her fortune was confiscated after she accompanied her husband into exile.
2   Grapte's husband's name indicates that he is a freedman of the Egnatius family, the same household to which Grapte belongs.

Tombstone of the ornatrix Gnome Pierinis, another slave hairdresser like Psamate (CIL 6.9730; ILS 7419), National Museum of Rome at the Baths of Diocletian, Rome. Photo courtesy of the Ministero per i Beni e le Attività Culturali Soprintenza Archeologica di Roma.

50. *Psamate, Hairdresser*

CIL 6.9732; *ILS* 7420a   Rome
Tombstone   1st Century AD

PSAMATE · FVRIAE
ORNATRIX · V · A · XIIX
MITHRODATES · PISTOR
FLACCI · THORI · FECIT

* * *

Psamate, Furiae ornatrix, v(ixit) a(nnos) XIIX; Mithrodates, pistor Flacci Thori, fecit.

* * *

Psamate, hairdresser[1] of Furia, lived 18 years; Mithrodates,[2] the baker of Thorius Flaccus,[3] made this.

1   Presumably the equivalent of a *tonstrix* (a female barber). There were also male *ornatores* who took care of their master's hair.
2   Mithrodates (perhaps a mistake for "Mithridates") is possibly her husband. If the Furia and Flaccus Thorius mentioned in the inscription were husband and wife, then Psamate and Mithrodates may have been from the same household.
3   Governor of Pontus and Bithynia under Augustus.

51. *Carpimus,*
in Charge of Household Expenses

CIL 6.33912; *ILS* 7391   Rome
Tombstone   1st Century AD

Carpimus was the slave of Pompeius Macer, a name shared by two important senators of the early Julio-Claudian period. This tombstone, a small marble stele, was discovered outside the city, between the *Via Salaria* and the *Via Pinciana* in the northern part of Rome.

CARPIMO
POMPEI · MACRI
SVMPTVARIO

* * *

Carpimo, Pompei Macri (servo), sumptuario.

* * *

To Carpimus, slave of Pompeius Macer, slave in charge of monitoring household expenses.

---

52. *Zethus, Barber*

CIL 6.9939; *ILS* 7414   Rome
Tombstone   1st Century AD

ZETHO · A · PLAVTI
TONSORI

* * *

Zetho A(uli) Plauti (servo), tonsori.

* * *

To Zethus, slave of Aulus Plautius,[1] barber.

1   The man who led the invasion of Britain for Claudius in 43 and served as its first governor.

53.   *Urbana, Pedagogue*

CIL 6.9758   Rome
Tombstone   Unknown

    The pedagogue was a slave who was in charge of the children of aristocratic families. Pedagogues accompanied children to and from school and took care of them in the household. Most were men, but this inscription records a female pedagogue. This marble tablet was found just outside the city on the *Via Ostiensis*. It was originally from a *columbarium*, a large tomb in which members of the household (especially the slaves and freedmen) were buried (see below for other *columbarium* inscriptions).

VRBANA
PAEDAGOGA
V • AN • XXV

* * *

Urbana, paedagoga, v(ixit) an(nos) XXV.

* * *

Urbana, pedagogue, lived 25 years.

54.   *Italia, Dressmaker*

CIL 6.9980; *ILS* 7428   Rome
Tombstone   2nd Century AD

ITALIAE
COCCEIAE • PHYLLIDIS • VESTIFICAE
VEIXSIT • ANNEIS • XX
ACASTVS • CONSERVOS • PRO
PAVPERIE • FECIT • SVA

* * *

Italiae, Cocceiae Phyllidis vestificae, v{e}ix{s}it ann{e}is XX; Acastus conservos pro pauperie fecit sua.

* * *

To Italia, dressmaker of Cocceia Phyllis,[1] lived 20 years; Acastus, her fellow-slave, made this because of her poverty.

1   Her name indicates that she was probably a freedwoman of the emperor Nerva.

55. *Burial Society for the Slaves of the Household of the Statilii*

CIL 6.6215, 6216; *ILS* 7360, 7360a   Rome
Tombstone   1ˢᵗ Century AD

This and the next two inscriptions come from the *columbarium* of the Statilius family. Funeral clubs and large households often buried their dead in a building called a *columbarium*. These *columbaria* (dovecotes) were places for group burial of the members of a burial club or family. Each person or couple had their own niche (*nidus*, pigeonhole), in which their funerary urn or urns were placed. Below each urn was a small plaque recording the person to whom the urn belonged. A number of *columbaria* are known throughout the Empire, especially in Rome and Ostia.

The *columbarium* of the Statilii is outside of the city limits, near the *Porta Praenestina*. The Statilii were an important Julio-Claudian family, several of whom were consuls (in 37 BC, 26 BC, AD 11, 16, 44 and 45); they were even related to the imperial family. Their *familia* (slaves and freedmen in their household) was very large. This *columbarium* has space for hundreds of people. This first inscription to the freedwoman Statilia Ammia was dedicated by a number of property managers for the Statilii.

STATILIA · AMMIA · HIC
SEPVLTA · EST · QVOIVS · SEPVLT
CVRAM · EGERVNT · CONLEG
COMMORIENT · CERDO · INS[VL]
VIR · EIVS · BATHYLLVS · ATRIENS[IS]
MVSAEVS · OST · EROS · INS · PHILOCAL[VS]
VNCTOR

* * *

Statilia Ammia hic sepulta est, [c]u{o}ius sepult(urae) curam egerunt conleg(ae) commorient(es): Cerdo ins[ul(arius)] vir eius, Bathyllus atriens[is], Musaeus ost(iarius), Eros ins(ularius), Philocal[us] unctor.

* * *

Statilia Ammia is buried here, whose burial the funeral club[1] took care of: Cerdo, the caretaker of the apartment block[2] and her husband, Bathyllus the steward of the house, Musaeus the janitor, Eros, the other caretaker of the apartment block, and Philocalus the masseur.[3]

1   Funeral clubs were associations that provided for the burial of members of their club. Members were required to pay a fee upon entering the club. Many such clubs had their own *columbaria* or cemeteries.
2   Looked after the apartment building for the wealthy owner, probably a member of the Statilii family.
3   An odd addition to the staff of an apartment building, but it is possible that he served in the house of the owner of all of the slaves listed.

56.   *Philologus, Butler of the Statilius Family*

CIL 6.6215, 6216; *ILS* 7360, 7360a   Rome
                  Tombstone   1ˢᵗ Century AD

This second inscription from the *columbarium* of the family of the Statilii records a *cellarius*, a slave who looked after the storerooms. It was dedicated by the same funeral club that dedicated the previous inscription to Statilia Ammia.

PHILOLOGVS
CELLARIVS
EX · CONLEGIO
COMMORIENTES

* * *

Philologus, cellarius; ex conlegio commorientes.

* * *

Philologus, butler; his fellow-members of the funeral club dedicated this to him.

57.   *Phyllis, Seamstress*

CIL 6.6351; *ILS* 7435b   Rome
                  Tombstone   Unknown

As this inscription shows, not all of the people buried in the *columbarium* of the Statilii were members of the burial club. Here, the husband dedicates an inscription to his wife, a seamstress (*sarcinatrix*). A male *sarcinator* named Attalus appears in the same *columbarium* (*CIL* 6.6348; *ILS* 7435a)

PHYLLIS · STATILIAE
SARCINATR
SOPHRO · CONIVGI · SVAE
MERENTI

* * *

Phyllis, Statiliae sarcinatr(ici); Sophro coniugi suae merenti.

* * *

To Phyllis, seamstress of Statilia; Sophro dedicated this to his deserving wife.

Public Slaves

Not all slaves were in the possession of a specific master (or the emperor). Some slaves belonged to the state. These so-called "public slaves" performed low-level duties in an ancient city. In the next inscription, a town patron has paid not only for a clock and the surrounding structure, but also a slave to take care of the clock.

58.   *C. Blaesius Gratus gives his Town a Clock*

CIL 12.2522; *ILS* 5624   Talliores, Gallia Narbonensis
Tombstone   1ˢᵗ Century AD

HOROLOGIVM · CVM · SVO · AEDIFICIO · ET
SIGNIS · OMNIBVS · ET · CLATRIS
C · BLAESIVS · C · FIL · VOLTINIA · GRATVS · EX · HS · N · X
ET · EO · AMPLIVS · AD · ID · HOROLOGIVM · ADMINIS
TRANDVM · SERVM · HS · N · IIII · D · S · P · D

* * *

Horologium cum suo aedificio et signis omnibus et clatris C(aius) Blaesius C(ai) fil(ius) Voltinia (tribu) Gratus ex HS n(ummum) X et eo amplius ad id horologium administrandum serv(u)m HS n(ummum) IIII d(e) s(ua) p(ecunia) d(edit).

* * *

This clock¹ with the accompanying building and all of the pictures and railings Gaius Blaesius Gratus, son of Gaius, of the Voltinia tribe, dedicated with 10,000 sestertii including another 4,000 sestertii to provide for a slave to take care of the clock,² all of this money came out of his own funds.

1   Probably some form of water clock that was kept in the forum or other public place.
2   The slave's duties would have been to keep the clock clean, filled, and operational.

Freedmen and their Patrons

Although freedmen were legally removed from their former master's ownership, it was expected that freedmen would maintain a close relationship with them. The relationship, however, changed from that of a master and slave to a patron and dependent client. As demonstrated on numerous inscriptions, freedmen often shared their patron's tomb. Outside of Rome, inscriptions frequently mention guilds of freedmen called *augustales*. Although prohibited from holding municipal office because of their servile past, wealthy freedmen, a product of the expansion of wealth in the early Empire, could still form *collegia* and benefit their local communities by engaging in public works, especially ones connected with the imperial cult. The children of *augustales* frequently went on to hold municipal office or entering the imperial service as equestrians.

59.   *The Friends A. Memmius Clarus and A. Memmius Urbanus*

CIL 6.22355a; *ILS* 8432   Rome, on the Via Appia
Tombstone   Unknown

This charming dedication demonstrates how fellow slaves could continue their friendship even after manumission.

A · MEMMIO · CLARO
A · MEMMIVS · VRBANVS
CONLIBERTO · IDEM · CONSORTI
CARISSIMO · SIBI
INTER · ME · ET · TE · SANCTISSIME · MI
CONLIBERTE · NVLLVM · VNQVAM
DISIVRGIVM · FVISSE · CONSCIVS
SVM · MIHI · HOC · QVOQVE · TITVLO
SVPEROS · ET · INFEROS · TESTOR · DEOS
VNA · ME · TECVM · CONGRESSVM
IN · VENALICIO · VNA · DOMO · LIBEROS
ESSE · FACTOS · NEQVE · VLLVS · VNQVAM
NOS · DIVNXISSET · NISI · HIC · TVVS
FATALIS · DIES

* * *

A(ulo) Memmio Claro; A(ulus) Memmius Urbanus conliberto idem consorti carissimo sibi. Inter me et te, sanctissime mi conliberte, nullum unquam disiurgium fuisse conscius sum mihi. Hoc quoque titulo superos et inferos testor deos, una me tecum congressum in venalicio, una domo liberos esse factos, neque ullus unquam nos diunxisset nisi hic tuus fatalis dies.

* * *

To Aulus Memmius Clarus; Aulus Memmius Urbanus dedicated this for his fellow freedman[1] and dearest companion. Between you and me, my most esteemed fellow freedman, I am not aware that there was ever any quarrel. With this inscription, I call to witness the gods of heaven and the underworld: a single day witnessed you and I together being sold into slavery, a single day witnessed us made freedmen from our household.

There was never a single day that saw us apart until the day of your death.

1   Their joint master is also indicated by the common *praenomen* and *nomen*, Aulus Memmius.

60.   *M. Aurelius Zosimus is Honored by his Former Master*

CIL 14.2298; *ILS* 1949   Rome, on the *Via Appia*
Tombstone   1ˢᵗ Century AD

In the years of his life after manumission, Zosimus and his former master, Maximus, remained close. Maximus helped Zosimus' family and even aided Zosimus' son in achieving the rank of equestrian.

M · AVRELIVS · COTTAE
MAXIMI · L · ZOSIMVS
ACCENSVS · PATRONI
LIBERTINVS · ERAM, · FATEOR
SED · FACTA · LEGETVR
PATRONO · COTTA · NOBILIS · VMBRA · MEA
QVI · MIHI · SAEPE · LIBENS · CENSVS · DONAVIT
EQVESTRIS · QVI · IVSSIT · NATOS
TOLLERE · QVOS · ALERET
QVIQVE · SVAS · COMMISIT · OPES
MIHI · SEMPER · ET · IDEM · DOTAVIT
NATAS · VT · PATER · IPSE · MEAS
COTTANVMQVE · MEVM · PRODVXIT
HONORE · TRIBVNI · QVEM · FORTIS
CASTRIS · CAESARIS · EMERVIT
QVID · NON · COTTA · DEDIT · QVI · NVNC
ET · CARMINA · TRISTIS · HAEC · DEDIT
IN · TVMVLO · CONSPICIENDA · MEO
AVRELIA · SATVRNIA · ZOSIMI

* * *

M(arcus) Aurelius Cottae Maximi l(ibertus) Zosimus, accensus patroni. Libertinus eram, fateor, sed facta legetur patrono Cotta nobilis umbra mea. Qui mihi saepe libens census donavit equestris; qui iussit natos tollere; quos aleret quique suas commisit opes mihi semper, et idem dotavit natas ut pater ipse meas, Cottanumque meum produxit honore tribuni, quem fortis castris Caesaris emeruit. Quid non Cotta dedit? Qui nunc et carmina tristis haec dedit in tumulo conspicienda meo. Aurelia Saturnia Zosimi.

* * *

Marcus Aurelius Zosimus, freedmen of Marcus Aurelius Cotta Maximus[1]
and personal attendant of his patron.[2] I was a freedmen, I admit, but my
noble shade is grieved by my patron Cotta. He often willingly gave me
the wealth equivalent to that required for admission to the equestrian
order;[3] he ordered me to raise my children; he helped raise them and
always gave to me from his own money. He provided dowries for my
daughters as though he were their father.[4] He obtained for my son
Cottanus the rank of military tribune;[5] in this position, he served bravely
in the army of Caesar.[6] What did Cotta not give us? He now sadly
provides for the message that can be read on my tombstone.[7] Aurelia
Saturnina, wife of Zosimus (made this).[8]

1   M. Aurelius Cotta Maximus (afterwards also called Messalinus), was
     consul in AD 20.
2   Zosimus' title of *accensus* would indicate that his duties as a slave had
     kept him close to his master.
3   The money may have been enough to enter the equestrian order, but
     Zosimus, like all those who had formerly been slaves, was prohibited
     from the higher social status. His children, however, were not bound
     by that restriction.
4   Paying for a daughter's dowry was one of the more difficult aspects of
     raising children. It was not infrequent that families would expose baby
     girls to avoid having to eventually pay for their dowries.
5   Therefore, the son had reached the rank of equestrian.
6   This probably means that he was tribune of a cohort of the Praetorian
     Guard.
7   Interestingly, the patron paid for this tombstone, which in turn praises
     his generosity. It is also very likely that the patron composed the
     dedicatory inscription which praises him.
8   Her name indicates that she was also freed by Maximus.

61.   *M. Aemilius Artema*
and his Freedman Hermes

CIL 6.11027; *ILS* 8285   Rome
      Tombstone   Unknown

Not all freedmen had a good relationship with their former masters. Hermes,
in this text, has offended his former master and has subsequently been barred from
the family tomb. This inscription was found on the other side of the Tiber from
Rome.

M · AEMILIVS · ARTEMA
FECIT

M · LICINIO · SVCCESSO · FRATRI
BENE · MERENTI · ET
CAECILIAE · MODESTAE · CONIVGI
SVAE · ET · SIBI · ET · SVIS · LIBERTIS
LIBERTABVSQ · POSTERISQ · EORVM

EXCEPTO · HERMETE · LIB · QVEM · VETO
PROPTER · DELICTA · SVA · ADITVM · AMBITVM · NE
VLLVM · ACCESSVM · HABEAT · IN · HOC · MONVMENTO

* * *

M(arcus) Aemilius Artema fecit M(arco) Licinio Successo, fratri bene merenti, et Caeciliae Modestae, coniugi suae, et sibi et suis libertis libertabusq(ue) posterisq(ue) eorum.

Excepto Hermete lib(erto), quem veto propter delicta sua aditum ambitum ne ullum accessum habeat in hoc monumento.

* * *

Marcus Aemilius Artema made this for Marcus Licinius Successus, his well-deserving brother,[1] and for Caecilia Modesta, his (Artema's) wife, and for himself and his freedmen, freedwomen, and their descendants.

From this right, the freedman Hermes is to be excluded. Because of his offenses, I forbid him from entering, walking around, or even coming close to this monument.

1   Evidently, they were not natural brothers as their *nomina* are different.

---

62.   *Cn. Statilius Crescens Crescentianus,* **Augustalis**

CIL 14.421; *ILS* 6159	Ostia, Latium, Italy
Tombstone	Unknown

Augustales were wealthy freedmen who, although barred from political office, could enjoy prestige derived from serving as an elected member of the *augustales*. In this role, the *augustales* became patrons of the town by using their collective wealth to benefit the town by sponsoring public building projects and games in the emperor's honor, often on the birthdays of the imperial family. This exposure and prestige would often prove helpful to the children of the *augustales*, who did not have the restrictions upon the holding of political office which had limited their fathers' careers. In this text, Crescentianus was an active member of two towns' *augustales*. He served as one of Ostia's six official *augustales* for five years, including time served as the head of the order (*curator*). He performed the same function in the town of Tusculum. This inscription was discovered in Ostia, outside the *Porta Romana*, on the road leading to Rome.

CN · STATILIVS
CRESCENS
CRESCENTIANVS
VIVIR · AVG · Q · Q · ET · CVRAT · ORDIN
AVGVSTAL · ET · VI · VIR · AVG · TVSCVLIS
FECIT · SIBI · ET · STATILIAE · ATALANTE · CONIVG
ET · LIB · LIBERT · POST · EOR · IN · F · P · XXI · IN · A · P · XXXII

* * *

Cn(aeus) Statilius Crescens Crescentianus, VIvir Aug(ustalis) q(uin)q(uennalis) et curat(or) ordin(is) Augustal(ium) et VIvir Aug(ustalis) Tusculis, fecit sibi et Statiliae Atalante, coniug(i) et lib(ertis) libert(abusque) post(erisque) eor(um); in f(ronte) p(edes) XXI, in a(gro) p(edes) XXXII.

* * *

Gnaeus Statilius Crescens Crescentianus, one of the six men in the guild of the Augustales,[1] *elected for five years and head of the order of the* augustales *and one of the six men in the guild of the* Augustales *at Tusculum, made this for himself and for Statilia Atalas,[2] his wife, and for his freedmen, freedwomen, and his descendants; this burial plot is 21 feet wide and 32 feet deep.*

1   Each town's group of *augustales* determined whether the organization was called *augustales* or *seviri augustales* (board of six *augustales*). Both Ostia and Tusculum employed the latter terminology. It is possible that, like the aristocracy of Rome, the wealthy freedman Crescentianus spent his summers in a villa at Tusculum.
2   The name both Crescentianus and his wife shared would indicate that they were freed from the same household.

Foreign Peoples at Rome

63.   *T. Flavius Alexander, Citizen*

CIL 3.6785; *ILS* 1979   Palaea Isaura, Cappadocia
Tombstone   1st Century AD

Well-connected members of the municipal aristocracy were also often granted citizenship. This inscription commemorates Alexander, a freeborn non-Roman from the town of Palaea Isaura. He was granted the citizenship by Vespasian. As in the case of freedman, people who received the citizenship in this way also took the *praenomen* and *nomen* of the emperor who granted them the citizenship.

> T · FLAVIO · CASTORIS
> F · CYR · ALEXANDRO
> CIVITATE · DONATO · AB
> IMP · CAES · VESPASIANO
> F · HERMES · LIB

> * * *

T(ito) Flavio Castoris f(ilio) [Quir(ina tribu)] Alexandro, civitate donato ab imp(eratore) Caes(are) Vespasiano, f(ecit) Hermes lib(ertus).

> * * *

To Titus Flavius Alexander, son of Castor, of the Qurina tribe, granted citizenship by the emperor Caesar Vespasian, Hermes, freedman, made this.

64. *C. Julius Mygdonius, Parthian Captive Turned Roman Citizen*

CIL 11.137; *ILS* 1980	Ravenna, Aemilia, Italy
Tombstone	1st Century AD

Capturing a portion of a conquered populace as slaves was a time-honored tradition of ancient Rome. By the first century AD, the Romans had conquered the majority of the civilized nations in the Mediterranean region. Although Rome fought frequent wars with Parthia, the empire to the east of Roman Syria, it was never fully annexed by Rome. Mygdonius was most likely captured during campaigns conducted by Augustus in the early years of the 1st century AD. He was incorporated into the imperial household as a slave but later was given the citizenship either by Augustus or, less likely, Caligula (as both are named Gaius Julius). He appears to have been financially well-off and was commemorated by the following inscription after his death:

> C · IVL · MYGDONIVS
> GENERI · PARTHVS
> NATVS · INGENVVS · CAPT
> PVBIS · AETATE · DAT · IN · TERRA
> ROMANA · QVI · DVM · FACTVS
> CIVES · R · IVVENTE · FATO · CO
> LOCAVI · ARKAM · DVM · ESSE
> ANNOR · L · PETI · VSQ · A · PVB
> ERTATE · SENECTAE · MEAE · PERVENI
> RE · NVNC · RECIPE · ME · SAXE · LIBENS
> TECVM · CVRA · SOLVTVS · ERO

* * *

C(aius) Iul(ius) Mygdonius, generi Parthus, natus ingenuus, capt(us) pubis aetate, dat(us) in terra(m) Romana(m); qui, dum factus cives R(omanus), iu[b]ente fato colocavi arkam, dum esse(m) annor(um) L. Peti usq(ue) a pubertate senectae meae pervenire; nunc recipe me, saxe, libens; tecum cura solutus ero.

* * *

Gaius Julius Mygdonius, Parthian by nationality, free-born, was captured in his youth and taken to Roman territory;[1] when I was made a free Roman citizen, with fate helping me, I set aside a retirement fund for when I became 50 years old. I have been heading for old age since my birth; now, receive me, stone, as I am willing; with you, I will be freed from care.

1   Mygdonius' Latin is not the best. "In terra Romana" should read "in terram Romanam"; "iuvente" should be "iubente"; "esse" should be "essem"; "peti" is an incorrectly formed perfect tense from the verb *peto* and should be "petii"; "senectae meae" should be "ad senectam meam".

THE IMPERIAL HOUSEHOLD

The imperial house was built on the model of an aristocratic household, but on a truly grand scale. The emperor had tens of thousands of slaves and freedmen scattered across the empire. Many worked on imperial estates or in offices in the provinces, others lived in Rome and operated out of the imperial palace. The following texts illustrate some members of the imperial household. Many positions are reminiscent of those seen in the aristocratic households, others, however, reflect the emperor's unique needs.

65.   *M. Ulpius Thaumastus, Record-Keeper*

CIL 11.3860; *ILS* 1603   Capua, Italy
Dedicatory Plaque   2nd Century AD

This is the marble dedicatory inscription from the base of a statue of Jupiter. It was put up by a freedman of Trajan who served as "*a commentariis*", a secretary who dealt with the personal property of the emperor. The property consisted mainly of land which was farmed for profit. The same officer also handled new property left to the emperor in wills and bequests. Thaumastus seems to have returned to his hometown after his service.

IOVI · OP · MAX
M · VLPIVS · AVG · LIB
THAVMASTVS
A · COMMENTARIIS
OPERVM · PVBLICORVM
ET · RATIONIS · PATRIMONI
D · D

* * *

Iovi op(timo) max(imo); M(arcus) Ulpius Aug(usti) lib(ertus) Thaumastus, a commentariis operum publicorum et rationis patrimoni; d(ecreto) d(ecurionum).

* * *

To Jupiter best and greatest; Marcus Ulpius Thaumastus, freedman of the emperor, record-keeper of the office of public works and of the financial office of the imperial inheritance; dedicated by decree of the town council.

66.   *Claudius Optatus,*
Procurator of the Port of Ostia

CIL 14.163; *ILS* 1533   Ostia
Round piece of metal   1st Century AD

    The emperor Claudius constructed a new harbor in Ostia, the port city of Rome. Originally, goods destined for Rome had been imported into Puteoli, in Campania, a good distance south of Rome. Optatus must have been one of the first imperial agents in charge of the new harbor as he was a freedman of Claudius.

Tombstone of the imperial freedman and invitator *Aphetus (CIL 6.7010), National Museum of Rome at the Baths of Diocletian, Rome. Photo courtesy of the Ministero per i Beni e le Attività Culturali Soprintenza Archeologica di Roma.*

The original findspot of this inscription is not known. It is currently in the Berlin museum, but probably originated in Ostia.

CLAVDI
OPTATI
AVG · L
PROC · PORTVS
OSTIESIS

* * *

Claudi Optati, Aug(usti) l(iberti), proc(uratoris) portus Ostie(n)sis.

* * *

(Tomb) of Claudius Optatus, freedman of Augustus, procurator[1] of the port of Ostia.

1   Freedmen procurators were officials put in charge of imperial estates or buildings across the empire. Equestrian procurators who were of higher social status (see the section on the equestrian aristocracy, above), governed smaller, less importrant provinces.

67.   *Alexander Pylaemenianus, Librarian*

CIL 6.5188; *ILS* 1589   Rome
Tombstone   1st Century AD

This and the following three inscriptions come from a single *columbarium* that was discovered in Rome between the *Via Appia* and the *Via Latina*. It apparently was the burial place of both imperial slaves and freedmen. Most of these lived during the reigns of Tiberius, Caligula and Claudius. This first inscription records the slave Alexander Pylaemenianus. Judging by his name, Pylaemenianus was originally from the Greek East. He was an imperial slave of the emperor Caligula. He was in charge of the Greek library in the temple of Apollo which stood on the Capitoline Hill, near the imperial palace. This inscription shows that some slaves were highly educated, despite their social status.

ALEXANDER · C · CAE
SARIS · AVG · GERMANICI · SER
PYLAEMENIANVS · AB · BYBLI
OTHECE · GRAECA · TEMPLI · APOLLI
NIS · VIX · ANNIS · XXX

* * *

Alexander C(ai) Caesaris Aug(usti) Germanici ser(vus) Pylaemenianus, ab bybliothece Graeca templi Apollinis, vix(it) annis XXX.

* * *

*Alexander Pylaemenianus, slave of Gaius Caesar Augustus Germanicus,[1]
in charge of the Greek library in the temple of Apollo,[2] lived 30 years.*

1   This is the emperor Caligula.
2   Augustus built two libraries on the Palatine hill near the new temple of
     Apollo, one containing Latin books, the other Greek.

68.   *Household of Musicus Scurranus*

CIL 6.5197; *ILS* 1514   Rome
        Tombstone   1st Century AD

This second inscription from the *columbarium* near the *Via Appia* records the
household of Musicus Scurranus, a slave of the emperor Tiberius. Although slaves
were not allowed to own slaves themselves, slaves from very large households
and the imperial *familia* did sometimes have *vicarii*, who were slaves working in
the bureau (in the case of public or imperial slaves) or household of another slave
(in the case of slaves in private ownership), but actually owned by that slave's
master (in this case the emperor). This inscription demonstrates the surprisingly
independent lifestyles some slaves enjoyed, despite their servile status.

MVSICO · TI · CAESARIS · AVGVSTI
SCVRRANO · DISP · AD · FISCVM · GALLICVM
PROVINCIAE · LVGDVNENSIS
EX · VICARIS · EIVS · QVI · CVM · EO · ROMAE · CVM
DECESSIT · FVERVNT · BENE · MERITO
VENVSTVS · NEGOT
DECIMIANVS · SVMP
DICAEVS · A · MANV
MVTATVS · A · MANV
CRETICVS · A · MANV
AGATHOPVS · MEDIC
EPAPHRA · AB · ARGENT
PRIMIO · AB · VESTE
COMMVNIS · A · CVBIC
POTHVS · PEDISEQ
TIASVS · COCVS
FACILIS · PEDISEQ
ANTHVS · AB · ARG
HEDYLVS · CVBICV
FIRMVS · COCVS
SECVNDA

* * *

Musico Ti(beri) Caesaris Augusti Scurrano, disp(ensatori) ad fiscum
Gallicum provinciae Lugdunensis, ex vicari(i)s eius, qui cum eo Romae

cum decessit fuerunt, bene merito: Venustus, negot(iator); Decimianus, sump(tuarius); Dicaeus, a manu(ensis); Mutatus, a manu(ensis); Creticus, a manu(ensis); Agathopus, medic(us); Epaphra, ab argent(o); Primio, ab veste; Communis, a cubic(ulo); Pothus, pediseq(uus); Tiasus, cocus; Facilis, pediseq(uus); Anthus, ab arg(ento); Hedylus, cubicu(larius); Firmus, cocus; Secunda.

* * *

To Musicus Scurranus, slave of Tiberius Caesar Augustus, administrator of the Gallic treasury of the province of Gallia Lugdunensis,[1] dedicated to him, well-deserving, by his own slaves, who were with him at Rome when he died:[2] Venustus, salesman; Decimianus, household expenses; Dicaeus, secretary; Mutatus, secretary; Creticus, secretary; Agathopus, medical doctor; Epaphra, financial advisor; Primio, wardrobe; Communis, chamberlain; Pothus, manservant; Tiasus, cook; Facilis, manservant; Anthus, financial advisor; Hedylus, minor chamberlain; Firmus, cook; Secunda.

1   The treasury would have contained funds belonging to the emperor. It would have included revenue from the imperial estates as well as money sent to him from the emperor in Rome. The treasury would have been controlled by a freedman procurator. As a slave, Scurranus was, however, merely a high-level administrator in that bureau.
2   Scurranus' post had ended and he had returned to Rome by the time of his death. The list of *vicarii* are those who were still in his household at the time of his death.

69. *Crescens, Chamberlain of the Second Station*

CIL 6.5195; *ILS* 1746   Rome
Tombstone   1st Century AD

This is the third inscription from the *columbarium* near the *Via Appia*. It records a certain Crescens who was a *cubicularius* ("chamberlain"), a high-ranking slave who originally supervised the emperor's bedroom, but later came to be in charge of much of the emperor's private staff. It is interesting to note that the office of *cubicularius* had expanded and in turn had been transformed into its own bureaucracy. Crescens was the junior chamberlain.

D · M
CRESCENTI · VERNAE
CAESARIS · N
CVBICVLARIO · STATIONIS · II
VIXIT · ANNIS · XXVII
MESIBVS · XI · DIEBVS · XI

* * *

D(is) m(anibus); Crescenti, vernae Caesaris n(ostri), cubiculario stationis II, vixit annis XXVII, me(n)sibus XI, diebus XI.

* * *

To the spirits of the dead; to Crescens, born a slave of our Caesar, chamberlain of the second level, lived 27 years, 11 months, 11 days.

70. *Papia Julia Jucunda, Nurse*

CIL 6.5201; *ILS* 1837   Rome
Tombstone   1st Century AD

This is the fourth and final inscription selected from the imperial *columbarium* from near the *Via Appia*. It records Gaius Papius Asclepiades. Among the dedicators of the inscription is Julia Jucunda, a nurse (nanny) of two children of Germanicus, who was the nephew of the emperor Tiberius. A number of slaves and freedmen took care of the children of the imperial family.

C · PAPIVS · ASCLEPIADES
PAPIA · EROTIS · L
IVLIA · IVCVNDA · NVTRIX
DRVSI · ET · DRVSILLAE

* * *

C(aius) Papius Asclepiades; Papia Erotis l(iberta), Iulia Iucunda, nutrix Drusi et Drusillae.

* * *

(Tomb of) Gaius Papius Asclepiades; (tomb of) Papia, freedwoman of Eros,[1] Julia Jucunda,[2] nurse of Drusus and Drusilla.[3]

1 The Eros is probably a Gaius Papius Eros. He was also presumably the former master of Papius Asclepiades as well. The names Asclepiades and Eros are Greek.
2 Iucunda was probably an imperial freedwoman, since she has the *nomen* Iulia. Her connection to the Papius family of freedmen is uncertain. It is possible that she was married to Asclepiades.
3 This seems to refer to two of the children of Germanicus. Germanicus was the elder son of Drusus, the brother of the emperor Tiberius (and the brother of the future emperor Claudius).

71.   *Protoctetus, Census Official in Gaul*

CIL 6.8578; *ILS* 1511   Rome
Tombstone   Unknown

Protoctetus is an example of a low-level bureaucratic slave in imperial service in the provinces. His inscription was found on the road between Rome and Ostia.

D · M
IANVARIO
VERNAE · DVLCISSIMO
Q · V · A · XIIII · M · IIII · D · XIIII
FECIT · PROTOCTETVS
AVG · DISPENSATOR
AD · CENSVS
PROVINCIAE
LVGDVNENSIS
B · M

* * *

D(is) m(anibus); Ianuario, vernae dulcissimo, q(ui) v(ixit) a(nnos) XIIII, m(enses) IIII, d(ies) XIIII; fecit Protoctetus Aug(usti) dispensator ad census provinciae Lugdunensis, b(ene) m(erenti).

* * *

To the spirits of the dead; to Ianuarius, the sweetest boy, born a slave, who lived 14 years, 4 months, 14 days; Protoctetus, accounts manager[1] of the emperor for the census in the province of Lugdunensis[2] made this for the well-deserving dedicatee.

1   The *dispensator* was a slave who managed financial accounts. They appear in private houses as well as state offices (as here).
2   Protoctetus was an official in the office in charge of the administration of the census in the province of Gallia Lugdunensis. The office would have been under the control of a freedman procurator, but numerous other slaves (like Ianuarius) worked in the office and performed various tasks.

72.   *Calamus Pamphilianus,*
Steward of the Lollian Warehouses

CIL 6.4226; *ILS* 1620   Rome
Tombstone   1st Century AD

This inscription was discovered in the *columbarium* of the empress Livia on the *Via Appia*. Like the *columbarium* between the *Via Appia* and *Via Latina* discussed above, the *columbarium* of Livia housed the remains of freedmen and slaves from the imperial household. In this inscription, a slave of the emperor Claudius is commemorated.

DIS · MANIBVS · SAC
CALAMVS
TI · CLAVDII · CAESARIS
AVGVSTI · GERMANICI
PAMPHILIANVS
VILICVS · EX · HORREIS
LOLLIANIS
EX · D · D · D · S · D · D

* * *

Dis manibus sac(rum); Calamus Ti(beri) Claudii Caesaris Augusti Germanici (servus) Pamphilianus, vilicus ex horreis Lollianis, ex d(ecreto) d(ecurionum) d(e) s(uo) d(onum) d(edit).

* * *

Sacred to the spirits of the dead; Calamus Pamphilianus, slave of Tiberius Claudius Caesar Augustus Germanicus,[1] steward[2] of the Lollian warehouses,[3] gave this gift out of his own funds by decree of the town council.[4]

1   The emperor Claudius.
2   A *vilicus* was anyone who acted as an overseer or director of the property of another. The term would seem to be equivalent to *procurator*. The title *vilicus* was generally used of imperial estates in the country (*villae*).
3   The Lollian warehouses stood on the river not far from the warehouses of Galba. This inscription indicates that, by the reign of Claudius, the warehouses were under imperial control. They had originally been privately built and owned by the family of Lollius (in the late Republic).
4   More commonly seen on building dedications and statue bases, this formula is an unusual addition to a tombstone. It probably signals some special privilege allowed to Calamus.

73.   *Sulpicius Fastus, in Charge of Admission to Imperial Audiences*

CIL 6.8699; *ILS* 1691   Rome
Tombstone   1st Century AD

Fastus was a freedman of the short-lived emperor Galba. The *ab admissione* official stood at the entrance to the emperor's chamber and allowed people to enter once the emperor had consented to see the person.

SER · SVLPICIO
AVG · L · FASTO
AB · ADMISSIONE
SER · SER · SVLPICI
AGATHEMER
ET · THALLVS
CONLIBERTO

* * *

Ser(vio) Sulpicio Aug(usti) l(iberto) Fasto, ab admissione; Ser(vius) Ser(vi) Sulpici (libertus) Agathemer(us) et Thallus conliberto.

* * *

To Servius Sulpicius Fastus, freedman of the emperor, in charge of admitting people to imperial audiences; Servius Agathemerus, freedman of Servius Sulpicius,[1] and Thallus to their fellow freedman.

1   He was also presumably a freedman of the emperor, but is not listed as such (Galba's *praenomen* and *nomen* are given instead: Servius Sulpicius). It is possible that Agathemerus was freed before Galba became emperor and Faustus after him. Agathemerus was perhaps inherited as a slave by Galba from Nero and then freed). The variation may also just be coincidental.

74.   *Ti. Claudius Bucolas, Taster*

CIL 11.3612; *ILS* 1567   Caere, Etruria, Italy
    Tombstone   1st Century AD

Bucolas is a good example of the bureaucracy which surrounded the private life of the emperor. His family also exemplifies the passage of the imperial bureaucracy from one imperial dynasty to the next. Bucolas was a freedman of Claudius. His wife, named Sulpicia, was probably a freedwoman of the emperor Galba. Their son, however, was named Quintus Claudius Flavianus, no doubt in honor of Vespasian, the first Flavian emperor.

TI · CLAVDIVS · AVG · LIB · BVCOLAS · PRAEGVSTATOR · TRICLINARC
PROC · A · MVNERIB · PROC · AQVAR · PROC · CASTRENSIS · CVM · Q · CLAVDIO
FLAVIANO · FILIO · ET · SVLPICIA · CANTABRA · MATRE · D · [D]

* * *

Ti(berius) Claudius Aug(usti) lib(ertus) Bucolas, praegustator, triclin(i)arc(hes), proc(urator) a munerib(us), proc(urator) aquar(um), proc(urator) castrensis, cum Q(uinto) Claudio Flaviano filio et Sulpicia Cantabra matre d(onum) [d(edit)].

* * *

Tiberius Claudius Bucolas, freedman of the emperor, taster,[1] servant in charge of the dining room,[2] procurator in charge of the games,[3] procurator in charge of the water supply, procurator in charge of military expenses;[4] he, along with Quintus Claudius Flavianus, his son, and Sulpicia Cantabra, his mother, gave this gift.

1   Presumably to test for poison, but probably also to check to ensure the food had been properly prepared.
2   The dining room was called the *triclinium* after its arrangement (three couches around a dining table). The tricliniarch was the freedman or slave who worked as an attendant at imperial meals.
3   The games (gladiatorial, theatrical and chariot racing) were called *munera*. Bucolas was probably in charge of overseeing expenses involved with holding the games. There was a large bureaucracy surrounding the games, and the procurator was probably the freedman in charge of the bureau which oversaw any expenditures. This office constituted a major step forward in Bucolas' career.
4   The imperial procurator in charge of military expenses probably oversaw the financial aspects of any incidental military expenditure or travel expenses which came from the emperor's personal funds.

75. *Ti. Claudius Classicus, Procurator of Delights*

AE 1972, 574; 1982, 862.   Ephesus, Asia Minor
        Statue Base   1st Century AD

Classicus enjoyed a long career which spanned the Julio-Claudian, Flavian, and adoptive emperors. No post is recorded for the reign of Domitian, between his service as chamberlain of Titus and procurator of delights of Nerva, possibly owing to the fact that Classicus fell out of favor in the reign of Domitian. It is also possible that Classicus chose to omit any mention of Domitian, since that emperor's memory was condemned after his death.

TI · CLAVDIO · AVG · LIB
CLASSICO
DIVI · T · A · CVBICVLO · ET · PROC
CASTRENSI · DIVI · NERVAE
PROC · A · VOLVPTATIBVS
IMP · NERVAE · TRAIANI · CAESARIS
AVG · GERMANICI · DACICI · PROC
A · VOLVPTATIBVS · ET · AD · LVDVM · MA
TVTINVM · ET · PROC · ALEXANDREAE
C · IVLIVS · PHOTINVS · CELER · ADIVTOR
IN · PROCVRATIONE · ALEXANDREAE
OB · MERITA · EIVS

* * *

Ti(berio) Claudio Aug(usti) lib(erto) Classico, divi T(iti) a cubiculo et proc(uratori) castrensi, divi Nervae proc(uratori) a voluptatibus, imp(eratoris) Nervae Traiani Caesaris Aug(usti) Germanici Dacici proc(uratori) a voluptatibus et ad Ludum Matutinum et proc(uratori) Alexandreae; C(aius) Iulius Photinus Celer, adiutor in procuratione Alexandreae, ob merita eius.

* * *

To Tiberius Claudius Classicus, freedman of the emperor,[1] chamberlain and procurator of the military expenses of the divine Titus, procurator of delights of the divine Nerva,[2] procurator of delights,[3] in charge of the Matutinus gladiatorial school,[4] and procurator of Alexandria of the emperor Nerva Trajan Caesar Augustus Germanicus Dacicus;[5] Gaius Julius Photinus Celer, aide in his procuratorship of Alexandria, put this up owing to Classicus' merits.

1   Classicus' career (if he had one) before his manumission is not mentioned. It is likely that his earlier career was omitted to save space on the stone for his more recent and important posts.
2   Probably a post which entailed arranging entertainment for the emperor during dinner parties.
3   The repetition of the post is a way of indicating that the post continued under Nerva's successor Trajan.
4   The *Ludus Matutinus* was one of the four gladiatorial training facilities which Domitian constructed. This one stood near the Colosseum, just south of the Ludus Magnus. It seems to have been a school for *venatores* and *bestiarii* who performed in the morning games.
5   Trajan's titulature indicates that the inscription was put up after Trajan received the title Dacicus (in 102/103), but before he received the title Parthicus (in 116). It is most likely, therefore, that Classicus died while Trajan was still alive, between 102/103 and 116.

76.   *M. Aurelius Bithus, in Charge of the Palace Cooks*

CIL 6.8752; *ILS* 1800   Rome
Tombstone   3rd Century AD

D · M
M · AVRELIVS · AVG · LIB · BIT[HVS]
PRAEPOSITVS · COCORVM · [SE]
VIVO · SIBI · ET · AVRELI · HERM[...]

* * *

D(is) m(anibus); M(arcus) Aurelius Aug(usti) lib(ertus) Bit[hus], praepositus cocorum, [se] vivo sibi et Aureli Herm[...]

* * *

To the spirits of the dead; Marcus Aurelius Bithus, freedman of the emperor, in charge of the palace cooks, while he was still alive, he made this for himself and for Aurelia Herm(?)...

77.   *M. Ulpius Valens,*
in Charge of the Emperor's Wardrobe

CIL 6.8550; *ILS* 1756   Rome
        Tombstone   2nd Century AD

This inscription appears on two matching marble tablets that were attached to each side of a tombstone *cippus*. The same Marcus Ulpius Valens also appears as the dedicator of a tombstone to Marcus Ulpius Phaedimus, another imperial freedman involved in the personal services of the emperor.

DIS • MANIBVS
COELIAE • DYNATE
M • VLPIVS • AVG • LIB
VALENS • A • VESTE • IMP
PRIVATA • CONIVG • KARISS
SANCTISSIMAE
CVM • QVA • VIXIT • AN • XXXVIII
SINE • CRIMINE • ET • SIBI
ET • SVIS • LIBERTIS
LIBERTABVSQVE
POSTERISQVE
EORVM

* * *

Dis minibus Coeliae Dynate; M(arcus) Ulpius Aug(usti) lib(ertus) Valens, a veste imp(eratoris) privata, coniug(i) [c]ariss(imae) sanctissimae, cum qua vixit an(nos) XXXVIII sine crimine, et sibi et suis libertis libertabusque posterisque eorum.

* * *

To the spirits of the dead of Coelia Dynate;[1] Marcus Ulpius Valens, freedman of the emperor, in charge of the private wardrobe of the emperor,[2] to his dearest and most venerable wife, with whom he lived 38 years without wrong, and to himself and his freedmen and freedwomen and to their posterity.[3]

1 Probably a freedwoman, but not imperial. Her *nomen* is Roman, but her *cognomen* is Greek.
2 The emperor had a large wardrobe. Similar inscriptions record slaves and freedmen who also chose and cared for his clothing worn in military and parade events, gladiatorial games, and other public appearances.
3 Dynate and Valens do not seem to have had children. As such, the survival of the family was in the hands of the freedmen. The inscription indicates that the tomb is provided for the couple as well as their freedmen, freedwomen, and their (the freedmen's) descendants. Several other inscriptions in this collection have the same formula.

78. *Dorcas, Hairdresser of the Empress Livia*

CIL 6.8958; *ILS* 1784   Rome
Tombstone   1st Century AD

Many imperial freedwomen and female slaves also held positions in the imperial household. Most were affiliated with the women of the imperial family. This inscription was found on a tomb on the *Via Salaria* in Rome.

IVNONI
DORCADIS
IVLIAE • AVGVSTAE • L
VERNAE • CAPRENSIS
ORNATRICIS
LYCASTVS • CONLIBERTVS
ROGATOR • CONIVGI
CARISSIMAE • SIBI

* * *

Iunoni; Dorcadis, Iuliae Augustae l(ibertae) vernae caprensis, ornatricis; Lycastus, conlibertus, rogator coniugi carissimae (et) sibi.

* * *

To Juno;[1] (tomb) of Dorcas, freedwoman, born a slave of Julia Augusta[2] on Capri,[3] hairdresser; Lycastus, her fellow-freedman, messenger(?)[4] dedicated this to his dearest wife and to himself.

1 A variant on the usual dedication to the spirits of the dead. It occurs most often on the tombs of women.
2 Livia, the wife of Augustus. Livia only received the name Augusta after Augustus' death. Therefore, the inscription must date to after AD 14 but before her death in 29.
3 There was an imperial palace on Capri, an island near the bay of Naples. The emperor Tiberius spent much of the later part of his reign there.

4   The duties of a *rogator* are not known. Literally, it should be a person who goes around asking for something. He therefore could be some kind of messenger or herald.

79.   *Extricata, Seamstress*

CIL 6.9037; *ILS* 1788   Rome
Tombstone   1ˢᵗ Century AD

Extricata was the seamstress of Octavia, the daughter of the emperor Claudius, who later married the future emperor Nero.

EXTRICATA
OCTAVIAE • AVG • F
SARCINATRIX
V • A • XX

* * *

Extricata, Octaviae Aug(usti) f(iliae serva), sarcinatrix, v(ixit) a(nnos) XX.

* * *

Extricata, slave of Octavia, the daughter of the emperor, seamstress, lived 20 years.

80.   *Chia, Masseuse*

CIL 6.9097; *ILS* 1790   Rome
Tombstone   1ˢᵗ Century AD

CHIAE
ANTONIAE • DRVSI
VNCTRIC

* * *

Chiae, Antoniae Drusi unctric(i).

* * *

To Chia, masseuse of Antonia, the wife of Drusus.[1]

1   Livia had two children by her first husband, Tiberius Claudius Nero: the future emperor Tiberius and Drusus. Antonia was the wife of Drusus, the brother of the emperor Tiberius. Antonia and Drusus had two sons (Germanicus and the future emperor Claudius), and a daughter (Livilla). Drusus died in 9 BC. Antonia, however, lived until the reign of Caligula.

81.   *Claudia Pthonge, Nurse*

Gordon 122   Rome
Tombstone   1st Century AD

CLAVDIAE • PTHONGE • NVTRICI • BRITTANNICI • APHNIVS
CAESARIS • AVG • AB • EPISTVLIS • CONTVBERNALI • OPTIME
DE • SE • MERITAE

* * *

Claudiae Pthonge, nutrici Brittannici; Aphnius Caesaris Aug(usti)
(servus), ab epistulis, contubernali optime de se meritae.

* * *

*To Claudia Pthonge,[1] nurse of Brittannicus;[2] Aphnius, slave of Caesar
Augustus, imperial secretary,[3] made this dedication to his wife who
deserved all the best from him.*

1   Either a freedwoman or a *verna* of Claudius. She probably died after
     Britannicus (who was poisoned by Nero).
2   Britannicus was the son of the emperor Claudius. After his marriage to
     Agrippina the Younger, Claudius overlooked Britannicus, his natural
     son, in favor of Agrippina's son, the future emperor Nero, who was
     her son by a previous marriage. Shortly after becoming emperor in 54,
     Nero poisoned Britannicus.
3   The *ab epistulis* was in charge of the emperor's correspondence.
     Letters to the emperor from across the empire occupied much of the
     emperor's time. This freedman helped the emperor compose letters.

82.   *M. Livius Prytanis, Pedagogue*

CIL 6.33787; *ILS* 1828   Rome
Tombstone   1st Century AD

In the imperial palace, a pedagogue was a slave or freedman who served as
the director of a school which trained the children of the slaves and freedmen of
the emperor to fulfill their future duties as members of the imperial *familia*.

M • LIVIVS
AVGVSTAE • LIB
PRYTANIS
LIVIAE • DRVSI • PAEDAG

* * *

M(arcus) Livius Augustae lib(ertus) Prytanis, Liviae Drusi paedagogus.

* * *

Marcus Livius Prytanis,[1] freedman of the empress,[2] pedagogue of Livia, the daughter of Drusus.[3]

1   His *cognomen* is Greek. Many pedagogues were Greek.
2   Either Livia, Augustus' wife, or Livilla (see the next note).
3   This is Livilla, the daughter of Antonia and Drusus.

83.   *T. Flavius Ganymede, Pedagogue*

CIL 6.8970; *ILS* 1831	Rome
Tombstone	2nd Century AD

Ganymede is another example of an imperial freedman who successfully made the transition from one imperial dynasty to another. He was a freedman of Vespasian, Titus or Domitian. His wife, however, was a freedwoman of Trajan, an indication that Ganymede continued in imperial service even after the murder of Domitian.

D · M
T · FLAVIO · AVG · LIB · GANYMEDI
PAEDAGOGO · PVERORVM
CAES · N · FEC · VLPIA · HELPIS
CONIVGI · OPTIMO · B · M · ET
LIB · LIBERTABVSQVE · SVIS

* * *

D(is) m(anibus); T(ito) Flavio Aug(usti) lib(erto) Ganymedi, paedagogo puerorum Caes(aris) n(ostri); fec(it) Ulpia Helpis coniugi optimo b(ene) m(erenti) et lib(ertis) libertabusque suis.

* * *

To the spirits of the dead; to Titus Flavius Ganymede, freedman of the emperor, pedagogue of the children of our Caesar; Ulpia Helpis made this for her best and well-deserving husband as well as to their freedmen and freedwomen.

ROMAN FAMILIES

Many private tombstones were dedicated to members of the lower and working classes. These do not list offices in a public career. Instead, they describe what the person (and sometimes his entire family) did in his or her lifetime. While the previous inscriptions tell us much about the careers of people in public positions, the tombstones of private individuals give us privileged glimpses into the everyday life of an ancient Roman. The first section here contains a number of examples of dedications which reveal information about not only the person to whom the inscription is dedicated, but also the rest of his family. It is from texts like these that we learn most about the structure of the ancient Roman family. They also provide data about life expectancy, infant mortality, naming conventions, and marriage practices.

Mattonius Restitutus' tombstone from Gaul records not only himself, but also his wife and two young children. Julius Alexander, also from Gaul, lived to be as old as 75. His inscription records with pride the three generations of his family which he left behind. The inscription of Clodia Secunda, the wife of a centurion in the urban cohorts in Rome, describes how she was born in 182, married at the age of 19, and died when she was 25. Personal wishes were sometimes recorded. Furia Spes put up a dedication to her husband Sempronius Firmus, which includes a plea to the spirits to reunite them as soon as possible. Similarly, the inscription of Pompeius Catussa to his wife Blandinia Martiola encourages the reader to bathe in the baths of Apollo, which was an activity they had enjoyed together before Martiola died. Some inscriptions record how a person died. Julius Timotheus had been fond of raising orphaned children. He had seven when he and his *alumni* were caught by bandits on the road and killed. Daizus Comozon, from Moesia Inferior, was fifty years old when the Castaboci, a Germanic tribe from the other side of the Danube, invaded Roman territory and killed him. Finally, the family of Germanius Valens is an excellent example of a family which benefited from the Roman citizenship granted after Germanius' discharge from the auxiliary forces.

84.   *The Family of Mattonius Restitutus*

CIL 13.2018; *ILS* 7530   Lugdunum, Gallia Lugdunensis
Tombstone   2nd century AD

D · M · ET
MEMORIAE · AETERNAE
MATTONI · RESTITVTI · CIVIS
TRIBOCI · NEGOTIATORIS
ARTIS · MACELLARIAE · HO
MINIS · PROBISSIMI · QVI · DE
FVNCTVS · EST · ANNOR · XXXX
MEN · III · D · XVIII
RVTTONIA · MARTIOLA · CON
IVNX · QVAE · CVM · EO · VIXIT
ANN · VIIII · D · VIIII · SINE · VL
LA · ANIMI · LAESIONE · ET
MATTONIVS · GERMANVS
RELICTVS · A · PATRE · ANN · III
M · I · D · XII · ET · MATTONIVS
RESPECTINVS · MENS · VIIII
FILI · ET · HEREDES · PONEN
DVM · CVRAVERVNT · ET · SI
BI · VIVI · SVB · ASCIA
DEDICAVERVNT

* * *

D(is) m(anibus) et memoriae aeternae Mattoni Restituti civis Triboci, negotiatoris artis macellariae, hominis probissimi, qui defunctus est annor(um) XXXX, men(sium) III, d(ierum) XVIII; Ruttonia Martiola, coniunx, quae cum eo vixit ann(os) VIIII, d(ies) VIIII sine ulla animi laesione, et Mattonius Germanus relictus a patre ann(orum) III, m(ensium) I, d(ierum) XII et Mattonius Respectinus, mens(es) VIIII, fili(i) et heredes ponendum curaverunt et sibi vivi sub ascia dedicaverunt.

* * *

To the spirits of the dead and the eternal memory of Mattonius Restitutus, citizen of the Triboci,[1] salesman of cured meats, a most decent man, who died at the age of 40 years, 3 months, 18 days;[2] Ruttonia Martiola, his wife, who lived with him 9 years, 9 days without any wounding of the heart, and Mattonius Germanus,[3] left by his father at the age of 3 years, 1 month, 12 days, and Mattonius Respectinus, 9 months, his children and heirs took the care of putting up this dedication and, still living, dedicated this for themselves while still under construction.

1   A Germanic tribe from the west bank of the Rhine River.
2   With an average life expectancy of 25 years, ancient Romans' lives were on average much shorter than they are today. The reasons for this

Tombstone of the freedman C. Julius Hermes depicting him and his wife (unnamed) (CIL 6.5326), National Museum of Rome at the Baths of Diocletian, Rome. Photo courtesy of the Ministero per i Beni e le Attività Culturali Soprintenza Archeologica di Roma.

are varied. For one, ancient medicine was not up to modern standards. Bad nutrition and hunger were common. Cities, especially the crowded streets of Rome, lacked adequate sanitation. War was a constant threat; it could bring death to soldier and civilian alike. With the threat of shipwreck and brigands, any travel could also be a life-threatening proposition. Infant mortality was common. In fact, nearly 50% of all babies died before the age of one. Children who reached their first birthday, however, had a good chance of reaching the age of 35. After 35, there was another sharp decline in the survival rate. Only about 25% reached the age of 45, and only about 5% reached 65.

3   Note the varied *cognomina* of the children. Neither had the same *cognomen* as their parents.

85.   *Three Generations of the Family of Julius Alexander*

CIL 13.2000; *ILS* 7648   Lugdunum, Gallia Lugdunensis
Tombstone   Unknown

Julius Alexander lived to the age of 75. His inscription records with pride the large number of descendants (three generations worth) which he had. Because it lists the names of all of those descendants, this inscription is an especially useful example of naming conventions.

D · M
ET · MEMORIAE · AETERNE · IV
LI · ALEXSADRI · NATIONE · AFRI · CIVI
CARTHAGINESI · OMINI · OPTIMO · OPIF
ICI · ARTIS · VITRIAE · QVI · VIX · ANOS · LXXV
MENSEN · V · DIES · XXIII · SENE · VLLA
LESIONE · ANIMI · CVM · CONIVGE
SVA · VIRGINIA · CVM · QVA · VIX
SIT · ANNIS · XXXXVIII · EX · QVA
CREAVIT · FILIO · III · ET · EILIAM
EX · QVIBVS · HIS · OMNIBVS · NE
POTES · VIDITE · DEOS · SVPEST
ITES · SIBI · RELIQVIT · HVNC
TVMVLVM · PONENDVM · CV
RAVERVNT · NVMONIA · BE
LLIA · VXSOR · ET · IVLIVS · AL
EXIVS · FILIVS · ET · IVLIVS · F
ELIX · FILIVS · ET · IVLIVS · GAL
LONIVS · FILIVS · ET · NVM[O]
NIA · BELLIOSA · FILIA · IT[EM]
NEPOTES · EIVS · IVLIVS · AV[CT]
VS · IVLIVS · FELIX · IVLIV[S · ALEX]
SANDER · IVLIVS · GALON[IVS · IVLI]
VS · LENTIVS · IVLIVS · GALL[................]
IVLIVS · EONIVS · P · P · CYR[.... · ET · SVB · ASC]
DEDICAV[ERVNT]

* * *

D(is) m(anibus) et memoriae aetern(a)e Iuli Alex{s}a(n)dri, natione Afri, civi carthaginesi, omini optimo, opifici artis vitriae, qui vix(it) an(n)os LXXV, mense{n}(s) V, dies XXIII s[i]ne ulla lesione animi cum coniuge sua virginia, cum qua vix{s}it annis XXXXVIII, ex qua creavit filio(s) III et [f]iliam, ex quibus his omnibus nepotes vidit{e} (et) {d}eos supestites sibi reliquit. Hunc tumulum ponendum curaverunt Numonia Bellia ux{s}or et Iulius Alexius filius, et Iulius Felix filius, et Iulius Gallonius filius, et Num[o]nia Belliosa filia, it[em] nepotes eius Iulius Au[ct?]us, Iulius Felix, Iuliu[s Alex?]sander, Iulius Galon[ius, Iuli]us

Lentius, Iulius Gall[................], Iulius Eonius p(arenti?) p(iissimo?) cur[averunt(?) .... et sub asc(ia)] dedicav[erunt].

* * *

To the spirits of the dead and the eternal memory of Julius Alexander, African by nationality, citizen of Carthage, in every way the best, artist in glass, who lived 75 years, 5 months, 23 days with his chaste wife without any injuring of spirit, with whom he lived 48 years and with whom he had three sons and a daughter; from all of these he saw grandchildren and left them all living after him. Numonia Bellia, his wife, took the care of putting up this tomb along with his sons Julius Alexius, Julius Felix, and Julius Gallonius, and his daughter Num[o]nia Belliosa,[1] likewise also his grandchildren Julius Auctus(?), Julius Felix, Julius Alexsander(?), Julius Galon[ius, Juli]us Lentius, Julius Gali[................], and Julius Eonius; all dedicated it while still under construction to their most dutiful father(?).

1   Named after her mother, Numonia Bellia.

86.   *The Family of Clodia Secunda*

AE 1901, 140	Rome
Sarcophagus	Early 3rd Century AD

This is one of the few inscriptions which include not only the age of a woman at death, but also the age at which she was married. Other inscriptions show that a marriage at 19 was quite late for a girl. More often, a girl would be married at 13 to 15.

D · M · S
CLODIAE · SE
CVNDAE · CONIV
GI · DVLCISSIMAE · ET · BENE
MERENTI · QVAE · VIXIT ·AN
XXV · MEN · X · DIEB · XIIII · IN
CONIVGIO · MECVM · FVIT · SI
NE · QVERELLA · AN · VII · M · IIII
DIEB · XVIII · L · CAELIVS · FLO
RENTINVS · 7 · COH · X ·
VRB · POSVIT
NAT · MAMERTINO · ET
RVFO · COS · PRI · NON
AVG · DEF · XV · KAL
IVL · APRO · ET · MAXIMO
COS

* * *

D(is) m(anibus) s(acrum); Clodiae Secundae, coniugi dulcissimae et bene merenti, quae vixit an(nis) XXV, men(sibus) X, dieb(us) XIIII, in coniugio mecum fuit sine querella an(nis) VII, m(ensibus) IIII, dieb(us) XVIII; L(ucius) Caelius Florentinus (centurio) coh(ortis) X urb(anae) posuit; nat(a) Mamertino et Rufo co(n)s(ulibus) pri(die) Non(as) Aug(ustas); def(uncta) XV Kal(endas) Iul(ias) Apro et Maximo co(n)s(ulibus).

* * *

Sacred to the spirits of the dead; to Clodia Secunda, the sweetest and well-deserving wife, who lived 25 years, 10 months, 14 days, who was married to me without any complaint for 7 years, 4 months, 18 days. Lucius Caelius Florentinus, centurion of the 10th urban cohort,[1] put this up for her. She was born on the day before the Nones of August when Mamertinus and Rufus were consuls.[2] She died on the 15th day before the Kalends of July while Aper and Maximus were consuls.[3]

1   See the section on the urban garrison of Rome for more on the urban cohorts.
2   August 4th, AD 182.
3   June 17th, AD 207.

87.   *Furia Spes and Sempronius Firmus, Childhood Sweethearts*

CIL 6.18817; *ILS* 8006   Rome
Tombstone   Unknown

Here, a wife commemorates her dead husband, who had been her childhood sweetheart. Her tombstone expresses her grief at their separation and prays that she might see her beloved once again in a dream so that they might be reunited once again.

ANIMAE · SANCTAE · COLENDAE
D · M · S
FVRIA · SPES · L · SEMPRONIO · FIRMO
CONIVGI · CARISSIMO · MIHI · VT · COGNOVI
PVER · PVELLA · OBLIGATI · AMORI · PARITER
CVM · QVO · VIXI · TEMPORI · MINIMO · ET
QVO · TEMPORE · VIVERE · DEBVIMVS
A · MANV · MALA · DISEPARATI · SVMVS
ITA · PETO · VOS · [MA]NES · SANCTISSIMAE
COMMENDAT[VM] · HABEATIS
MEVM · CA[RV]M · ET · VELLITIS

HVIC · INDVLGENTISSIMI · ESSE
HORIS · NOCTVRNIS
VT · EVM · VIDEAM
ET · ETIAM · ME · FATO · SVADERE
VELLIT · VT · ET · EGO · POSSIM
DVLCIVS · ET · CELERIVS
APVT · EVM · PERVENIRE

* * *

Animae sanctae colendae; d(is) m(anibus) s(acrum); Furia Spes l(iberta) Sempronio Firmo coniugi carissimo mihi. Ut cognovi, puer puella obligati amor[e] pariter; cum quo vixi tempori minimo, et quo tempore vivere debuimus, a manu mala diseparati sumus. Ita peto vos, [ma]nes sanctissimae, commendat[um] habeatis meum ca[ru]m et vellitis huic indulgentissimi esse horis nocturnis, ut eum videam et etiam me fato suadere vellit, ut et ego possim dulcius et celerius aput eum pervenire.

* * *

To a spirit both sacred and worshipful; a sacred thing to the spirits of the dead; I, Furia Spes, freedwoman, dedicate this to Sempronius Firmus, my husband, most dear to me. When I met him, as a boy and girl, we were joined equally in love; I lived with him for too short a time and in the time we should have lived, we were torn apart by an evil hand. Therefore, I ask you, most sacred spirits, that you protect my dear husband whom I entrust to you and that you be willing to be most indulgent to him in the night hours, that I might see him (in a dream?) and also that he might want me to persuade fate to allow me to come to him more sweetly and quickly.

88. *Blandinia Martiola and Pompeius Catussa*

CIL 13.1983; *ILS* 8158   Lugdunum, Gallia Lugdunensis
Tombstone   3rd Century AD

In addition to the formulae usually found on tombstones, the dedicator Pompeius Catussa directly addresses the reader to bathe in the baths of Apollo, as that had been a favorite pastime of this husband and wife prior to the wife's death. The lettering on this small *cippus* allows us to date the inscription to the third century.

D · ET · M
MEMORIAE · AETERN
BLANDINIAE · MARTIOLAE · PVELLAE
INNOCENTISSIMAE · QVAE · VIXIT
ANN · XVIII · M · VIIII · D · V · POMPEIVS

CATVSSA · CIVES · SEQVANVS · TEC
TOR · CONIVGI · INCOMPARABILI
ET · SIBI · BENIGNISSIME · QVAE · ME
CVM · VIXIT · AN · V · M · VI · D · XVIII
SINE · VLA · CRIMINIS · SORDE · VIVS
SIBI · ET · CONIVGI · PONENDVM · CV
RAVIT · ET · SVB · ASCIA · DEDICAVIT
TV · QVI · LEGIS · VADE · IN · APOLINIS
LAVARI · QVOD · EGO · CVM · CONIV
GE · FECI · VELLEM · SI · ADVC · POSSEM

* * *

D(is) {et} m(anibus) (et) memoriae aetern(ae) Blandiniae Martiola, puellae innocentissimae, quae vixit ann(os) XVIII, m(enses) VIIII, d(ies) V; Pompeius Catussa cives Sequanus, tector, coniugi incomparabili et sibi benignissim(a)e, quae mecum vixit an(nos) V, m(enses) VI, d(ies) XVIII sine u(l)la criminis sorde; vi(v)us sibi et coniugi ponendum curavit et sub ascia dedicavit. Tu qui legis vade in Apol(l)inis lavari, quod ego cum coniuge feci; vellem si ad(h)uc possem.

* * *

To the spirits of the dead and the eternal memory of Blandinia Martiloa, a most innocent girl, who lived 18 years, 9 months, 5 days; Pompeius Catussa, a citizen of the Sequani,[1] a plasterer, dedicated this to his wife, incomparable and most kind to him, who lived with me five years, 6 months, 18 days[2] without any hint of wrong-doing; while still alive, he took care of putting this up for himself and his wife and dedicated it while still under construction. You who reads this, go and bathe in the baths of Apollo,[3] which I used to do with my wife; I wish I still could.

1   The Sequani were a Gallic people who became heavily Romanized.
     They lived in the upper Rhône River, near the Rhine.
2   Thus, she was only 13 when she married Catussa. It was very common
     for girls to marry when very young.
3   In Lugdunum.

89. *The Unfortunate Family of Julius Timotheus*

CIL 6.20307; *ILS* 8505   Rome
Tombstone   Unknown

This unfortunate man was killed by bandits on the road while traveling with his seven foster-children. The wife was evidently not on the trip and dedicated the inscription to her dead husband and *alumni* (see below for *alumni*). The tombstone, a marble tablet, was discovered among a number of later Christian burials in the grove of Dea Dia on the *Via Portuensis*, near the grove of the priesthood of the Arval Brethren.

```
                IVLIO · TIMO
               THEO · QVI · VI
             XIT · P · M · ANNIS
            XXVIII · VITAE · IN
              NOCENTISSIME
           DECEPTO · A · LATR
             ONIBVS · CVM
           ALVMNIS · N · VII
           OTACILIA · NARCI
           SA · COIVGI · DVL
                CISSIMO
```

* * *

Iulio Timotheo, qui vixit p(lus) m(inus) annis XXVIII, vitae innocentissim(a)e, decepto a latronibus cum alumnis n(umero) VII; Otacilia Narcisa co(n)iugi dulcissimo.

* * *

To Julius Timotheus, who lived more or less 28 years, a man of most innocent life, deceived by bandits along with his seven foster-children;[1] Otacilia Narcisa (dedicated this) to her sweetest husband.

1   Alumni were orphaned children who had been taken in by a family. See the chapter on children below for more information and examples.

90.   *Daizus Comozon, Inhabitant of Dacia*

CIL 3.14214, 12; *ILS* 8501   Tropaeum Traiani, Moesia Inferior
        Tombstone   2nd Century AD

This inscription comes from the modern town of Adamklissi in Moesia Inferior, the site of a war memorial which the emperor Trajan erected to commemorate his victory over the Dacians on the other side of the Danube (the so-called *tropaeum Traiani*).

```
                   D · M
               DAIZI · CO
               MOZOI · VI
            XIT · AN · L · INTER
             FECTVS · A · CAS
              TABOCIS · IV
           S · TVS · ET · VAL · PA
           TRI · B · M · POSV
                  ERVNT
```

* * *

D(is) m(anibus) Daizi Comozoi, vixit an(nos) L, interfectus a Castabocis; Iustus et Val(erius) patri b(ene) m(erenti) posuerunt.

* * *

To the spirits of the dead of Daizus Comozon,[1] lived 50 years, killed by the Castaboci,[2] Iustus and Valerius[3] put this up to their well-deserving father.

1   Probably a non-citizen or, possibly, a retired auxiliary soldier.
2   The Castaboci were a hostile people living east of the new province of Dacia. The Castaboci streamed across the Danube in 170 after Marcus Aurelius tried to invade their territory but was defeated. It is known that the Castaboci had driven through Moesia Inferior and eventually sacked Eleusis in Greece before being pushed back across the Danube in 171.
3   Note the Roman names of Comozon's children. Although their Latin *cognomina* (Iustus and Valerius) may indicate that they were Roman citizens, it is more likely that they were non-citizens who had adopted them in order to appear Roman.

91.   *Germanius Valens and his Family*

AE 1983, 782b   Intercisa, Pannonia
Tombstone   3rd Century AD

D · M
AVRELIAE · BARACHAE · [V]IXIT
ANN · XXXV · ET · AVRHL · GER
MA[N]ILAE · VIXIT
ANN · IIII · ET · ALTERA
FILIA · AVRELIA · GER
MANILLA · VI[XIT] · ANN
II · ET · IMMOSTAE · MATRI · SV
E · VIXIT · ANN · LX · GERMAN
IVS · VALENS · MIL · COH · M · HEM
ES · VXORI · ET · MATRI · ET · FI
LIIS · POSVIT · ET · SIBI · VVIVS · FE
CIT

* * *

D(is) M(anibus); Aureliae Barachae [v]ixit ann(os) XXXV, et Aur{h}(e)l(iae) Germa[n]il(l)ae, vixit ann(os) IIII, et altera filia Aurelia Germanilla, vi[xit] ann(os) II, et Immostae matri su(a)e, vixit ann(os) LX; Germanius Valens, mil(es) coh(ortis) M(illiariae) Hemes(enorum), uxori et matri et filiis posuit et sibi {v}vi(v)us fecit.

* * *

To the spirits of the dead; to Aurelia Baracha,[1] lived 35 years, and Aurelia Germanilla, lived 4 years, and his second daughter Aurelia Germanilla,[2] lived 2 years, and Immosta, his mother, lived 60 years,

Germanius Valens,[3] soldier of the auxiliary cohort of 1000 Hemeseni;[4] dedicated this to his wife, mother and children as well as to himself while he was still alive.

1   She either became a citizen when the emperor Caracalla (Marcus Aurelius Antoninus) extended the citizenship to all freeborn people in the empire c. AD 212, or was descended from someone who had been granted citizenship at that time.

2   The second daughter received the same name as the first because the first must have died before the second was born. They both had the same *nomen* as their mother (Aurelia), but their *cognomen* (Germanilla) was derived from the *nomen* of their father. It is most likely that the family (mother and daughters) received the citizenship from Caracalla after Valens' discharge from the auxiliaries.

3   His name would indicate that he was a citizen. Other inscriptions indicate that this cohort was composed of Roman citizens. On discharge, his family would have received the citizenship.

4   The Hemeseni were a people from the region of Emesa in Roman Syria. This cohort was stationed in Intercisa, on the Danube, south of the town of Aquincum.

ROMAN WOMEN

While inscriptions frequently record a man's role in the public realm, women were most often mentioned in relation to their family and household. Men's virtues (strength, moderation, devotion) were noted in relation to their activities in both the public and private spheres of daily life. Women's virtues, however, were tied almost exclusively to the private, domestic sphere: *e.g.* childbirth, housekeeping, chastity, and devotion to husband and family. From childhood, girls learned how to run the household. Marriage generally took place in the early teens. The infant mortality rate, short life expectancy, and the dangers of childbirth dictated that girls begin to produce children as early in their lives as possible. Husbands and wives generally enjoyed very close relationships. While the husband was engaged in his public life, the wife had *de facto* control over the household. Despite the patriarchal nature of Roman society, and women's exclusion from public careers, funeral inscriptions (such as those given in the previous chapter on Roman families) illustrate the significance of women in daily life. The inscriptions in this section illustrate how Romans wished to remember the women in their lives. For instance, the delightful tombstone of Claudia shows her close relationships to her children, as well as her ability to keep an orderly home. While they did not hold office, some women did become visible in public, through public benefaction. Paccia Valeria was honored by her hometown in the Greek East with a statue in the center of town because of her beneficence.

92.   *Claudia's Lament*

CIL 1.1007 and 6.15346; *ILS* 8403   Rome
Tombstone   2nd Century BC

This is the oldest inscription in this collection. It reports the words of Claudia, a woman of the 2nd century BC. Note the many archaic forms in the text. The

Latin long "i" is represented as "ei" as in "deico", "heic", "mareitum", "deilexit", and "abei". Two "u"s together are represented as "uo" or "ou" as in "suom" and "souo". "Horum" is given as "horunc". This is a verse inscription based on an epigram by the Greek author Heraclitus. The writing of the epitaph in verse and the use of a Greek source is meant to place the woman in the realm of the cultured aristocracy. The epitaph also illustrates the two most important roles women played: the bearing of children, and the care of the household.

HOSPES · QVOD · DEICO · PAVLLVM · EST · ASTA · AC · PELLEGE
HEIC · EST · SEPVLCRVM · HAV · PVLCRVM · PVLCRAI · FEMINAE
NOMEN · PARENTES · NOMINARVNT · CLAVDIAM
SVOM · MAREITVM · CORDE · DEILEXIT · SOVO
GNATOS · DVOS · CREAVIT · HORVNC · ALTERVM
IN · TERRA · LINQVIT · ALIVM · SVB · TERRA · LOCAT
SERMONE · LEPIDO · TVM · AVTEM · INCESSV · COMMODO
DOMVM · SERVAVIT · LANAM · FECIT · DIXI · ABEI

* * *

Hospes, quod d{e}ico paullum est, asta ac pellege. H{e}ic est sepulcrum hau pulc[h]rum pulc[h]ra[e] feminae. Nomen parentes nominarunt Claudiam. Su[u]m mar{e}itum corde d{e}ilexit s{o}uo. [G]natos duos creavit, horu[m] alterum in terra linquit, alium sub terra locat. Sermone lepido, tum autem incessu commodo. Domum servavit, lanam fecit. Dixi. Ab{e}i.

* * *

Friend, what I say is short; stop and read it.[1] This is the tomb, by no means pretty, of a pretty girl.[2] Her parents named her Claudia. She loved her husband in her heart. She gave birth to two children; one of them remains on earth, the other she placed under the earth. She was pleasant of conversation and also proper in manner. She kept house and made wool. I have spoken. Be on your way.

1   Frequently, inscriptions called out to be read by the passerby. Here, Claudia urges a hypothetical reader to stop and read her story.
2   This is a play on the words for pretty "pulcra" and tomb "sepulchrum".

---

93.   *L. Paccia Valeria Saturnina,*
                 Honored by her Town

CIL 3.12149; *ILS* 7203   Comama Pisidia, Asia Minor
      Statue Base   3rd Century AD

This was the base of one of four statues dedicated to Lucia Paccia Valeria by her daughter Aurelia Valeria Scriboniana. Each of the four bases (of which only one is extant) was headed by a part of her name written in Greek (Lucia, Paccia, Valeria, Saturnina). This base is the "Valeria" base. The four bases were probably placed on four sides of a public area, such as the forum, to maximize its visibility to the local citizenry. The occasion of the dedication (paid for by the daughter) was an honor bestowed upon Paccia by the town of Comama Pisidia in Asia Minor. Paccia's praiseworthy public benefaction is not recorded, but her inscription presents an interesting contrast to that of Claudia.

L • PACCIAM • VALE
RIAM • SATVRNINAM
HONORAVIT • COL
IVL • AVG • PRIMA • FI
DA • COMAMA • STATV
AMQVE • POSVIT • AV
RELIA • VALERIA
SCRIBONIANA • FRON
TINA • FILIA • EIVS

* * *

L(uciam) Pacciam Valeriam Saturninam honoravit col(onia) Iul(ia) Aug(usta) Prima Fida Comama statuamque posuit Aurelia Valeria Scriboniana Frontina filia eius.

* * *

The colony of Julia Augusta Prima Fida Comama[1] honored Lucia[1] Paccia Valeria Saturnina; Aurelia Valeria Scroboniana Frontina, her daughter, put up this statue.

1   This town of Asia Minor was originally named Comama (in the region of Pisidia) but was re-established as a Roman colony with the name *colonia Julia Augusta Prima Fida.*
2   Most women did not have *praenomina.* It is probably an indication of her importance in her town.

Women's Occupations

Women's roles, however, were not limited only to the household. Because of the widespread poverty among the lower classes of Rome, it was often necessary for both the husband and wife of the family to work. Children also sometimes took jobs (see the section on Roman children). The following inscriptions illustrate the kinds of jobs women held. Examples include women who worked in the houses of the aristocracy either as caretakers of children or housekeepers (Crispina the nurse of two senators, Flavia Sabina the midwife, and the wet-nurse Terentia Thisbe) or as secretaries (Pyrrhe the scribe and Hapate the short-hand writer). Some women even worked as professionals (Julia Saturnina the medical doctor, and Gallonia Paschusa the barber). Others worked as artisans (Irene the spinner of wool) and saleswomen (Data who sold silk, and Aurelia Nais the seller of fish).

94.   *Crispina, Nurse of Two Senators*

CIL 6.16592; *ILS* 8531   Rome
Tombstone   Unknown

Crispina was married at 13 and went to work in the house of a senator. There is no record of any children of her own, but her tombstone proudly announces that she was the nurse (*nutrix*) of two senators.

D · M · S
CRISPINAE · COIVGI
DIVINAE · NVTRI
CI · SENATORVM
DVVM · ALBVS
CONIVNX · C · Q · F
AN · XVII · H · VIX
AN · XXX · M · II
B · M · F

* * *

D(is) m(anibus) s(acrum); Crispinae co(n)iugi divinae, nutrici senatorum duum; Albus coniunx c(um) q(uo) [v(ixit)] an(nos) XVII; h(aec) vix(it) an(nos) XXX, m(enses) II; b(ene) m(erenti) f(ecit).

* * *

To the spirits of the dead; to Crispina, a divine wife, nurse of two senators; Albus was her husband, with whom she lived 17 years; she lived 30 years, 2 months; her husband made this for her, well-deserving.

95.   *Pyrrhe, Scribe*

CIL 6.9525; *ILS* 7400   Rome
Funerary Urn   Unknown

This inscription is on the side of a funerary urn from Rome. On either side of the inscription are pictures of a ram's head. Beneath the inscription are pictures of two birds.

PYRRHE · RVBRIAE
HELVIAE · LIBRARIAE
P · RVBRIVS · OPTATVS
CONTVBERNALI · SVAE

* * *

Pyrrhe, Rubriae Helviae librariae; P(ublius) Rubrius Optatus contubernali suae.

* * *

Pyrrhe, scribe of Rubria Helvia; Publius Rubrius Optatus[1] dedicated this to his wife.[2]

1   Probably a freedman since his *nomen* is the same as the family name of Pyrrhe's mistress. It is uncertain whether Pyrrhe is a slave or freedwoman.

2   The Latin here is *contubernalis* ("tent-mate"), the term often used to define marriages between slaves. The word, however, is also used more loosely even by freeborn persons.

96.   *Hapate, Short-Hand Writer*

CIL 6.33892; *ILS* 7760	Rome
Tombstone	Unknown

Hapate's inscription was discovered on the *Via Tiburtina*. She is another example of a literate woman who originally came from the Greek East and worked in the house of an aristocrat. It is unknown whether Hapate was a slave, a freedwoman, or freeborn. Her job was probably to take dictation in Greek.

[D] • M • S
HAPATENI
NOTARIAE
GRECE • QVE
VIX • ANN • XXV
PITTOSVS • FE
CIT • CONIVGI
DVLCISSIME

* * *

[D(is)] m(anibus) s(acrum); Hapateni, notariae Gr(a)ec(a)e, qu(a)e vix(it) ann(os) XXV; Pittosus fecit coniugi dulcissim(a)e.

* * *

Sacred to the spirits of the dead; to Hapate, short-hand writer of Greek, who lived 25 years; Pittosus made this for his sweetest wife.

97.   *Julia Saturnina, Medical Doctor*

CIL 2.497; *ILS* 7802   Emerita, Spain
Tombstone   Perhaps the 1st Century AD

D · M · S
IVLIAE · SATVRNINAE
ANN · XXXXV
VXORI · INCOMPARABILI
MEDICAE · OPTIMAE
MVLIERI · SANCTISSIMAE
CASSIVS · PHILIPPVS
MARITVS · OBMERITIS
H · S · E · S · T · T · L

* * *

D(is) m(anibus) s(acrum); Iuliae Saturninae, ann(orum) XXXXV, uxori incomparabili, medicae optimae, mulieri sanctissimae; Cassius Philippus, maritus ob meritis; h(ic) s(ita) e(st); s(it) t(ibi) t(erra) l(evis).

* * *

Sacred to the spirits of the dead; to Julia Saturnina, 45 years old, incomparable wife, a very good medical doctor and the most blameless wife; Cassius Philippus, her husband, dedicated this because of her merits. She is buried here. May the earth be light upon you.

98.   *Gallonia Paschusa, Barber*

CIL 6.9941   Rome
Tombstone   Unknown

GALLONIAE
C · L
PASCHVSAE
TOSTRICI

* * *

Galloniae C(ai) l(iberta) Paschusae, to(n)strici.

* * *

To Gallonia Paschusa, freedwoman of Gaius, barber.

99.   *Flavia Sabina, Midwife*

CIL 6.6647	Rome
Tombstone	Unknown

This tomb was discovered in a *columbarium* close to the *Porta Praenestina* (it is also in the vicinity of the *columbarium* of the Statilius family, which was previously discussed). She was probably an imperial freedwoman. It is possible that after acquiring her freedom, she worked on her own or in the house of another aristocrat. Note that the husband, Marius Orthrus, was not an imperial freedman, but was either freeborn or the freed slave of a person named Marius.

HYGIAE
FLAVIAE · SABINAE
OPSTETR · VIXIT · ANN · XXX
MARIVS · ORTHRVS · ET
APOLLONIVS · CONTVBERNALI
CARISSIMAE

* * *

Hygiae; Flaviae Sabinae, opstetr(ici), vixit ann(os) XXX; Marius Orthrus et Apollonius contubernali carissimae.

* * *

To Hygia;[1] to Flavia Sabina, midwife, lived 30 years; Marius Orthrus and Apollonius dedicated this to his dearest wife.

1   The goddess of health.

100.   *Terentia Thisbe, Wet-Nurse*

CIL 6.27262; *ILS* 8536	Rome
Tombstone	Unknown

Terentia Thisbe was probably a Greek freedwoman from the aristocratic house of the woman Terentia Selicia. This marble tablet was discovered outside the *Porta Salaria.*

D · M
TERENTIAE · THISBE
TERENTIA · SELICIA
NVTRICI · LACTARIAE · F

* * *

D(is) m(anibus); Terentiae Thisbe; Terentia Selicia nutrici lactariae f(ecit).

* * *

To the spirits of the dead; to Terentia Thisbe; Terentia Selicia made this for her wet-nurse.

101.   Irene, Spinner of Wool

CIL 6.9497   Rome
Tombstone   Unknown

D · M
IRENES
LANIPENDAE
V · A · XXVIII
OLYMPVS
CONTVBERNALI
BENEMERENTI
FECIT

* * *

D(is) m(anibus) Irenes, lanipendae, v(ixit) a(nnos) XXVIII; Olympus contubernali bene merenti fecit.

* * *

To the spirits of the dead of Irene, spinner of wool, lived 28 years; Olympus made this for his well-deserving wife.

102.   Data, Seller of Silk

CIL 6.9891   Rome
Tombstone   Unknown

D · M
CLAVD · BACCHYLO
V · A · XLIX
DATA · SERICAR
CONT · B · M · ET · SIBI
CONS

* * *

D(is) m(anibus); Claud(io) Bacchylo, v(ixit) a(nnos) XLIX; Data, sericar(ia), cont(ubernali) b(ene) m(erenti) et sibi cons(ervo).

* * *

To the spirits of the dead; to Claudius Bacchylus, who lived 49 years; Data, a seller of silk, dedicated this to her well-deserving husband and fellow slave as well as to herself.

Tombstone of the freedwoman piscatrix *Aurelia Nais (CIL 6.9801; ILS 7500), National Museum of Rome at the Baths of Diocletian, Rome. Photo courtesy of the Ministero per i Beni e le Attività Culturali Soprintenza Archeologica di Roma.*

103.   *Aurelia Nais, Seller of Fish*

CIL 6.9801; *ILS* 7500   Rome
Tombstone   3rd Century AD

Here, two freedmen honor a fellow freedwoman who earned money by selling fish in the warehouse of Galba. A picture of a laurel wreath appears in the center of the front of the stone, with the words of the third, fourth and fifth lines appearing on either side of the wreath.

AVRELIA · C · L · NAIS
PISCATRIX · DE · HORREIS · GALBAE
C · AVRELIVS · C · L · PHILEROS
PATRONVS
L · VALERIVS · L · L · SECVNDVS

* * *

Aurelia C(ai) l(iberta) Nais, piscatrix de horreis Galbae; C(aius) Aurelius C(ai) l(ibertus) Phileros, patronus, L(ucius) Valerius L(uci) l(ibertus) Secundus.

* * *

Aurelia Nais, freedwoman of Gaius, seller of fish in the warehouse of Galba;[1] Gaius Aurelius Phileros, freedmen of Gaius, her patron,[2] and Lucius Valerius Secundus, freedmen of Lucius,[3] put this up.

1   The *Horrea Galbae* was an extensive warehouse complex in southwest
     Rome, between the southern face of the Aventine hill and the Tiber.
     The warehouses originally belonged to the family of the Sulpicii and
     were probably known as the *Horrea Sulpicia*. During the reign of the
     emperor Galba (Servius Sulpicius Galba), the *Horrea Sulpicia* became
     imperial property and were henceforth known as the *Horrea Galbae*.

2   The same owner freed both Aurelia Nais and C. Aurelius Phileros.
     Because Phileros (a Greek name) is described as Nais' *patronus*, he
     may have been named Nais' legal guardian (patron) due to her youth
     or unmarried status at the time of their manumission.

3   L. Valerius Secundus originates from a different household than Nais
     and Phileros. Although the inscription does not mention it specifically,
     he may be from the household of Nais' husband.

*Tombstone of the child Sex. Rufius Achilleus (CIL
6.25572), National Museum of Rome at the Baths of
Diocletian, Rome. Photo courtesy of the Ministero
per i Beni e le Attività Culturali Soprintenza Archeologica di Roma.*

CHILDREN

The Roman world was a dangerous place for children. The lack of modern healthcare and sanitation as well as difficult living conditions for the majority of the Roman populace resulted in a very high infant mortality rate. Documents, especially those found on papyri from Egypt, indicate that only about 50% of children born reached the age of one. Having children, while inherently joyous, often had tragic results, and families often suffered terribly when they lost an infant or child. The following texts illustrate some of the tender emotions expressed by parents on the tombstones of their children.

104.   *L. Aponius Abascantus, 4 Years Old*

CIL 6.12156; *ILS* 8544   Rome
Tombstone   1st Century AD

There are very few tombstones of children who died before the age of one. Most, as in the case of the following three, commemorate children two years and older. It is most likely that, because of the frequency of infant mortality, the majority of children who died in infancy were not commemorated with expensive tombstones.

L · APONIVS
ABASCAN
TVS · V · A · IIII · M
VI · T · FLAVIVS
ANICETVS · ET
APONIA · SYR
ILLA · ISSVLO

ET · DELICIO
SVO · FECER

* * *

L(ucius) Aponius Abascantus, v(ixit) a(nnos) IIII, m(enses) VI; T(itus) Flavius Anicetus et Aponia Syrilla issulo et delicio suo fecer(unt).

* * *

Lucius Aponius Abascantus,[1] lived 4 years, 6 months; T. Flavius Anicetus[2] and Aponia Syrilla made this for their little boy and delight.

1   The son was named after his mother (Aponia), not his father (Flavius). The child may have been illegitimate or born while Anicetus was still an imperial slave (without the name Titus Flavius).
2   His name indicates that he was probably an imperial freedmen from the Flavian dynasty.

105. *Pomponia Fortunula, 2 Years Old*

| *AE* 1975, 41 | Catacombs of S. Callisto, Rome |
| Tombstone | Unknown |

D · M
POMPONIAE · FORTVNV
LAE · QVE · DECESSET · IN · PACE
QVE · VIXIT · ANN · II · MEN · I · DIES · XX

* * *

D(is) m(anibus); Pomponiae Fortunulae, qu(a)e decesset in pace, qu(a)e vixit ann(os) II, men(sem) I, dies XX.

* * *

To the spirits of the dead; to Pomponia Fortunula, who died peacefully and who lived 2 years, 1 month, 20 days.

106. *Lutatia Secundina, 4 Years Old*

| *CIL* 6.21738 | Rome |
| Tombstone | Unknown |

D · M
LVTATIAE
SECVNDINAE
INFANTI · SVAVISSI
MAE · VIXIT · AN · IIII
MENS · VI · D · VIIII

* * *

D(is) m(anibus); Lutatiae Secundinae, infanti suavissimae, vixit an(nos) IIII, mens(es) VI, d(ies) VIIII.

* * *

To the spirits of the dead; to Lutatia Secundina, the sweetest baby, lived 4 years, 6 months, and 9 days.

---

107.   *Silvia, 3 Years Old*

CIL 6.36353; *ILS* 8548   Rome
Tombstone   1ˢᵗ Century AD

This inscription illustrates ancient Roman baby talk. Among the dedicators are a "tata" and a "mamma", names which reflected the child's names for her grandparents. As the parents are already mentioned (Claudius and Claudia), Epictetus was Silvia's grandfather and Aphrodisia her grandmother.

D · M · SILVIAE · VIX · ANNI · III · MENS · II · DIEB · IX
CLAVDIVS · PROTOMACHVS · ET · CLAVDIA · DAMAL
FILIAE · ET · SALONIVS · EPICTETVS · TATA · ET
APHRODISIA · MAMMA · FEC

* * *

D(is) m(anibus) Silviae, vix(it) anni(s) III, mens(ibus) II, dieb(us) IX; Claudius Protomachus et Claudia Damal(is) filiae et Salonius Epictetus tata et Aphrodisia mamma fec(erunt).

* * *

To the spirits of the dead; to Silvia, lived 3 years, 2 months, 9 days; Claudius Protomachus and Claudia Damalis made this for their daughter along with Salonius Epictetus, her grandpa, and Aphrodisia, her grandma.

---

108.   *Pieris, Hairdresser*

CIL 6.9731   Rome
Tombstone   Unknown

As this and other similar inscriptions demonstrate, children, including girls like Pieris, often went to work at very early ages in order to help their struggling families survive financially. This is a marble tablet from a *columbarium* discovered in the Campana gardens near the church of St. John Lateran.

PIERIS · ORNATRIX
VIXIT · AN · VIIII
HILARA · MATER · POSVIT

* * *

Pieris, ornatrix, vixit an(nos) VIIII; Hilara mater posuit.

* * *

Pieris, hairdresser, lived 9 years; Hilara, her mother, dedicated this to her.

109.   *Q. Sulpicius Maximus, Poet*

CIL 6.33976; *ILS* 5177	Rome
Tombstone	1st Century AD

Poetry competitions were open to poets of all ages. Here, the parents of one young poet recollect their deceased son's competition at the third Capitoline Games of AD 94 where his young age and skill won him the admiration of the competition. Maximus' inscription, a large marble *cippus*, was discovered outside of Rome on the *Via Salaria*, near the *Porta Collina*. The text is inscribed below the sculpted image of a boy. He wears a toga and holds a scroll in his left hand. The poem in Greek which Maximus delivered extemporaneously is included on the stone.

DEIS · MANIBVS · SACRVM
Q · SVLPICIO · Q · F · CLA · MAXIMO · DOMO · ROMA · VIX · ANN · XI · M · V · D · XII
HIC · TERTIO · CERTAMINIS · LVSTRO · INTER
GRAECOS · POETAS · DVOS · ET · L
PROFESSVS · FAVOREM · QVEM · OB · TENERAM
AETATEM · EXCITAVERAT
IN · ADMIRATIONEM · INGENIO · SVO · PERDVXIT · ET · CVM · HONORE ·
DISCESSIT · VERSVS
EXTEMPORALES · EO · SVBIECTI · SVNT · NE · PARENT · ADFECTIB · SVIS ·
INDVLSISSE · VIDEANT
Q · SVLPICIVS · EVGRAMVS · ET · LICINIA · IANVARIA · PARENT · INFELICISSIM ·
F · PIISSIM · FEC · ET · SIB · P · S

* * *

Deis manibus sacrum; Q(uinto) Sulpicio Q(uinti) f(ilio) Cla(udia tribu) Maximo, domo Roma, vix(it) ann(os) XI, m(enses) V, d(ies) XII. Hic tertio certaminis lustro inter Graecos poetas duos et L professus favorem, quem ob teneram aetatem excitaverat, in admirationem ingenio suo perduxit et cum honore discessit. Versus extemporales eo subiecti sunt ne parent(es) adfectib(us) suis indulsisse videant(ur). Q. Sulpicius

Eugramus et Licinia Ianuaria parent(es) infelicissim(i) f(ilio) piissim(o) fec(erunt) et sib(i) p(o)s(terisque).

* * *

Sacred to the Departed Spirits; to Quintus Sulpicius Maximus, son of Quintus, of the Claudian tribe, born in Rome, lived eleven years, five months and twelve days. This boy in a competition of fifty-two Greek poets, during the third holding of the games,[1] won favor on account of his young age. He induced everyone into admiration by his skill and left the competition with honor.[2] The verses he composed extemporaneously are inscribed below lest his parents seem to have indulged in their own affections. Quintus Sulpicius Eugramus[3] and Licinia Ianuaria, unlucky parents, made this for their most dutiful son, as well as for themselves, and their descendants.

1 A reference to the Capitoline Games, the *Ludi Capitolini*. The emperor Domitian instituted these games on the model of the Olympic Games in Greece. They were held in the early summer, every four years: in AD 86, 90 and 94. There were three categories of contests: chariot racing, athletics, and music/poetry/rhetoric. The games were very popular and attracted a large number of contestants (note the fifty-two competitors in Greek poetry in this inscription).
2 Quintus does not seem to have won the competition.
3 Quintus' father is a citizen, but the name Eugramus ("well-written" in Greek) might indicate that he was of Greek origin or descent.

110. *Florus, Child Charioteer*

CIL 6.10078; *ILS* 5300   Rome
Tombstone   Unknown

One of the worst aspects of the poverty in which so much of the population of ancient cities found themselves was the tendency to expose children at birth rather than go through the expense of raising them. Girls especially were exposed because they carried the added expense of a dowry at the time of their marriage. Children were left on dung heaps or on the street. These children, however, did not always die after exposure. Sometimes, they were picked up by slave traders or by other families. The children were raised by their new masters or parents and were called *alumni* or *alumnae* ("foster-children"). Florus is an example of an *alumnus*. It is not known whether this is a child with his own chariot or a young, professional charioteer. An image of a boy standing in a chariot pulled by a horse is carved on the stone. The boy holds the reins in one hand and a palm of victory in his other. Another person runs next to the chariot and holds a victory crown over the boy's head.

FLORVS · EGO · HIC · IACEO
BIGARIVS · INFANS · QVI · CITO
DVM · CVPIO · CVRRVS · CITO · DECIDI · AD · VMBR
IANVARIVS · ALVMNO · DVLCISSIMO

* * *

Florus ego hic iaceo bigarius infans qui, cito dum cupio currus, cito decidi ad umbr(as); Ianuarius alumno dulcissimo.

* * *

I, Florus, lie here, a child driver of a two-horse chariot, who, while I wanted to race my chariot quickly, quickly fell to the shades; Ianuarius made this for his sweetest foster-child.

111. *Ursinus, Victim of a Shipwreck*

CIL 3.1899; *ILS* 8516   Spalatum, Dalmatia
Tombstone   Unknown

Travel by ship was always dangerous. Here, an eleven-year-old victim of a shipwreck is commemorated. His body was never recovered.

D · M
M · ALLIVS
FIRMINVS
VRSINO · F
C · SEPTIMI
CARPOPO
RI · DELICA
TO · INFELI
CISSIMO · P
NAVFRAGIO
OBITO · AN · XI
CVIVS · MEM
BRA · CONSVM
SIT · MARIS · PER
SE · QVOT · NOMEN
TITVLVS · PRAESTAT
SVISQ · DOLO
REM

* * *

D(is) m(anibus); M(arcus) Allius Firminus Ursino f(ilio), C(ai) Septimi Carpopori delicato, infelicissimo p(uero), naufragio obito an(norum) XI, cuius membra consumsit mar[e] per se. Quot nomen titulus praestat suisq(ue) dolorem.

* * *

To the spirits of the dead; Marcus Allius Firminus dedicated this to
Ursinus, delight of Gaius Septimius Carpoporus, a most unlucky boy,
killed in a shipwreck at 11 years old, whose body alone the sea devoured.
How often an inscription displays a name and is responsible for bringing
grief to the family.

112. *Latro, Bitten by a Snake*

CIL 11.2056; *ILS* 8521   Perusia, Umbria, Italy
Tombstone   Unknown

LATRO · C · PETRONI · C [...]
SER · ANNORVM · XII · A · VIPE[RA]
PERCVSSVS · SEPTVMO · DIE · PER[IT]
MODESTVS · FRATER · PHILARGVRVS
CONSERVOS · POSVERVNT

* * *

Latro C(ai) Petroni C[...] ser(vus), annorum XII, a vipera percussus,
septumo die perit; Modestus frater, Philargurus conserv[i] posuerunt.

* * *

[Gaius?] Latro, slave of Gaius Petronius C[?], 12 years old, bitten
by a snake, he died on the seventh day. Modestus, his brother, and
Philargurus, his fellow-slaves, put this up.

113. *Parthenope Fructosa, Foster-Child*

CIL 6.27009; *ILS* 8543   Rome
Tombstone   Unknown

In this inscription, Parthenope's mother died and left her (as an orphaned
alumna) in the care of another woman, Sulpicia. Parthenope, however, only lived
another 22 days.

D · M
SVLPICIA · PARTH
ENOPAE · FRVCTOSAE
ALVMNE · SVAE · B · M
QVAE · VIXIT · ANNOS
VIIII · M · II · D · XV · QVAE · SV
PRA · MONNVLAM · SV

AM · SVPRA · VIXIT · DIES · XXII

* * *

D(is) m(anibus); Sulpicia Parthenopae Fructosae, alumne suae b(ene) m(erenti), quae vixit annos VIIII, m(enses) II, d(ies) XV, quae supra monnulam suam supravixit dies XXII.

* * *

To the spirits of the dead; Sulpicia dedicated this to Parthenope Fructosa, her well-deserving foster-child, who lived 9 years, 2 months, 15 days, who outlived her mamma[1] by only 22 days.

1   Another example of affectionate names children use for their parents (see 107 above for an additional example).

THE GAMES

Entertainment was big business in Rome. There were many types of spectacles, each with its own professional entertainers and dedicated building. Within the amphitheater beast hunts and gladiatorial combats were held. Highly trained beast hunters (*venatores*), beast handlers (*bestiarii*), and gladiators used their skills in contests of man against animal, animal against animal, and man against man, even at great personal risk, for the enjoyment of the crowd. Within the theater, various types of actors (and actresses) performed dramatic and comedic works. Finally, within the *circus*, charioteers raced chariots pulled by teams of two, four or even eight horses. A tremendous number of people were involved with the production of each type of spectacle, either as entertainers, administrators, or other personnel. Training of performers was another source of employment. Gladiatorial training was highly specialized, since gladiators were trained in the use of a specific combination of armor, weaponry and tactics. A wide assortment of actors trained in theatrical troupes for the performance of specific types of plays and scenes. The inscriptions of charioteers do not indicate specialization, but more training and experience were required for chariots drawn by larger teams of horses, or for more difficult races. Particularly good charioteers were noted as appearing in more unusual and difficult races (such as in eight-horse chariot races, races which used various handicaps such as mismatched teams, or races without whips).

The games originated as obligatory shows paid for by members of the aristocracy. Although expensive, sponsoring games was a good way of gaining political support from the lower classes. The emperors eventually took over sponsorship of the majority of the games in the city of Rome, not only because of the expense, but also to monopolize the popularity which the games generated. In the provinces, however, games on a smaller scale were mainly paid for by local magistrates and priests.

The Amphitheater

Gladiatorial combat was held in the amphitheater, a large central arena surrounded by bleacher-style seating. Pairs of equally matched gladiators fought with real weapons in a demonstration of skill and endurance. The desire for variety in these combats led to the creation of many types of gladiators who specialized in a wide variety of weapons and armor. These types were then mismatched in order to create interesting pairings of fighters. Gladiators became extremely popular with the population.

Despite their popularity, however, gladiators were considered to be of slave status. Although most were slaves, many freeborn persons subjugated themselves willingly to the *munerarius* (the aristocratic sponsor of the games), out of a desire for the popularity generally bestowed upon successful gladiators. All, however, were compelled to take an oath submitting themselves to the possibility of death at the behest of the *munerarius* and the crowd. This oath placed their bodies at the disposal of the *munerarius* and made the gladiators no better than slaves, whose bodies belonged to their masters. Even members of the aristocracy participated in the games (the most famous example of this is the emperor Commodus), thus diminishing the dignity of their social order. As a result, the emperors passed laws prohibiting the aristocracy from fighting as gladiators. The following inscriptions illustrate some of the varieties of gladiatorial specialties.

114.   *Thelyphus, Samnite*

CIL 6.10187; *ILS* 5085   Rome
        Tombstone   Unknown

The Samnite gladiator was equipped like Rome's native Italic adversary of the same name. The Samnite wore heavy armor, including an oblong shield, and fought with a short sword. Thelyphus fought as a Samnite, but was originally from the province of Thrace. Many gladiators originated in the provinces, some even as prisoners of war.

THELYPHVS · SAMNES
NATIONE · TRAEX

* * *

Thelyphus, samnes, natione T(h)raex.

* * *

Thelyphus, Samnite, Thracian by nationality.

115.   *Beryllus, Essedarius*

CIL 12.3323; *ILS* 5095   Nemausus, Gallia Narbonensis
Tombstone   Unknown

An *essedarius* was a type of gladiator who fought from a war chariot.

> BERYLLVS • ESSE
> LIB • XX • NAT
> GRAECVS • ANN • XXV
> NOMAS • CONIVNX
> VIR • B • MER

* * *

Beryllus, esse(darius), lib(ertus), (pugna) XX, nat(ione) Graecus, (vixit) ann(os) XXV; Nomas coniunx vir(o) b(ene) mer(enti).

* * *

Beryllus, chariot fighter, freed in his 20[1] fight,[1] Greek by nationality, lived 25 years;[2] Nomas, his wife,[3] put this up for her well-deserving husband.

1   Gladiators had a social status equal to that of slaves. Those that fought well, however, and pleased the crowd could be given the *rudis*, a small wooden training sword which was a symbol of the gladiator's freedom.
2   Inscriptions have revealed much about how often gladiators fought. Gladiators in Rome seem to have fought only once or twice a year. Gladiators in the provinces, far from the famous schools in the heart of the empire, usually fought more often. Beryllus, a gladiator in Gaul, fought two or three times a year.
3   Many gladiators were married and even had children, an indication that life in the *ludus* (the gladiatorial training school and dormitory), was not as oppressive as once thought.

116.   *Antigonus, Provocator*

CIL 5.4502; *ILS* 5108a   Brixia, Po Valley, Italy
Tombstone   Unknown

Provocator literally means "challenger". Gladiators of this type usually fought other *provocatores*. Their equipment included a full helmet, breastplate, rectangular shield, and broadsword.

> D • M
> ANTIGONI
> PROVOK
> VERVS • DOCTOR
> POSVIT

* * *

D(is) m(anibus) Antigoni, provok(atoris); Verus, doctor, posuit.

* * *

To the spirits of the dead of Antigonus, provocator; *Verus, his trainer, put this up.*

117.   *Prior, Retiarius of the Ludus Magnus*

CIL 6.10169; *ILS* 5124	Rome
Tombstone	Unknown

The *retiarius* was one of the most common types of gladiators. They were lightly armored, wearing only a tunic and light armor on one arm. As weapons, they carried a trident and a net. The net was to entangle or trip up their more heavily armored opponents (like the *murmillo* and *secutor*). Prior's inscription was found near the church of St. John Lateran in Rome.

D · M
PRIORI
RETIARIO
LVD · MAG
IVVENIS
MVRMILLO
LVD · MAG
CONVCTORI
B · M · F

* * *

D(is) m(anibus); Priori, retiario lud(i) mag(ni); Iuvenis, murmillo lud(i) mag(ni), conv(i)ctori b(ene) m(erenti) f(ecit).

* * *

To the spirits of the dead; to Prior, retiarius *of the* Ludus Magnus; Iuvenis, murmillo *of the* Ludus Magnus,[1] *made this to his well-deserving co-victor.*[2]

1   The *Ludus Magnus* was the largest imperial training school in Rome. It was situated just outside of the Colosseum.
2   Gladiators who dedicated texts to fellow gladiators of the same *familia* or *ludus* use the term co-victor more often than other terms of endearment.

118.   *Urbicus, Secutor*

CIL 5.5933; *ILS* 5122   Milan, Po Valley, Italy

Tombstone   3rd Century AD?

The following three texts illustrate *secutores*, heavily armed swordsmen who normally fought the *retiarius*. As the name implies, the *secutor* would pursue the more lightly-armored *retiarius*, especially after the *retiarius* had thrown his trident and missed. Their equipment included a small, round helmet and shield and a short sword. Urbicus' inscription includes, under the "D M", a picture of a gladiator holding a sword and shield.

D · M
VRBICO · SECVTORI
PRIMO · PALO · NATION · FLO
RENTIN · QVI · PVGNAVIT · XIII
VIXSIT · ANN · XXII · OLYMPIAS
FILIA · QVEM · RELIQVIT · MESI · V
ET · FORTVNESIS · FILIAE
ET · LAVRICIA · VXSOR
MARITO · BENEMERENTI
CVM · QVO · VIXSIT · ANN · VII
TE · MONEO · VT · QVIS · QVEM · VIC[E]
RIT · OCCIDAT
COLANT · MANES · AMATORES · IPSI
VS

* * *

D(is) m(anibus); Urbico, secutori, primo palo, nation(e) florentin(o), qui pugnavit XIII, vix{s}it ann(os) XXII; Olympias filia quem reliquit me(n)si(bus) V, et Fortunesis filiae (serva), et Lauricia ux{s}or marito bene merenti, cum quo vix{s}it ann(os) VII. Te moneo, ut quis quem vicerit occidat. Colant manes amatores ipsius.

* * *

To the spirits of the dead; to Urbicus, secutor, *highest-ranking gladiator in the* ludus,[1] *from Florence, who fought 13 times, lived 22 years; Olympias, his daughter, whom he left at 5 months, and Fortunesis, the slave of his daughter,[2] and Lauricia, his wife, dedicated this to her well-deserving husband, with whom she lived for 7 years.[3] I warn you, he killed whomever he defeated (in the arena).[4] His fans celebrate his spirit.*

1   On the analogy of the highest-ranking centurion in a legion (the *primus pilus*), the highest-ranking gladiator in a *ludus* was named the *primus palus*. The *palus* was the wooden stake with which gladiators trained.
2   Fortunesis was most likely a nurse or caretaker of the child.
3   Urbicus was probably already fighting as a gladiator at the age of 15, when he and Lauricia were married.

4   This statement is surprising, seeing how the object of the contest was not to kill the other gladiator. Such bloodlust was frowned upon by those who paid to train gladiators and sponsored the games. It is also possible that the quality of gladiators was lower outside of Rome, and thus they may have been killed in the arena more frequently than those at Rome. The statement could also be an exaggeration to make Urbicus seem more exciting.

119.   *Flamma, Secutor*

CIL 10.7297; *ILS* 5113   Sicily
Tombstone   Unknown

FLAMMA · SIC · VIX · AN · XXX
PVGNAT · XXXIIII · VICIT · XXI
STANS · VIIII · MIS · IIII · NAT · SRVS
HVI · DELICATVS · COARMIO · MERENTI · FECIT

* * *

Flamma, s[e]c(utor), vix(it) an(nos) XXX, pugna(vi)t XXXIIII, vicit XXI, stans VIIII, mis(sus) IIII, nat(ione) S[y]rus; hui(c) Delicatus coarmio merenti fecit.

* * *

Flamma,[1] secutor, lived 30 years, fought 34 times,[2] won 21 times, fought to a draw 9 times,[3] defeated 4 times,[4] a Syrian by nationality; Delicatus made this for his deserving comrade-in-arms.[5]

1   Gladiators often took stage names in preference to their native names. Flamma means "flame". See below for Amabilis ("loveable").
2   Flamma is another example of a provincial gladiator who fought more often than his counterparts in Rome.
3   Fairly often, fights between gladiators lasted so long that the contests were called a draw. The Latin term for that is *stans missus* ("released standing").
3   The end of the fight was termed the *missio*, when one gladiator was sent away in defeat (*missus*). As shown by this text and many others like it, not every defeated gladiator died in the arena. During the first two centuries, it has been estimated that only about 10% of defeated gladiators actually died in the arena.
4   An interesting variation of the co-victor term (see above).

120. *Amabilis, Secutor*

CIL 3.14644; *ILS* 5111   Epetium, Dalmatia
Cinerary Urn   Unknown

This inscription comes from a four-sided funerary urn. The ashes of Amabilis were still inside of it when it was discovered. One interesting feature of this text is the description of his death as being "deceived by fate". It was relatively common for gladiators, especially in the Greek East, to ascribe their death in the arena to having been "deceived by fate" rather than admit being killed by an opponent.

AMABILI · SECVTORI
NAT · DACVS · PVG · XIII
FATO · DECEPTVS
NON · AB · HOMINE

* * *

Amabili, secutori, nat(ione) Dacus, pug(navit) XIII, fato deceptus, non ab homine.

* * *

To Amabilis, secutor, Dacian by nationality, fought 13 times, deceived by fate, not by his opponent.

121. *Lycus, Murmillo*

CIL 6.10180; *ILS* 5105   Rome
Tombstone   Unknown

The *murmillo* acquired his name from the type of helmet he wore: a Gallic helmet with a fish-shaped crest. They were also equipped with a breastplate, a rectangular Gallic shield, and a short sword. The *murmillo*'s most frequent opponents were the Thracian and *retiarius*.

D · M
LYCO · LIB · MVR
SCAEV · PVGNA · IIII
FEC · LONGINAS
LIB · CONTRARETE
FRATRI · B · M

* * *

D(is) m(anibus); Lyco, lib(erato), mur(milloni) scaev(a manu), pugna(vit) IIII; fec(it) Longinas, lib(eratus), contrarete, fratri b(ene) m(erenti).

* * *

To the spirits of the dead; to Lycus, freed, left-handed myrmillo,[1] *fought four times; Longinas, freed,* contra-retiarius,[2] *made this for his well-deserving brother.*

1   The emperor Commodus, when he fought as a gladiator in games two months before his murder in 192, fought as a left-handed Thracian (Dio 72.22). Fighting left-handed was a special treat for the crowd and presented a more difficult fight to his opponent as gladiators were trained to fight with and oppose very specific moves. The stigma attached to left-handed people (the left hand, in Latin, was the *sinister manus*) may have also made such a gladiator appear to be a more difficult or even evil opponent.

2   The *contra-retiarius* was a type of gladiator that fought against a *retiarius*. He was probably the equivalent of a *secutor*.

122.   *M. Antonius Exochus, Thracian*

CIL 6.10194; *ILS* 5088   Rome
Tombstone   2nd Century AD

The Thracian gladiator, like the Samnite, was named after and resembled in armor and weaponry an old enemy of Rome. The Thracian gladiator used a large helmet, greaves on both legs, a small round shield, and a curved short sword or dagger. The majority of this stone is taken up by a picture of a Thracian gladiator. He raises his left arm to his head, and holds a palm branch in his right hand. A laurel crown appears at his side. The inscription appears on the bottom of the stone, next to his right foot.

THR
M · ANTONIVS
EXOCHVS · NAT
ALEXANDRINVS
ROM · OB · TRIVMP
DIVI · TRAIANI · DIE · II
TIR · CVM · ARAXE · CAE
ST · MISS
ROM · MVN · EIVSD
DIE · VIIII · FIMBRIAM
LIB · VIIII · MISS · FE
ROM · MVN · EIVSD
[DIE ....]

* * *

Thr(aex), M(arcus) Antonius Exochus, nat(ione) Alexandrinus, Rom(ae) ob triump(hum) divi Traiani, die II tir(o) cum Araxe Cae(saris servus)

st(ans) miss(us); Rom(ae) mun(eris) eiusd(em) die VIIII Fimbriam
lib(ertum pugna) VIIII miss(um) fe(cit); Rom(ae) mun(eris) eiusd(em)
[die....]

* * *

*The Thracian Marcus Antonius Exochus,[1] Alexandrian in nationality; at
Rome, during the triumph of the divine Trajan,[2] on the second day (of the
games), as a recruit, he fought with Araxes, slave of Caesar, to a draw;
at Rome, on the 9th day of the same games, he fought Fimbria, a freed
gladiator of nine fights,[3] and defeated him;[4] at Rome on the ? day of the
same games ...[6]*

1   As his name implies, Exochus was a descendant of someone who
    received the citizenship (either as a freedman or native) from Marcus
    Antonius (the infamous Marc Antony), who had a love affair with
    Cleopatra in Alexandria, Egypt.
2   The games in honor of the triumph of the divine Trajan probably refer
    to games given after Trajan's death in 117, in honor of his victories
    over Parthia.
4   *Missum fecit* is a variation of *vicit*, indicating a victory in a fight.
5   Fimbria had received his freedom. He was also a veteran of nine fights
    which made him substantially more experienced than Exochus.
6   The text is broken and the remainder of his account of the games in
    honor of Trajan has been lost.

123.   *A Gladiatorial Familia*

CIL 6.631; *ILS* 5084   Centumcellae, near Rome
Marble Tablet   AD 177

This inscription documents the members of a typical gladiatorial *familia*
(troop). The emperor probably owned this *familia*, which was based in a relatively
small *ludus*.

IMP · CAES · L · AVRELIO · COMMODO · M · PLAVTIO · QVINTILLO · COS
INITIALES · COLLEGI · SILVANI · AVRELIANI
CVRATORES · M · AVRELIVS · AVG · LIB · HILARVS · ET · COELIVS ·
MAGNVS · CRYPTARIVS

DEC · I
BORYSTHENES · THR · VET
CLONIVS · HOPL · VET
CALLISTHENES · THR · VET
ZOSIMVS · ESS · VET
PLVTION · ESS · VET
PERTINAX · 7 · RET · VET
CARPOPHORVS · MVR · VET

CRISPINVS · MVR · VET
PARDVS · PROV · VET
MILETVS · MVR · VET

DEC · II
VITVLVS · MVR · VET
DEMOSTHENES · MANICAR
FELICIANVS · RET · TIR
SERVANDVS · RET · TIR
IVVENIS · MVR · SP
RIPANVS · 7 · RET · TIR
SILVANVS · 7 · RET · TIR
SECVNDINVS · PROV · TIR
ELEVTHER · THR · TIR
PIRATA · VNCT

DEC · III
BAROSVS · 7 · RET · TIR
AEMILIANVS · 7 · RET · N
VLPIVS · EVPORAS
PROSHODVS · 7 · RET · TIR
AVRELIVS · FELICIANVS
AVRELIVS · FELIX
ZOILVS · PAGAN
FLAVIVS · MARISCVS
FLAVIVS · SANCTVS
DIODORVS · PAGAN

DEC · IIII
APRILIS · PAEGNIAR
ZOSIMVS · THR · SP

* * *

Imp(eratore) Caes(are) L(ucio) Aurelio Commodo, M(arco) Plautio Quintillo co(n)s(ulibus), initiales collegi Silvani Aureliani, curatores M Aurelius Aug(usti) lib(ertus) Hilarus et Coelius Magnus, cryptarius.

Dec(urio) I: Borysthenes, thr(ex), vet(eranus); Clonius, hopl(omachus), vet(eranus); Callisthenes, thr(ex), vet(eranus); Zosimus, ess(edarius), vet(eranus); Plution, ess(edarius), vet(eranus); Pertinax, [contra]ret(e), vet(eranus); Carpophorus, mur(millo), vet(eranus); Crispinus, mur(millo), vet(eranus); Pardus, prov(ocator), vet(eranus); Miletus, mur(millo), vet(eranus).

Dec(urio) II: Vitulus, mur(millo), vet(eranus); Demosthenes, manicar(ius); Felicianus, ret(iarius), tir(o); Servandus, ret(iarius), tir(o); Iuvenis, mur(millo), sp(ectatus?); Ripanus, [contra]ret(e), tir(o); Silvanus, [contra]ret(e), tir(o); Secundinus, prov(ocator), tir(o); Eleuther, thr(ex), tir(o); Pirata, unct(rix).

Dec(urio) III: Barosus, [contra]ret(e), tir(o); Aemilianus, [contra]ret(e), n(ovicius); Ulpius Euporas; Proshodus, [contra]ret(e), tir(o); Aurelius Felicianus; Aurelivs Felix; Zoilus, pagan(us); Flavius Mariscus; Flavius Sanctus; Diodorus, pagan(us).

Dec(urio) IIII: Aprilis, paegniar(ius); Zosimus, thr(ex), sp(ectatus?).

* * *

While the emperor Caesar Lucius Aurelius Commodus and Marcus Plautius Quintillus were consuls,[1] the founding members[2] of the college of Silvanus Aurelianus, the caretakers Marcus Aurelius Hilarus, freedman of the emperor, and Coelius Magnus, in charge of the practice ground.[3]

1st Decurion:[4] Borysthenes, Thracian, veteran[5]; Clonius, hoplomachus, veteran; Callisthenes, Thracian, veteran; Zosimus, essedarius, veteran; Plution, essedarius, veteran; Pertinax, contra-retiarius, veteran; Carpophorus, murmillo, veteran; Crispinus, murmillo, veteran; Pardus, provocator, veteran; Miletus, murmillo, veteran.

2nd Decurion: Vitulus, murmillo, veteran; Demosthenes, armor-maker[6]; Felicianus, retiarius, recruit; Servandus, retiarius, recruit; Iuvenis, murmillo, trial member[7]; Ripanus, contra-retiarius, recruit; Silvanus, contra-retiarius, recruit; Secundinus, provocator recruit; Eleuther, Thracian, recruit; Pirata, masseur.

3rd Decurion: Barosus, contra-retiarius, recruit; Aemilianus, contra-retiarius, novice; Ulpius Euporas; Proshodus, contra-retiarius, recruit; Aurelius Felicianus; Aurelivs Felix; Zoilus, non-combatant[8]; Flavius Mariscus; Flavius Sanctus; Diodorus, non-combatant.

4th Decurion; Aprilis, comic gladiator[9]; Zosimus, Thracian, trial member;

1　These were the ordinary consuls of the year AD 177, the year in which the dedication was made.

2　The *initiales* were probably the first members of the *collegium*.

3　The *crypta* was the open area in the middle of the *ludus* where the gladiators trained.

4　Note how each decurion, except the fourth, had ten members (as the name decurion "group of ten" implies). The gladiators were organized in the decurions according to seniority.

5　As has been seen in the tombs of individual gladiators, there were three categories of gladiators: novice (*novicius*, a gladiator still in training), recruit (*tiro*, a gladiator who was ready for his first fight), and veteran (*veteranus*, a gladiator who had survived his first fight).

6　*Manicae* were metal arm guards that went up the arm and covered the shoulder. They were worn on the sword-arm, which was not protected by the shield.

7　The abbreviation "sp" is not clear. It could be *sp(ectatus)* or *sp(ectator)* indicating someone who had not yet entered training. Iuvenis, a rather senior member of the *familia* in the second decurion may have been originally another type of gladiator, but had decided to train instead as a *murmillo*.

8   The *paganus* no longer fought in the arena but continued to live at the *ludus*. Most seem to have received the *rudis* and their freedom. Many recipients of the *rudis*, or even retired gladiators, continued on in the *ludus* either as trainers or as *pagani*.

9   Comic gladiators probably did some kind of comedy routine between individual gladiatorial combats.

124.   *Gladiatorial Graffiti*

CIL 4.4345, 4356, 4353	Pompeii, Campania, Italy
Wall Graffiti	1st Century AD

The following three texts are graffiti scratched onto some columns of a peristyle inside a private house in the Reg. V.5 area of Pompeii. A number of gladiatorial graffiti were discovered in this house.

PVELLARVM · DECVS
CELADVS · TR

* * *

Puellarum decus Celadus t(h)r(ex).

* * *

Celadus, Thracian, the charm of the girls.

* * *
TR
CELADVS · RETI
CRESCENS
PVPARRV · DOMNVS [....]

* * *

T(h)r(ex) Celadus. Reti(arius), Crescens, pupar{r}u(m) dom(i)nus [...]

* * *

Celadus, Thracian. The retiarius Crescens, master of the girls ...[1]

1   The remainder of the text is illegible.

* * *
CRESCES · RETIA
PVPARVM · NOCTVRNARVM [...]

* * *

Cresce(n)s, retia(rius) puparum nocturnarum

* * *

Crescens, retiarius, (delight?) of the girls of the night...[1]

1   The sense of these words is not known.

125.   *C. Cassius Gemellus,* *Trainer of the* Hoplomachi

CIL 6.10181; *ILS* 5099	Rome
Tombstone	Unknown

As demonstrated by the *familia* text given above, the gladiators' supporting cast could be extensive. Here is an example of a trainer of *hoplomachi*, a type of gladiator who fought in full armor with a round, Greek-like shield (the *hoplon*).

C · CASSIVS
GEMELVS
DOCTOR
OPLOMACHOR

* * *

C(aius) Cassius Gemel[l]us, doctor oplomachor(um).

* * *

Gaius Cassius Gemellus, trainer of the hoplomachi.

126.   *Felix will Fight the Bears!*

CIL 4.1989; *ILS* 5147	Pompeii, Campania, Italy
Wall Graffiti	1st Century AD

Gladiators were not the only performers on display in the arena. On the morning of the games, the *venationes* took place, which were the beast hunts in which humans (*venatores*, hunters) fought animals, or animals fought animals. The *bestiarii* were animal handlers who directed the animals in the arena. *Bestiarii* were also employed when condemned criminals were exposed to animals during the noon intermission, between the *venationes* and the gladiatorial combat. Neither *venatores* nor *bestiarii* also fought as gladiators. This inscription is another example of graffiti from Pompeii. It was discovered on the northern wall in the House of Apollo e Coronis on the Strada delle Scuole.

HEC · VENATIO · PVGNABET · V · K · SEPTEMBRES
ET · FELIX · AD · VRSOS · PVGNABET

* * *

H(a)e{i}c venatio pugnabet V k(alendas) Septembres, et Felix ad ursos pugnabet.

* * *

The beast hunt will be played out on the fifth day before the Kalends of September,[1] and Felix will fight the bears.[2]

1   August 28th.
2   Bears were among the most popular type of animal used in the *venatio*. We have examples of inscriptions, graffiti and mosaics on which famous bears were named. The historian Ammianus Marcellinus records how the emperor Valentinian had two savage man-eating she-bears named *Mica* and *Innocentia* (Gold-dust and Innocence).

127. *Cn. Maetius Felix, Contractor of Gladiators*

CIL 10.1733; *ILS* 5151   Neapolis, Campania, Italy
Tombstone   Unknown

For each set of games, gladiators would be rented to a *munerarius* (i.e., an aristocratic sponsor of games) by a *lanista*, who worked for the *ludus*. The *lanista* was responsible for coming up with the rental price (as well as the fees for gladiators killed or freed in the arena). An extremely interesting document from AD 177 (the so-called *Aes Italicense*) describes a tax on gladiatorial rentals which Marcus Aurelius had levied on the *lanistae*. Unfortunately for the local priests of the imperial cult in Gaul (who were compelled by their office to offer annual games), the local *lanistae* were attempting to increase their profits by passing on the expense of the tax to the priests. The priests wrote to the emperor and complained. The document outlines the remission of the tax as well as the placement of a salary cap on the rental price for gladiators. The following is an example of a *lanista*.

CN • MAETIVS
FELIX • LANISTA
AVGVST

* * *

Cn(aeus) Maetius Felix, lanista, August(alis).

* * *

Gnaeus Maetius Felix, contractor of gladiators, priest of Augustus.[1]

1   A mark of significant status in his hometown.

128. *Ti. Claudius Speclator, Procurator of an Elephant Farm*

CIL 6.8583; *ILS* 1578   Rome
Tombstone   1st Century AD

Speclator, a freedman of the emperor Claudius, was in charge of an elephant farm at Laurentum (near Rome). As the games became a more important part of life in Rome, it was useful for the emperor to raise his own animals in Italy, rather than have to rely upon the animal trade from the provinces. Elephants were also used in parades and triumphal processions.

D · M
TI · CLAVDIO · SPECLATORI
AVG · LIB · PROCVRATOR
FORMIS · FVNDIS · CAIETAE
PROCVRATOR · LAVRENTO · AD
ELEPHANTOS
CORNELIA · BELLICA · CONIVGI
B · M

* * *

D(is) m(anibus); Ti(berio) Claudio Speclatori, Aug(usti) lib(erto), procurator Formis Fundis Caietae, procurator Laurento ad elephantos; Cornelia Bellica coniugi b(ene) m(erenti).

* * *

To the spirits of the dead; to Tiberius Claudius Speclator, freedman of the emperor, procurator at Formi, Fundi and Caieta,[1] procurator at Laurentum[2] of the imperial elephant farm; Cornelia Bellica dedicated this to her well-deserving husband.

1   These three towns were on the coast of Campania, north of the bay of Naples.
2   This town was on the coast of Latium, just south of Ostia.

129. *M. Ulpius Callistus,* in Charge of the Armory of the **Ludus**

CIL 6.10164; *ILS* 5153   Rome
Tombstone   2nd Century AD

While not a gladiator, Callistus was an imperial freedman who was in charge of the armory of the *Ludus Magnus*. The job seems to have been quite prestigious, and Callistus was wealthy enough to have his own freedmen and freedwomen. This inscription was discovered close to the first milestone on the *Via Appia*.

DIS · MANIBVS
CORNELIAE · FRONTINAE
VIXIT · ANNIS · XVI · M · VII
M · VLPIVS · AVG · LIB · CALLISTVS
PATER · PRAEPOSITVS · ARMAMENTARIO
LVDI · MAGNI · ET · FLAVIA · NICE · CONIVXS
SANCTISSIMA · FECERVNT · SIBI
LIBERTIS · LIBERTABVSQ · POSTERISQ · EOR

* * *

Dis manibus; Corneliae Frontinae, vixit annis XVI, m(ensibus) VII;
M(arcus) Ulpius Aug(usti) lib(ertus) Callistus, pater, praepositus
armamentario Ludi Magni et Flavia Nice, coniu(n)x{s} sanctissima
fecerunt sibi libertis libertabusq(ue) posterisq(ue) eor(um).

* * *

*To the spirits of the dead; to Cornelia Frontina, lived 16 years, 7 months;
Marcus Ulpius Callistus, freedman of the emperor, her father, in charge
of the armory of the* Ludus Magnus, *and Flavia Nice,[1] his most devout
wife, made this for themselves and their freedmen and freedwomen and
their freedmen's descendants.*

1   Callistus and Nice were imperial freedmen. Frontina, Callistus'
    daughter, is probably also a freedwoman, but from the household of
    a Cornelius. It is odd that their child ended up in another household.
    The child could have been illegitimate, not Nice's daughter but the
    daughter of another woman who was in the house of Cornelius, or a
    foster daughter.

The Theater

The theater was a structure which consisted of a stage with hemispherical
rows of bleacher-style seats radiating around it. Professional actors performed
traditional tragic and comic plays. Another category of actor was the mime; mimes
were organized into troops, and performed both literary and dramatic scenes in
the theater. A pantomime was a dancer/actor who, on his own, dramatized scenes
from mythology without speaking but with musical accompaniment. Mimes and
pantomimes generally had reputations for loose morals; their performances often
involved very bawdy, lewd and violent themes, which they depicted as graphically
as possible.

130.   *P. Publilius Ingenuus, Comic Actor*

CIL 3.375; *ILS* 5180   Parium, Asia Minor
Tombstone   Unknown

Ingenuus was an actor of comic plays and scenes. His hometown honored him with this statue, a very rare honor for an actor.

COLONIA
P • PVBLILIVM
INGENVVM
COMOEDVM
PROPTER • SINGVLAREM
ARTIS • PRVDENTIAM • ET
MORVM • PROBITATEM

* * *

Colonia P(ublium) Publilium Ingenuum, comoedum, propter singularem artis prudentiam et morum probitatem.

* * *

The colony[1] honored Publius Publilius Ingenuus, comic actor, because of the singular proficiency of his art and the uprightness of his morals.

1   The colony was named *colonia Gemella Julia.*

131.   *M. Ulpius Apolaustus, Pantomime*

CIL 6.10114; *ILS* 5184   Rome
Statue Base   2nd Century AD

Apolaustus was one of the most skilled and famous pantomimes of the second century. He was probably originally a slave who received his freedom (probably for an especially good performance) by the emperor. This is a large base on which the statue of Apolaustus was displayed.

M • VLPIVS • AVG • LIB • APOLAVSTVS
MAXIMVS • PANTOMIMORVM
CORONATVS • ADVERSVS • HISTRIONES
ET • OMNES • SCAENICOS
ARTIFICES • XII

* * *

M(arcus) Ulpius Aug(usti) lib(ertus) Apolaustus, maximus pantomimorum, coronatus adversus histriones et omnes scaenicos artifices XII.

* * *

Marcus Ulpius Apolaustus, freedman of the emperor, greatest of pantomimes, crowned in competitions of pantomimes[1] and other theatrical entertainers twelve times.

1   The Latin terms *pantomimus* and *histrio* are synonyms for the same thing: a pantomime.

132.   *Luria Privata, Mime*

CIL 6.10111; *ILS* 5215	Rome
Tombstone	Unknown

In legitimate theater, men played all of the roles, even those which represented women. Women in the theater were denigrated as little more than prostitutes. Privata was a mime from Rome who died when she was still quite young. This is a small marble tablet which probably originated in a *columbarium*.

LVRIA · PRIVATA
MIMA · V · A · XIX · BLEPTVS
FECIT

* * *

Luria Privata, mima, v(ixit) a(nnos) XIX; Bleptus fecit.

* * *

Luria Privata, mime, lived 19 years; Bleptus made this.

133.   *Claudia Hermiona, Mimic Actress*

CIL 6.10106; *ILS* 5211	Rome
Cinerary Urn	1st Century AD

The *archimimus/archimima* was the chief mime of the company. They often trained their own mimes and wrote or modified scenes for performance. Like many mimes and pantomimes, Hermiona was Greek (as her name implies).

DORMI
CLAVDIAE
HERMIONAE
ARCHIMIMAE · SV
I · TEMPORIS · PRI
MAE · HERE
DES

* * *

Dormi. Claudiae Hermionae, archimimae sui temporis primae; heredes.

* * *

Sleep on! To Claudia Hermionae, chief mimic actress of her time; her heirs dedicated this to her.

134. *L. Axius Daphnus, Flute-Player in the Chorus*

CIL 10.10119; *ILS* 5235	Rome
Tombstone	Unknown

There were also numerous musicians associated with theatrical performances. Daphnus, a flute-player, would have played the musical accompaniment in plays and mimes. Some theatrical companies had their own musical groups.

L · AXIVS
DAPHNVS
CHORAVLES

* * *

L(ucius) Axius Daphnus, choraules.

* * *

Lucius Axius Daphnus, flute-player in the chorus.

The Circus

The chariot races were held in the *circus*, an oblong racetrack with starting gates at one end, a dividing barrier running down the middle, and seating on all sides. The *Circus Maximus*, the largest *circus* in Rome, was a truly enormous structure, which may have held as many as 250,000 spectators on race days. The charioteers and their teams were organized into factions (teams). Each faction was designated by color: red, green, blue, and white. In the *Circus Maximus*, chariots made seven laps around the track before reaching the finish line in front of the emperor's box.

135. *Epaphroditus, Charioteer of the Red Faction*

CIL 6.10062; *ILS* 5282   Rome
             Tombstone   Late 1st Century AD

Epaphroditus seems to have been one of the great charioteers of his day. He won 178 races for the red faction. The emperor Domitian, a great fan of the *circus*, established two new factions: the purple and gold factions (Suetonius, *Domitian* 7; Dio 67.4). Epaphroditus was transferred to the new purple faction. The new teams, however, did not last very long. Epaphroditus had only eight wins with his new team before his retirement or return to the red faction. Unlike gladiators who generally fought once or twice a year, charioteers raced frequently; thus, very successful charioteers could become extremely wealthy.

D · M
EPAPHRODITVS
AGITATOR · F · R
VIC · CLXXVIII · ET
AT · PVRPVREVM
LIBER · VIC · VIII
BEIA · FELICVLA
F · CONIVGI · SVO
[B] · MERENTI

* * *

D(is) m(anibus); Epaphroditus, agitator f(actionis) r(ussatae), vicit CLXXVIII, et at purpureum liber(atus) vic(it) VIII; Beia Felicula f(ecit) coniugi suo [b](ene) merenti.

* * *

To the spirits of the dead; Epaphroditus, charioteer of the red faction, won 178 times, and, having been freed,[1] as a member of the purple faction, he won 8 times; Beia Felicula made this for her well-deserving husband.

1   Like gladiators, charioteers were also occasionally freed by the emperor or the aristocrat holding the games (the *munerarius*). Like Epaphroditus, however, they often continued their lucrative careers as charioteers.

136. *M. Aurelius Polynices, Charioteer of the Red Faction*

CIL 6.10049; *ILS* 5286,1   Rome
Tombstone   3rd Century AD

This tombstone was found on the *Via Praenestina*, about one mile from the city. It was discovered together with a second inscription to a Marcus Aurelius Mollicius Tatianus. Both were born slaves, but won an extraordinary amount of prize money by racing in the *circus*. Polynices won more than 43 million *sestertii* in the course of his career, making him one of the richest Romans in history. Despite his fabulous wealth, however, the fact that he was a charioteer gave him the social status of a slave. He and his friend Tatianus' tombs are reported to have had colossal statues of themselves alongside their chariots and horses.

M · AVR · POLYNICES · NAT · VER
NA · QVI · VIXIT · ANN · XXIX · MENS
IX · DIEBVS · V · QVI · VICIT · PALMAS
N · DCCXXXIX · SIC · IN · RVSSEO · N
DCLV · IN · PRASINO · LV · IN · VENE
TO · XII · IN · ALBO · N · XVII · PRAE
MIA · XXXX · N · III · XXX · XXVI · PV
RA · N · XI · OCTOIVG · N · VIII · DEC · N
VIIII · SEIVG · N · III

* * *

M(arcus) Aur(elius) Polynices, nat(us) verna, qui vixit ann(is) XXIX, mens(ibus) IX, diebus V, qui vicit palmas n(umero) DCCXXXIX, sic: in russeo n(umero) DCLV, in prasino LV, in veneto XII, in albo n(umero) XVII; praemia XXXX n(umero) III, XXX XXVI, pura n(umero) XI; octoiug(e) n(umero) VIII, dec(emiuge) n(umero) VIIII, seiug(e) n(umero) III.

* * *

Marcus Aurelius Polynices, born a slave, who lived 29 years, 9 months, 5 days, won 739 palms as follows: 655 in the red faction, 55 in the green faction, 12 in the blue faction, 17 in the white faction.[1] *He won prizes of 40,000 sestertii 3 times, prizes of 30,000 sestertii 26 times, lesser prizes (15,000 sestertii?) 11 times; he won in eight-horse chariots 8 times, in ten-horse chariots 9 times, in six-horse chariots 3 times.*[2]

1   While most charioteers spent their whole career in one faction, Polynices spent some time in all four (but mainly in the red faction).
2   These were specialty races which were more dangerous and exciting than four-horse chariots. Only the most famous and experienced charioteers would race in such events.

137.   *Claudius Aurelius Polyphemus, Owner and Charioteer*

CIL 6.10060; *ILS* 5297   Rome
Tombstone   AD 275

On the Front:

CL · AVRELIO · POLYPHEMO
DOMINO · ET · AGITATORI
FACTIONIS · RVSSATAE · TOGENI
CAESAREVS · SVI · TEMPORIS · PRIMO
ET · SOLO · FACTIONARIO · OB · GLORIA
[...]

On the Side:

DEDICATA
D · N · AVRELIANO · AVG · III
MARCELLINO · COS
XIII · KAL · FEBRAR

* * *

Cl(audio) Aurelio Polyphemo, domino et agitatori factionis russatae, togeni Caesareus, sui temporis primo et solo factionario ob gloria [...]

Dedicata d(omno) n(ostro) Aureliano Aug(usto) III, Marcellino co(n)s(ulibus) XIII Kal(endas) Febr(u)ar(ias).

* * *

To Claudius Aurelius Polyphemus, owner and charioteer of the red faction, born in the imperial house,[1] the foremost charioteer of his time and the only head of his faction because of his glory ...

Dedicated on the 13th day before the Kalends of February while our lord Aurelian Augustus for the third time and Marcellinus were consuls.[2]

1   The "togeni" is Latinized Greek for "in origin". His name would indicate that his parent (or grandparent) received the citizenship under the name M. Aurelius (Polyphemus). As he does not have the *praenomen* Marcus, he was not the one who originally received the citizenship, nor was he the eldest son of the one who had been freed. More than likely, his father was a freedman in the imperial household who had remained in the service of Caesar after his freedom.

2   January 20th, 275.

138. *A Circus Faction*

CIL 6.10046; *ILS* 5313   Rome
Marble Tablet   1st Century AD

Like the gladiatorial *familia* text given above, this text records the members of a chariot faction in Rome. The form of the letters has led to the belief that the inscription dates to the reign of Augustus (if not earlier) making it very early in the development of the factions at Rome. As with the gladiatorial *familia*, note the large number of people other than charioteers who were associated with the races.

> FAMILIAE · QVADRIGARIAE · T · AT · CAPITONIS
> PANNI · CHELIDONI · CHRESTO · QVAESTORE
> OLLAE · DIVISAE · DECVRIONIBVS · HEIS · Q · IF · S · S
> M · VIPSANIO · MIGIONI
> DOCIMO · VILICO
> CHRESTO · CONDITORI
> EPAPHRAE · SELLARIO
> MENANDRO · AGITATORI
> APOLLONIO · AGITATORI
> CERDONI · AGITATORI
> LICCAEO · AGITATORI
> HELLETI · SVCCONDITORI
> P · QVINCTIO · PRIMO
> HYLLO · MEDICO
> ANTEROTI · TENTORI
> ANTIOCHO · SVTORI
> PARNACI · TENTORI
> M · VIPSANIO · CALAMO
> M · VIPSANIO · DAREO
> EROTI · TENTORI
> M · VIPSANIO · FAVSTO
> HILARO · AVRIG
> NICANDRO · AVRIG
> EPIGONO · AVRIG
> ALEXANDRO · AVRIG
> NICEPHORO · SPARTOR
> ALEXIONI · MORATORI
> [......] · VIATORI

* * *

familiae quadrigariae T(iti) At(ei) Capitonis panni chelidoni, Chresto quaestore, ollae divisae decurionibus heis q(ui) i(n)f(ra) s(ubscripti) s(unt): M(arco) Vipsanio Migioni; Docimo, vilico; Chresto, conditori; Epaphrae, sellario; Menandro, agitatori; Apollonio, agitatori; Cerdoni, agitatori; Liccaeo, agitatori; Helleti, succonditori; P(ublio) Quinctio Primo; Hyllo, medico; Anteroti, tentori; Antiocho, sutori; Parnaci, tentori; M(arco) Vipsanio Calamo; M(arco) Vipsanio Dareo; Eroti, tentori; M(arco) Vipsanio Fausto; Hilaro, aurig(ae); Nicandro, aurig(ae); Epigono, aurig(ae); Alexandro, aurig(ae); Nicephoro, spartor; Alexioni, moratori; [.......], viatori.

* * *

The charioteer organizations of Titus Ateius Capito[1] of the swallow-colored faction,[2] while Chrestus was the financial officer, organized in the decurions as written below: Marcus Vipsanius Migio;[3] Docimus, director; Chrestus, head of the stables; Epaphra, head of the storerooms; Menander, charioteer; Apollonius, charioteer; Cerdo, charioteer; Liccaeus, charioteer; Helles, assistant to head of the stables; Publius Quinctius Primus; Hyllus, physician; Anteros, operator of the starting gates;[4] Antiochus, cobbler; Parnacus, operator of the starting gates; Marcus Vipsanius Calamo; Marcus Vipsanius Dareo; Eros, operator of the starting gates; Marcus Vipsanius Faustus; Hilarus, charioteer; Nicander, charioteer; Epigonus, charioteer; Alexander, charioteer; Nicephorus, spartor;[5] Alexio, delayer;[6] [.......], announcer.

1   This T. Ateius Capito may be related to the C. Ateius Capito who was a famous lawyer in the reign of Augustus and was a suffect consul in AD 5.
2   The color represented by the word "chelidonius" is not certain. The word often refers to the color of a bird: the swallow. It is possible that this inscription was put up before the four factions had been firmly established.
3   The fact that several charioteers have the *praenomen* and *nomen* Marcus Vipsanius is another possible indication of date. The name may be derived from Marcus Vipsanius Agrippa, the good friend and one-time heir of Augustus (he also married Augustus' only daughter).
4   This was the person who maintained the mechanical starting gates in the *circus*. A system of pulleys connected the starting gates to a single lever. The door on each starting gate was spring-loaded and was kept closed by a latch. When the lever was thrown, the latches were removed and all of the doors sprung open simultaneously. It was important that the starting gates work correctly in order to assure a fair start to the race.
5   The word *spartor* would seem to indicate someone who splashed the horses as they ran by during the race. It may have been a way to keep the horses cool. There were pools in the barrier down the middle of the track (the *spina*), perhaps for this purpose.
6   The delayer (*morator*) was perhaps the slave who kept the horses under control while they were standing inside the starting gates.

MEN'S OCCUPATIONS

The very numerous inscriptions of the working class of ancient Rome demonstrate the high degree of specialization and variety of Roman occupations. The following texts illustrate just a few of the jobs which appear on inscriptions: salesmen, craftsmen, architects, bankers, artists, doctors, orators, teachers and philosophers. Many of the men listed below were freedmen, as indicated by the large number of non-Roman *cognomina*.

139. *L. Lepidius Hermes, Salesman of Bronze and Iron*

CIL 6.9664; *ILS* 7536	Rome
Tombstone	Unknown

D · M
L · LEPIDIVS · L · LIB · HERMES
NEGOTIATOR · AERARIVS · ET
FERRARIVS · SVB · AEDE · FORTVNAE
AD · LACVM · ARETIS · ET
OBELLIA · THREPTE
FECERVNT
L · LEPIDIO · L · F · PAL · HERMEROTI
QVI · VIXIT · ANNIS · VIII · MENSE · DIEBVS · XXII · ET
LEPIDIAE · L · F · LVCILLAE
QVAE · VIXIT · ANNIS · V · DIEBVS · VIIII
FILIS · DVLCISSIMIS · ET · PIISSIMIS · ERGA · SE · ET
LIB · LIBERTABVSQVE · POSTERISQVE · EORVM

* * *

D(is) m(anibus); L(ucius) Lepidius L(uci) lib(ertus) Hermes, negotiator aerarius et ferrarius sub aede fortunae ad lacum Aretis, et Obellia Threpte fecerunt L(ucio) Lepidio L(uci) f(ilius) Pal(atina tribu) Hermeroti, qui vixit annis VIII, mense, diebus XXII et Lepidiae L(uci) f(iliae) Lucillae, quae vixit annis V, diebvs VIIII, filiis dulcissimis et piissimis erga se, et lib(ertis) libertabusque posterisque eorum.

* * *

To the spirits of the dead; Lucius Lepidius Hermes, freedman of Lucius, salesman of bronze and iron whose shop is near the temple of Fortune at the basin of Ares,[1] and Obellia Threpte made this dedication for Lucius Lepidus Hermeros, son of Lucius, of the Palatina tribe, who lived 8 years, 1 month, 22 days, and to Lepidia Lucilla,[2] daughter of Lucius, who lived 5 years, 9 days, the sweetest and most dutiful children toward their parents, and to their freedmen and freedwomen.

1   The temple is probably that in the *Forum Boarium*, the cattle market to the west of the Forum between the *Circus Maximus* and the river.
2   A feminine version of the father's *praenomen*.

---

140.   *Cucumio, Worker at the Baths of Caracalla*

CIL 6.9232; *ILS* 7621	Rome
Tombstone	3rd Century AD

CVCVMIO · ET · VICTORIA
SE · VIVOS · FECERVNT
CAPSARARIVS · DE · ANTONIANAS

* * *

Cucumio et Victoria se vivos fecerunt, capsararius de antonianas (thermas).

* * *

Cucumio and Victoria made this dedication for themselves while still alive. He was in charge of the clothes of the bathers[1] in the baths of Caracalla.[2]

1   People going to the public baths undressed in the *apodyterium* ("locker room"), which were usually located near the entrance. Because thieves stealing clothing was a problem, larger baths hired attendants like Cucumio to protect the bather's property.
2   These baths were built by the emperor Caracalla in the 210s AD. These baths were located near the Aventine hill, to the southeast of the Colosseum. At the time of their construction, they were the largest in the Roman Empire.

141. *C. Julius Posphoro, Architect of the Emperor*

CIL 6.8724; *ILS* 7733   Rome
Tombstone   1ˢᵗ Century AD

C · IVLIO
LVCIFERI · FILIO
POSPHORO
ARCHITECT · AVG
CLAVDIA · STRATONICE
VXOR · VIRO
OPTVMO

* * *

C(aio) Iulio Luciferi filio Posphoro, architect(o) Aug(usti); Claudia Stratonice, uxor viro opt[i]mo.

* * *

To Gaius Julius Posphorus, son of Luciferus,[1] architect of the emperor; Claudia Stratonice,[2] his wife dedicated this to her excellent husband.

1   The father was possibly a freedman of Augustus, judging by the name of his son (Gaius Julius). His son was still an employee of the emperor.
2   She may be a freedwoman of the emperor Claudius or Nero.

142.   *Q. Caelius Vivius, Naval Architect*

CIL 10.5371; *ILS* 7734   Minturnae, Campania, Italy
Tombstone   Unknown

VIVIT
Q · CAELIVS · SP · F · VIVI
ARCHITECTVS · NAVALIS
VIVIT
VXOR · CAMIDIA · M · L
APRHODISIA
HOSPES · RESISTE · ET · NISI · M
OLESTVST · PERLEGE · NOLI
STOMACARE · SVADEO
CALDVM · BIBAS
MORIV
NDVST · VALE

* * *

Vivit, Q(uintus) Caelius Sp(uri) f(ilius) Vivi(us?), architectus navalis. Vivit, uxor Camidia M(arci) l(iberta) Aphrodisia. Hospes resiste et nisi molestu[m e]st, perlege. Noli stomacare. Suadeo, caldum bibas. Moriundu[m e]st. Vale.

* * *

He lives: Quintus Caelius Vivius(?), son of Spurius,[1] naval architect.[2]
She lives: his wife, Camidia Aphrodisia, freedwoman of Marcus. Friend,
stop and read unless it is annoying (to stop). Do not be irritated. I ask
that you drink a hot beverage. It is the kind of thing that passes away.[3]
Goodbye.

1   Vivius was freeborn, but he married a freedwoman.
2   Vivius designed and built ships.
3   It was quite common on tombstones to encourage the reader to enjoy
    life in some particular way which the deceased enjoyed, because life
    was seen as fleeting.

143.   *Sex. Clodius Amoenus, Worker in Ivory*

CIL 6.7655; *ILS* 7707   Rome
        Tombstone   Unknown

This inscription was found on the *Via Appia*, but the exact original findspot is not known. It probably was placed in a *columbarium*.

SEX · CLODIVS · SEX · L · AMOENVS
EBORARIVS · AB · HERCVLE
PRIMIGENIO

* * *

Sex(tus) Clodius Sex(ti) l(ibertus) Amoenus, eborarius ab Hercule primigenio.

* * *

Sextus Clodius Amoenus, freedman of Sextus, worker in ivory near the
temple of Hercules the Firstborn.[1]

1   The location of this temple (mentioned only in this and one other
    inscription) is not known.

144.   *M. Balonius Lariscus,*
Wool-Worker and Felt-Maker

CIL 6.9494; *ILS* 7558   Rome
Tombstone   Unknown

D · M
BALONIAE
LIVITTIANAE
M · BALONIVS
M · LIB · LARIS
CVS · LANARIVS
COACTILIARIVS
CONIVGI · CARISSI
MAE · B · M · FEC

* * *

D(is) m(anibus); Baloniae Livittianae; M(arcus) Balonius M(arci) lib(ertus) Lariscus, lanarius coactiliarius, coniugi carissimae b(ene) m(erenti) fec(it).

* * *

To the spirits of the dead; to Balonia Livittiana; Marcus Balonius Lariscus, freedman of Marcus,[1] wool-worker and felt-maker, made this for his dearest, well-deserving wife.

1   Both the husband and wife were freed by the same master, a Marcus Balonius.

145.   *C. Cacius Heracla, Banker*

CIL 6.9179; *ILS* 7503   Rome
Tombstone   Unknown

C · CACIVS · C · L · HERACLA
ARGENTARIVS · DE · FORO
ESQVILINO · SIBI · ET · LIBE
ET · LIBERTABVS

* * *

C(aius) Cacius C(ai) l(ibertus) Heracla, argentarius de foro esquilino, sibi et libe(rtis) et libertabus.

* * *

Gaius Cacius Heracla, freedman of Gaius, banker in the Esquiline forum,[1] dedicated this to himself and his freedmen and freedwomen.

1   This was a marketplace on the main road leading from the eastern gates to the Forum. As its name implies, it was on the Esquiline Hill. It was just outside of the *Porta Esquilina* in the Servian Wall.

146.   *L. Furius Diomedes, Stone-Engraver*

CIL 6.9221; *ILS* 7694   Rome
            Tombstone   Unknown

L · FVRIVS
L · L · DIOMEDES
CAELATOR · DE
SACRA · VIA
CORNELIAE · L · F
TERTVLLAE · VXORI

* * *

L(ucius) Furius L(uci) l(ibertus) Diomedes, caelator de sacra via, Corneliae L(uci) f(iliae) Tertullae, uxori.

* * *

Lucius Furius Diomedes, freedman of Lucius, stone-engraver on the Via Sacra,[1] dedicated this to Cornelia Tertulla, daughter of Lucius, his wife.[2]

1   The *Via Sacra* was the main street which ran through the length of the Forum.
2   She was freeborn, but was probably not many generations removed from slave status. She married a freedman.

147.   *A. Hirtius Felix, Locksmith*

CIL 6.9260; *ILS* 7639   Rome
            Tombstone   Unknown

A · HIRTIVS
FELIX
CLOSTRARIVS

* * *

A(ulus) Hirtius Felix, clostrarius.

* * *

Aulus Hirtius Felix, locksmith.

148.   *C. Julius Epaphra,* *Fruit Seller in the* Circus Maximus

CIL 6.9822; *ILS* 7496   Rome

Tombstone   1st Century AD

C · IVLIVS · EPAPHRA
POMAR · DE · CIRCO
MAXIMO · ANTE
PVLVINAR · SIBI · ET
VENVLEIAE
CN · CN · L
HELENAE
CONIVGI · SVAE

* * *

C(aius) Iulius Epaphra, pomar(ius) de Circo Maximo ante pulvinar(em), sibi et Venuleiae Cn(aei), Cn(aei fili), l(ibertae) Helenae, coniugi suae.

* * *

Gaius Julius Epaphra, fruit-seller in the Circus Maximus, *in front of the imperial box,[1] made this for himself and for Venuleia Helena, freedwoman of Gnaeus, son of Gnaeus,[2] his wife.*

1   When there were no races, the *Circus Maximus* was converted into a giant market. Epaphra can boast that his stand is at the finish line, right in front of the imperial box.
2   It is unusual to give the filiation of a former master.

149.   *L. Marcleius Philargurus, Sword-Maker*

CIL 9.3962; *ILS* 7640   Alba Fucens, Latium, Italy

Tombstone   Unknown

L · MARCLEIVS · L · L
PHILARGVRVS
GLADIARIVS

* * *

L(ucius) Marcleius L(uci) l(ibertus) Philargurus, gladiarius.

* * *

Lucis Marcleius Philargurus, freedman of Lucius, a sword-maker.

150.   *P. Clodius Metrodorus, Boiler of Glue*

CIL 6.9443; *ILS* 7657   Rome
         Tombstone   Unknown

This inscription was found in a tomb near the *Porta di S. Giovanni.*

P · CLODIVS · P · L
METRODORVS
GLVTINARIVS

* * *

P(ublius) Clodius P(ubli) l(ibertus) Metrodorus, glutinarius.

* * *

Publius Clodius Metrodorus, freedman of Publius, boiler of glue.

151.   *P. Curius Euporus, Flute-Maker*

CIL 6.9935; *ILS* 7645   Rome
         Tombstone   Unknown

This marble tablet was discovered on the *Via Appia,* not far from the first milestone.

P · CVRIVS
EVPOR
TIBIARIVS · DE · SACRA · VIA

* * *

P(ublius) Curius Eupor(us), tibiarius de sacra via.

* * *

Publius Curius Euporus, flute-maker on the sacred way.

152.   *P. Cornelius Philomusus, Scene-Painter*

CIL 6.9794; *ILS* 7672   Rome
         Tombstone   Unknown

This inscription was found near Piazza del Popolo, in the northwestern part of Rome.

P · CORNELIVS · P · L
PHILOMVSVS · PICTOR
SCAENARIVS · IDEM · REDEMPT

MONIMENTVM · FECIT · H · C
CORNELIAE · P · L · LYCCE · LIBE
[RT]AE · CASTAE · ANNOR · NATA · XIIX · HIC · SI[TA · EST]
SIBI · ET · SVIS · POSTERISQVE · EORV

* * *

P(ublius) Cornelius P(ubli) l(ibertus) Philomusus, pictor scaenarius idem redempt(or), mon[u]mentum fecit h(ic) c(onditus); Corneliae P(ubli) l(ibertae) Lycce, libe[rt]ae castae, annor(um) nata XIIX hic si[ta est], sibi et suis posterisque eoru(m)

* * *

Publius Cornelius Philomusus, freedman of Publius, scene-painter and also contractor, made this monument constructed here; dedicated to Cornelia Lycce, freedwoman of Publius,[1] a chaste freedwoman, 18 years old, who is here buried, and to himself and to his family and posterity.

1   Philomusus and his wife were freed by the same master, a Publius Cornelius.

---

153.   *C. Mestrius Alapa, Seller of Sponges*

CIL 11.2931; *ILS* 7652   Musignanum, Italy
    Tombstone   Unknown

C · MESTRIO · C · F · ALAPAE
SPONGIARIO
V · CHIA · L · FECIT · SIBI · ET · SVIS

* * *

C(aio) Mestrio C(ai) f(ilio) Alapae, spongiario; V(iva) Chia l(iberta) fecit sibi et suis.

* * *

To Gaius Mestrius Alapa, son of Gaius, seller of sponges; Chia, freedwoman, still alive, made this for herself and her family.

---

154.   *A. Cornelius Priscus, Cloak-Salesman*

CIL 6.33906; *ILS* 7584   Rome
    Tombstone   After the 1st Century AD

A · CORNELIVS · A · L
PRISCVS · SAGARIVS
DE · HORREIS · GALBIANIS

V · F · SIBI · ET
CORNELIAE · DEXTRI · LIBER
EROTIDI · CONIVGI · SVAE · ET
A · CORNELIO · A · L · ROMANO
CONLIBERTO · SVO · ET
A · CORNELIO · A · L · CORINTHO
LIBERTO · SUO · ET
CETERIS · LIBERTIS
LIBERTABVSQVE · OMNIBVS
SVIS · POSTERISQVE · EORVM

* * *

A(ulus) Cornelius A(uli) l(ibertus) Priscus, sagarius de horreis Galbianis, v(ivus) f(ecit) sibi et Corneliae Dextri liber(ta) Erotidi, coniugi suae, et A(ulo) Cornelio A(uli) l(iberto) Romano, et A(ulo) Cornelio A(uli) l(iberto) Corintho liberto suo, et conliberto suo et ceteris libertis libertabusque omnibus suis posterisque eorum.

* * *

Aulus Cornelius Priscus, freedman of Aulus, cloak-salesman in the warehouses of Galba, made this while still alive for himself, for Cornelia Eros, freedwoman of Dexter,[1] his wife, and for Aulus Cornelius Romanus, freedman of Aulus, and Aulus Cornelius Corinthus, freedman of Aulus, his fellow-freedman,[2] and all of the rest of their freedmen and freedwomen and their posterity.

1   Although her filiation is listed differently, she is probably from the same house as Priscus. Therefore, the name of their master was probably Aulus Cornelius Dexter.
2   These two freedmen were freed slaves of Priscus who were probably especially close and so were specifically mentioned as being allowed to be buried in the tomb of the family of their former master.

155.   *M. Fulvius Icarus, Eye Doctor*

CIL 2.5055; *ILS* 7808   Ipagrum, Baetica
Tombstone   1st Century AD

It is possible to date this inscription to the 1st century AD (or even the 1st century BC) because of the form of the letters.

M · FVLVIVS · ICARVS · PONTV
FICIENSIS · MEDICVS · OCV
LARIVS · SIBI · ET · SVIS · FEC[IT]

* * *

M(arcus) Fulvius Icarus Pontuficiensis, medicus ocularius sibi et suis fecit.

* * *

Marcus Fulvius Icarus, from (Obulco) Pontificiensis,[1] eye doctor, made this for himself and his family.

1   A town in Baetica (southern Spain).

---

156.   *Ti. Claudius Docimus, Salesman of Salted Fish and Wine*

CIL 6.9676; *ILS* 7486   Rome
Tombstone   1st Century AD

D · M
TI · CLAVDIVS · DOCIMVS
FECIT · SIBI · ET · SVIS · LIBERTIS
LIBERTABVSQVE
POSTERISQVE · EORVM
NEGOTIANS · SALSAMENTARIVS
ET · VINARIARIVS · MAVRARIVS

* * *

D(is) m(anibus); Ti(berius) Claudius Docimus fecit sibi et suis libertis libertabusque posterisque eorum; negotians salsamentarius et vinariarius Maurarius.

* * *

To the spirits of the dead; Tiberius Claudius Docimus[1] made this for himself and his freedmen, freedwomen and their descendants; he was a salesman of salted fish and wine from Mauretania.[2]

1   Probably an imperial freedman, although he was possibly the son (or grandson) of a freedman.
2   The westernmost African province, across the straits of Gibraltar from Spain. It is modern-day Morocco.

---

157.   *Q. Gavius Primus, Sandal-Maker*

CIL 6.9284; *ILS* 7547   Rome
Tombstone   Unknown

Q · GAVIVS · Q · L · PRIMVS
CREPIDARIVS · DE · SVBVRA
VIXIT · ANN · XXV

* * *

Q(uintus) Gavius Q(uinti) l(ibertus) Primus, crepidarius de Subura, vixit ann(os) XXV.

* * *

Quintus Gavius Primus, freedman of Quintus, sandal-maker in the Subura,[1] lived 25 years.

1   The *Subura* was the district in the valley between the Viminal and Esquiline hills along the heavily-used road from the Esquiline Forum to the Forum. The satirists Juvenal and Martial complained of it as a noisy, dirty, wet and crowded area. The district was filled with large apartment buildings and shops (including the sandal store of Primus).

158.   *C. Atilius Iustus, Cobbler of Military Boots*

CIL 5.5919; *ILS* 7545   Mediolanum, Po Valley, Italy
Tombstone   Unknown

A picture of a cobbler has been carved beneath the text. Such images are not terribly common and added considerably to the price of the tombstone. Iustus must have been very proud of his occupation. It is very likely that the will contained detailed instructions for the tombstone.

C · ATILIVS · C · F
IVSTVS
SVTOR · CALIGARIVS
SIBI · ET
CORNELIAE · EXORAT
VXORI · T · P · I

* * *

C(aius) Atilius C(ai) f(ilius) Iustus, sutor caligarius, sibi et Corneliae Exorat(ae) uxori; t(estamento) p(onere) i(ussit).

* * *

Gaius Atilius Iustus, son of Gaius, cobbler of military boots, dedicated this to himself and his wife Cornelia Exorata; he ordered this to be put up in his will.

159.   *Q. Publicius Aemilianus,*
Professional Orator

CIL 3.2127a; *ILS* 7774   Salone, Dalmatia
Tombstone   Unknown

D · M · S
Q · PVBLICI
VS · AEMILI
ANVS · RHETOR
NATIO
NEM · AFER
VIXIT · AN
XLVII · MENSES
VIIII · DIES · VII · HOR
AS · NOCTIS · V

* * *

D(is) m(anibus) s(acrum); Q(uintus) Publicius Aemilianus, rhetor, nationem afer, vixit an(nos) XLVII menses, VIIII, dies VII, horas noctis V.

* * *

Sacred to the spirits of the dead; Quintus Publicius Aemilianus, professional lawyer,[1] African by nationality, lived 47 years, 9 months, 7 days, (died in the) 5th hour of the night.[2]

1   Professional orators were primarily hired to act as defense or prosecution attorneys.
2   It is rare for a tombstone to be so precise about the time of death.

160.   *M. Mettius Epaphroditus,* *Greek* Grammaticus

CIL 6.9454; *ILS* 7769   Rome
Statue Base   1st Century AD

    This inscription was discovered on the base of a statue of Epaphroditus. The statue represented him sitting on a chair and holding a book in his hand. The *Suda*, a Byzantine collection of information from the earlier Roman world, gives an account of his life. It describes how he was born as a slave in the house of Archias of Alexandria. He was then purchased by Marcus Mettius Modestus, a prefect of Egypt early in the reign of Nero. Epaphroditus served as the *grammaticus* of Modestus' son, Pelelinus. He was one of the most important *grammatici* in Rome during the 1st Century AD. He was a bibliophile and the *Suda* reports that he owned 30,000 books. As this inscription demonstrates, Modestus freed Epaphroditus. Epaphroditus then had slaves of his own, one of whom, Germanus, as a freedman, dedicated the inscription.

M · METTIVS
EPAPHRODITVS
GRAMMATICVS · GRAECVS
M · METTIVS · GERMANVS · L · FEC

* * *

M(arcus) Mettius Epaphroditus, grammaticus Graecus; M(arcus) Mettius Germanus l(ibertus) fec(it).

* * *

Marcus Mettius Epaphroditus, Greek grammaticus;[1] *Marcus Mettius Germanus, freedman, dedicated this.*

1   The *grammaticus* was a school teacher of boys (and sometimes girls) in their early teens. The students had already learned basic reading, writing and arithmetic from a *litterator* or a *ludi magister*. The *grammaticus* taught Greek and Latin literature in preparation for further training in rhetoric (for public careers involving oratory) by the *rhetor*.

161.   *C. Tutilius Hostilianus, Stoic Philosopher*

CIL 6.9785; *ILS* 7779   Rome
Tombstone   Unknown

This inscription was discovered on the *Via Labicana*.

C · TVTILIO · HOSTILIANO
PHILOSOPHO · STOICO
DOMO · CORTONA
PATRI · OPTIMO
C · TVTILIVS · IVSTINVS
FILIVS
TVTILIA · QVINTA
TVTILIA · QVARTA
FILIAE

* * *

C(aio) Tutilio Hostiliano, philosopho stoico, domo Cortona, patri optimo; C(aius) Tutilius Iustinus, filius, Tutilia Quinta, Tutilia Quarta, filiae.

* * *

Gaius Tutilius Hostilianus, stoic philosopher, from the town of Cortona;[1] Gaius Tutilius Iustinus, his son, and Tutilia Quinta and Tutilia Quarta, his daughters,[2] dedicated this to their excellent father.

1   Cortona was a town in Italy.
2   Note the numerical *cognomina*. There may have been three other daughters who had died before the stone was dedicated.

162.   *T. Flavius Apsens, Land-Surveyor*

CIL 8.12638; *ILS* 7738a   Carthage, Africa Proconsularis
Tombstone   Unknown

This tombstone was discovered in a tomb containing imperial freedmen and employees. Therefore, Apsens probably surveyed land on the immense imperial estates in Africa Proconsularis.

D · M · S
T · FLAVIVS · APSENS
MESOR · AGROR
PIVS · V · A · XXVI
H · S · E

* * *

D(is) m(anibus) s(acrum); T Flavius Apsens, me(n)sor agr[a]r(ius), pius v(ixit) a(nnos) XXVI; h(ic) s(itus) e(st).

* * *

To the spirits of the dead; T. Flavius Apsens, land-surveyor, a pious man, who lived 26 years. He is buried here.

---

163.   *C. Vergilius Martanus, Farmer*

CIL 6.9275; *ILS* 7454   Rome
Tombstone   Unknown

By the second century AD, the small, independent farmer had all but disappeared and much of the empire's agricultural land was divided into huge rural estates belonging to wealthy landowners. Dependent tenant farmers (*coloni*) did most of the actual farming. These tenants, like serfs in the Middle Ages, gave a portion of their crop to the landowner, who then sold the excess for a profit.

D · M
C · VERGILIVS · MARTA
NVS · COLONVS · AGRI · CAE
LI · AENEI · ANVLENAE · CER
TAE · COLONAE · AGRI · S · S · ANO
RVM · XXII · COIVGI · COIVGALI
CASTAE · CARAE · BONE · PIAE
FIDELI · DVLCI · CARE · AMAN
TISSIME · DESIDERANTISSIME
SODALICIARIA · CONSILI · BONI · B · M

* * *

D(is) m(anibus); C(aius) Vergilius Martanus, colonus agri Caeli Aenei, Anulenae Certae, colonae agri s(upra) s(cripti), an(n)orum XXII, co(n)iugi coiugali castae carae bon(a)e piae fideli dulci car(a)e amantissim(a)e desiderantissim(a)e, sodaliciaria(e) consili boni, b(ene) m(erenti).

* * *

To the spirits of the dead; Gaius Vergilius Martanus, farmer on the property of Caelius Aeneius,[1] dedicated this to Anulena Certa, a farmer on the same property, 22 years old, his conjugal, chaste, dear, good, dutiful, loyal, sweet, dear, most beloved, most desired wife, a companion in his good councils, well-deserving.[2]

1   One of the wealthy aristocrats. The term used for these large estates is *ager* ("property" or "land").
2   Martanus uses an unusually long list of epithets to describe his wife.

Altar dedicated to the future emperor Marcus Aurelius, while still Caesar under his adoptive father Antoninus Pius (CIL 14, 4366), barracks of the fire brigade, Ostia (courtesy of the Archivio Fotografico della Soprintendenza por i Beni Archeologici di Ostia).

SELECTED BIBLIOGRAPHY OF FURTHER READING

General Reference

Adkins, L. and R. *Handbook to Life in Ancient Rome*. New York, 1994.
Balsdon, J. P. V. D. *Life and Leisure in Ancient Rome*. London, 1969.
Carcopino, J. *Daily Life in Ancient Rome: the People and the City at the Height of the Empire*. New Haven, 1968.
Cornell, T., Matthews, J. *Atlas of the Roman World*. New York, 1982.
Harris, W. V. *Ancient Literacy*. Cambridge, 1989.
Hornblower, S., Spawforth, A. (eds.) *The Oxford Classical Dictionary*. Oxford, 1999.
Le Glay, M., Voisin, J.-L., Le Bohec, Y. *A History of Rome*. Oxford, 2001.
Matyszak, P. *Chronicle of the Roman Republic: the Rulers of Ancient Rome from Romulus to Augustus*. London, 2003.
Potter, D. (ed.) *Life, Death, and Entertainment in the Roman Empire*. Ann Arbor, 1999.
Richardson, L. *A New Topographical Dictionary of Ancient Rome*. Baltimore, 1992.
Scarre, C. *Chronicle of the Roman Emperors*. London, 1995.
Stambaugh, J. *The Ancient Roman City*. Baltimore, 1988.
Talbert, R. (ed.) *Atlas of Classical History*. London, 1985.

Epigraphy

Bodel, J. (ed.) *Epigraphic Evidence: Ancient History from Inscriptions*. London, 2001.
Courtney, E. *Musa Lapidaria: A Selection of Latin Verse Inscriptions*. Atlanta, 1995.

Egbert, J. *Introduction to the Study of Latin Inscriptions.* New York, 1923.

Gordon, A. *Illustrated Introduction to Latin Epigraphy.* Berkeley, 1983.

Keppie, L. *Understanding Roman Inscriptions.* Baltimore, 1991.

MacMullen, R. "The Epigraphic Habit in the Roman Empire," *American Journal of Philology,* 103 (1982), 233-246.

Meyer, E.A. "Explaining the Epigraphic Habit in the Roman Empire: the Evidence of the Epitaphs," *Journal of Roman Studies,* 80 (1990), 74-96.

Miller, M.C.J. *Abbreviations in Latin.* Chicago, 1998.

Sandys, J. *Latin Epigraphy.* Cambridge, 1927.

Susini, G. *The Roman Stonecutter: an Introduction to Latin Epigraphy.* Translated by Dabrowski, A.M. Totowa, 1973.

Epigraphic Collections

L'Année Épigraphique (AE). Paris, 1888-present.

Cagnat, R. *Inscriptiones Graecae ad Res Romana Pertinentes.* Paris, 1906-1927.

Corpus Inscriptionum Latinarum (CIL).

Dessau, H. *Inscriptiones Latinae Selectae (ILS).* Berlin, 1892-1916.

Gordon, A.E. and J.S. *Album of Dated Latin Inscriptions.* Berkeley/Los Angeles, 1958-1965.

General Sourcebooks

Friggeri, R. *The Epigraphic Collection of the Museo Nazionale Romano at the Baths of Diocletian.* Milan, 2001.

Lewis, N., Reinhold, M. *Roman Civilization, Volume 1: The Republic and the Augustan Age.* New York, 1990.

Lewis, N., Reinhold, M. *Roman Civilization, Volume 2: the Empire.* New York, 1990.

Maxfield, V., Dobson, B. *Inscriptions of Roman Britain.* London, 1995.

Shelton, J. *As the Romans Did: A Sourcebook on Roman Social History.* Oxford, 1997.

Sherk, R. *The Roman Empire: Augustus to Hadrian, Translated Documents of Greece and Rome.* Cambridge, 1988.

Warmington, B., Miller, S. *Inscriptions of the Roman Empire, AD 14-117.* London, 1996.

Burial and Funerary Practices

Champlin, E. *Final Judgments: Duty and Emotion in Roman Wills, 200 BC – AD 250.* Berkeley, 1991.

Flower, H. *Ancestor Masks and Aristocratic Power in Roman Culture.* Oxford, 1996.

Bibliography 187

Shore, P. *Rest Lightly: An Anthology of Latin and Greek Tomb Inscriptions.* Wauconda, 1997.

Roman Government: Senators, Equestrians and the Municipal Aristocracy

Arnold, W. T. *The Roman System of Provincial Administration.* Chicago, 1914.
Balsdon, J.P.V.D. *Rome: the Story of an Empire.* New York, 1970.
Birley, A. *The* Fasti *of Roman Britain.* Oxford, 1981.
Brunt, P. "*Princeps* and *Equites*," *Journal of Roman Studies*, 73 (1983), 42-75.
Levick, B. *The Government of the Roman Empire: A Sourcebook.* London, 1985.
Meiggs, R. *Roman Ostia.* Oxford, 1973.
Rives, J. "Civic and Religious Institutions," in Bodel, J. (ed.) *Epigraphic Evidence: Ancient History from Inscriptions.* London, 2001, 118-136.
Sherwin-White, A.N. *The Roman Citizenship.* Oxford, 1973.
Talbert, R. *The Senate of Imperial Rome.* Princeton, 1984.

Roman Religion

Adkins, L. and R. *Dictionary of Roman Religion.* New York, 1996.
Beard, M., North, J., Price, S. *Religions of Rome.* Cambridge, 1998.
Gradel, I. *Emperor Worship and Roman Religion.* Oxford, 2002.
Potter, D. "Roman Religion: Ideas and Actions," in Potter, D. (ed.) *Life, Death, and Entertainment in the Roman Empire.* Ann Arbor, 1999, 113-170.
Rives, J. "Civic and Religious Institutions," in Bodel, J. (ed.) *Epigraphic Evidence: Ancient History from Inscriptions.* London, 2001, 118-136.
Taylor, L. R. *The Divinity of the Roman Emperor.* Middletown, 1931.
Warrior, V. *Roman Religion: a Sourcebook.* Newburyport, 2001.

The Roman Army

Anderson, A. *Roman Military Tombstones.* Aylesbury, 1984.
Bowman, A. *Life and Letters on the Roman Frontier: Vindolanda and its People.* London, 1994.
Campbell, B. *War and Society in Imperial Rome, 31 BC – AD 284.* London, 2002.
Campbell, B. *The Roman Army: 31 BC – AD 337: A Sourcebook.* London, 1994.
Cheesman, G.L. *The Auxilia of the Roman Imperial Army.* Chicago, 1914.
Davies, R., David B., Maxfield, V. *Service in the Roman Army.* Edinburgh, 1989.
Goldsworthy, A. *The Roman Army at War, 100 BC - AD 200.* Oxford, 1996.
Keppie, L. *The Making of the Roman Army: from Republic to Empire.* New York, 1984.
Le Bohec, Y. *The Imperial Roman Army.* New York, 1994.
Parker, H.M.D. *The Roman Legions.* Chicago, 1923.

The Roman Family

Frier, B. "Roman Demography," in Potter, D. (ed.) *Life, Death, and Entertainment in the Roman Empire*. Ann Arbor, 1999, 85-112.

Hanson, A. "The Roman Family," in Potter, D. (ed.) *Life, Death, and Entertainment in the Roman Empire*. Ann Arbor, 1999, 19-66.

Rawson, B. (ed.) *The Family in Ancient Rome: New Perspectives*. Ithaca, 1986.

Saller, R. "The Family and Society," in Bodel, J. (ed.) *Epigraphic Evidence: Ancient History from Inscriptions*. London, 2001, 95-117.

Salomies, O. "Names and Identities: Onomastics and Prosopography," in Bodel, J. (ed.) *Epigraphic Evidence: Ancient History from Inscriptions*. London, 2001, 73-94.

The Games

Dodge, H. "Amusing the Masses: Buildings for Entertainment and Leisure in the Roman World," in Potter, D. (ed.) *Life, Death, and Entertainment in the Roman Empire*. Ann Arbor, 1999, 205-255.

Humphrey, J. *Roman Circuses: Arenas for Chariot Racing*. Berkeley, 1986.

Mahoney, A. *Roman Sports and Spectacles; a Sourcebook*. Newburyport, 2001.

Potter, D. "Entertainers in the Roman World," in Potter, D. (ed.) *Life, Death, and Entertainment in the Roman Empire*. Ann Arbor, 1999, 256-326.

Wiedemann, T. *Emperors and Gladiators*. London, 1992.